Black Musical Theatre

BLACK MUSICAL THEATRE

From *Coontown* to *Dreamgirls*

ALLEN WOLL

A DA CAPO PAPERBACK

The author is grateful to the copyright holders for permission to quote the following songs: "It's Getting Dark on Old Broadway," by Louis A. Hirsch, Gene Buck and Dave Stamper, © 1922 Warner Bros. Inc. (Renewed). All Rights Reserved. Used by Permission. The lyric is on page 76.

"Dixie Dreams," "Mandy, Make Up Your Mind," and "I'm a Little Blackbird," words by Grant Clark and Roy Turk, music by George W. Meyer and Arthur Johnston. Copyright © 1924 by Irving Berlin, Inc., now Bourne Co. International copyright secured. All rights reserved. Lyrics printed by permission. The lyrics are on pages 102, 104, and 107–108, respectively.

"My Handy Man Ain't Handy No More"
© 1930 Shapiro Bernstein & Co. Inc. NY. Renewed
Used by permission. Lyrics by Andy Razaf, music by Eubie Blake.
The lyric is on page 145.

The Langston Hughes poem that begins "You've done taken my blues and gone" is reprinted by permission of Harold Ober Associates Incorporated. Copyright 1940 by Crisis Publishing Company.

Library of Congress Cataloging in Publication Data

Woll, Allen L.
Black musical theatre: from Coontown to Dreamgirls / Allen Woll.
p. cm.—(A Da Capo paperback)
Reprint. Originally published: Baton Rouge: Louisiana State University Press, c1989.
Includes bibliographical references and index.
ISBN 0-306-80454-9
1. Musicals—United States—History and criticism. 2. Revues—United States—History and criticism. 3. Afro-Americans—Music—History and criticism. 4. Afro-American entertainers. I. Title.
[ML1711.W64 1991] 91-18959
782.1′4′08996073—dc20 CIP

This Da Capo Press paperback edition of Allen Woll's *Black Musical Theatre* is a republication of the edition published in Baton Rouge, Louisiana in 1989. It is reprinted by arrangement with the Louisiana State University Press.

Published by Da Capo Press, Inc.
A Subsidiary of Plenum Publishing Corporation
233 Spring Street, New York, N.Y. 10013

Manufactured in the United States of America

To My Parents

CONTENTS

ILLUSTRATIONS

PREFACE

During the 1970s, virtually every New York newspaper hailed the talents of Eubie Blake, ragtime pianist and composer of the most popular black musical of the 1920s, *Shuffle Along*. He was revered as the first black to compose a score for the Broadway theatre, the first black to produce a show for Broadway, and the first black to conduct an orchestra for a Broadway show. When he died in 1983, at the age of one hundred, obituaries repeated these tributes. While no one doubts the importance of Eubie Blake's contribution to the Broadway theatre, it is unfortunate that all these statements are false. Blake was praised for a variety of historic "firsts" that were clearly not his.[1]

These oft-repeated errors are certainly not Blake's fault; he continually apprised scholars and journalists of the facts. Blake cautioned a New York *Times* reporter about this problem in 1978 as he sketched the early history of the black musical theatre: "Now remember those names—Walker and Williams. They were great. My people forget the great ones they had. Everyone remembers Al Jolson. Who remembers Walker and Williams? Who remembers Cole and Johnson? Miller and Lyles? Ernest Hogan? I'd never abuse the word 'great.' I couldn't. These men were great and now nobody remembers them."[2]

These "great ones" all wrote and appeared in black Broadway musicals prior to Blake's 1921 hit *Shuffle Along*. In 1898, Bob Cole and Billy Johnson presented *A Trip to Coontown*, the first musical written, directed, and performed by black artists, at the Third Avenue Theatre. George Walker and Bert Williams starred in several Broadway shows between 1900 and 1910, and even appeared before the king of England in their smash hit *In Dahomey* (1903). Cole and J. Rosamond Johnson wrote countless songs for Broadway musicals during the

1. For example, see New York *Daily News*, October 31, 1973, p. 73, and February 3, 1978, p. 5, which proclaim *Shuffle Along* the first black musical on Broadway. The New York *Times* repeats similar errors in Blake's obituary, February 4, 1983, C-1. Newspapers oriented toward black audiences supply erroneous accounts as well (see *Amsterdam News*, March 10, 1979, p. 45).

2. New York *Times*, December 1, 1978, C-2.

same decade and were in two shows of their own creation, *The Shoo-Fly Regiment* (1907) and *The Red Moon* (1909). Ernest Hogan, a talented songwriter and performer, established a touring company for black musicals and appeared on Broadway in *Rufus Rastus* (1906) and *The Oyster Man* (1907). Flournoy Miller and Aubrey Lyles, who are generally unknown today, were the comic talents behind several of the black (and white) musical revues and comedies of the 1920s. Indeed, they appeared on Broadway in almost every season during the entire decade, a record few white performers could match.

Eubie Blake knew the true history of the black musical and never misled his interviewers. Yet this history has been either forgotten or mangled beyond recognition. As a result, most theatregoers are familiar with the names of musical comedy pioneers Victor Herbert, George M. Cohan, Irving Berlin, and Jerome Kern, but the fathers of black musical theatre remain virtually unknown.

The causes for this blurring of the historical record are complex. Some might cite racism to explain why relatively recent books on the musical comedy have ignored or underestimated black contributions to the American theatre.[3] Yet this cannot explain the entire problem, as black writers and critics have also tended to look away from the early period of the black theatrical experience.

A recent incident may provide some clarification. Ben Vereen was invited to appear at Reagan's Inaugural Gala in 1981, and he decided to present a tribute to the great black performer, Bert Williams. Vereen prepared a brief historical introduction to explain Williams' great talents. Unfortunately, due to time constraints, this portion of the sequence was cut, and all that remained was Vereen's extremely accurate impersonation of Williams. The character who appeared wore baggy clothes and blackface makeup, and shuffled about the stage. His speech and song seemed slow, and his grammar woefully inadequate. Without a historical setting for the performance, it seemed a classic gaffe: Vereen presenting the epitome of a stereotypical black before the members of a presidential administration with little interest in the problems of America's black citizens. Black critics lambasted Vereen

3. For example, see Stanley Green, *Ring Bells! Sing Songs! Broadway Musicals of the 1930's* (New Rochelle, N.Y., 1971). This otherwise excellent survey virtually ignores black contributions to musical theatre except in shows written by whites. In a similar fashion, Lawrence W. Levine's major work, *Black Culture and Black Consciousness: Afro-American Thought from Slavery to Freedom* (New York, 1977), discusses all varieties of black song except those written for Broadway musicals. In a chapter entitled "Secular Song and Cultural Values—Black and White," Levine places Eubie Blake's *Shuffle Along* hit "Love Will Find a Way" in a list of white popular songs (p. 277).

for his insensitivity, and Williams' supposed contributions to black musical theatre were again hushed up.

Vereen later explained that he had intended to pay tribute to Williams. Although he swiftly became a Broadway star, he often had to perform under the most humiliating conditions. For example, as a light-skinned black, he had to conform to the stage conventions of the time and don burnt cork makeup. Even as a Ziegfeld star, he found himself barred from most hotels while the show was on tour. Williams should be honored, argued Vereen, for the success he achieved against considerable odds in a time of great racial prejudice. Indeed, this is what makes Williams a hero in Afro-American history and in black theatrical history. Thus it seems that the early history of the black musical theatre has been both passively and actively avoided. White authors have tended to dismiss or underestimate black contributions, and black critics have found the stage persona of Williams, Hogan, or Miller and Lyles to be something of an embarrassment.[4]

An additional complication is that *black musical* has defined a variety of theatrical presentations. At times the words connote an entirely Afro-American creation: blacks onstage and behind the scenes shaped the final work for black audiences. On other occasions (particularly in the context of the Broadway stage), black artists created these shows for predominantly white audiences. Furthermore, as these musical shows became financially successful, white producers, directors, writers, and composers assumed control of the genre and presented their vision of black life. Consequently, it has been difficult to establish historical continuity since the creation, evolution, and shape of the black musical has changed so abruptly and so often since the turn of the century. This situation, which mirrors the history of black theatre in general, led Douglas Turner Ward, playwright, director, and head of the Negro Ensemble Company, to adopt the broadest possible definition of *black theatre*. He concluded that *black theatre* is "by, about, with, for and related to blacks," but need not include every one of these attributes.[5] To narrow the definition even slightly would result in the

4. "Tony Brown's Journal," PBS, 1983. The reevaluation of Bert Williams' talents was evident shortly after the comedian's death. The *Messenger*'s obituary admitted that Williams was "the premier American comedian," but argued that he "rendered a disservice to black people. . . . He played in theatres that either barred or Jim-Crowed Negroes—a policy born of the conception that all men of color are inherently inferior to white men—and by a strange irony of fate, Bert Williams was himself a facile instrument of this insidious cult. His fun-making, of course, was what they wanted, the lowest form of intellection. They delight in visualizing a race of court-jesters" (*Messenger,* IV [April, 1922], 394).

5. New York *Times,* August 31, 1980.

elimination of a vital portion of the black experience. A similar notion must govern the approach to black musical theatre in this century. Unless the totality of the Afro-American experience is conveyed, the resilience of this black cultural effort would be either minimized or lost.

Although many have dismissed musical comedies as "frivolous entertainments for the tired businessman," black musical theatre retains a prime importance in Afro-American history. Around the turn of the century, musical theatre became one of the few avenues of black mobility in a white world. Within a short period, the barriers of burnt cork fell—black actors, writers, producers, choreographers, songwriters, and directors assaulted the musical theatre in order to achieve financial success but also to carve a niche for black theatrical artists and culture in a restricted field. The pace of change, though at times halting, was relatively swift as the black-performed play, an oddity in the nineteenth century, became the rage in the early twentieth. Musical theatre became a prime route to achievement for black performers in show business. Nonetheless, this Afro-American success story has rarely been analyzed by modern historians.

As a result of this incomplete vision of the past, the contemporary interest in black dramas and musicals lacks historical context. Without this perspective, the boom in black musical theatre seems to have come out of nowhere. Actually, the smashing success of such shows as *Purlie* (1970), *Raisin* (1973), *The Wiz* (1975), *Bubbling Brown Sugar* (1976), *Eubie!* and *Ain't Misbehavin'* (1978), *Sophisticated Ladies* and *Dreamgirls* (1981), and *The Tap Dance Kid* (1983) is the culmination of ninety years of blacks' experience on Broadway.

Eubie Blake's now-forgotten heroes gave birth to the modern black musical that is currently flourishing on Broadway. Their efforts produced a unique expression of Afro-American culture and a contribution to the growth of American musical theatre. This is the story of the evolution of the black musical, which, until now, has been hidden from history.

ACKNOWLEDGMENTS

The attempt to document and analyze the elusive history of black musical theatre was facilitated by the staffs of several archives, in particular the Theatre Collection at the Philadelphia Free Library and the Billy Rose Theatre Collection at the New York Public Library. David Schoonover, Curator of the American Literature Collection of the Beinecke Rare Book and Manuscript Library at Yale University, offered invaluable assistance with the James Weldon Johnson Papers. The scrapbooks of theatrical clippings yielded great insights into the early years of black musical theatre. The Schomburg Center for Research in Black Culture (the New York Public Library) and the Theatre Collection at the Museum of the City of New York also contained information on early black musicals. The Music Collection at the Library of Congress supplied several important early librettos, and the Music Collection at the New York Public Library at Lincoln Center offered the music and lyrics of many of the songs included in this text. The able staff of reference librarians at Rutgers University in Camden, New Jersey, provided important factual details with relative ease.

Martin Williams, of the Smithsonian Institution, provided encouragement during the early days of this project, while Robert Cogswell graciously supplied information and recordings of the important comedy team of Miller and Lyles. I would like to also thank the Research Council of Rutgers University for both leave and financial assistance for the completion of this project.

I would also like to praise Myra Woll's keen editorial ability, which nursed the text from a preliminary version to page proofs. Her invaluable and gracious assistance during the writing of this book hastened its completion considerably.

ABBREVIATIONS

The following are used in the footnotes:

JWJP	James Weldon Johnson Papers, Yale University
MC/LC	Music Collection, Library of Congress
MC/NYPL	Music Collection, New York Public Library
SCCF/NYPL	Schomburg Center Clipping File, New York Public Library
TC/NYPL	Billy Rose Theatre Collection, New York Public Library
TC/PFL	Theatre Collection, Philadelphia Free Library

Black Musical Theatre

I

THE FIRST BLACK MUSICALS

Clorindy and *A Trip to Coontown* (1898)

Before 1895, Broadway experienced only the image of the Afro-American and rarely the reality. Stage conventions demanded that white actors in blackface portray all Negro characters in the legitimate theatre. Even plays such as *The Octoroon* and *Uncle Tom's Cabin,* whose plots featured Negro characters in major roles, managed to avoid casting black performers for most of the nineteenth century. In this fashion "real" blacks with dramatic aspirations found all hopes of a stage career thwarted. While a few Afro-American actors such as Ira Aldridge and James Hewlett achieved some success in Shakespearean roles in minuscule stock companies or in overseas productions, drama remained strictly the province of white actors and actresses.[1]

Similar restrictions existed at first for musical presentations. From the moment T. D. Rice donned burnt cork and "jumped Jim Crow" in a New York City minstrel show in 1832, Broadway audiences saw a secondhand vision of black life created by white performers. The minstrel show, which featured "shuffling, irresponsible, wide-grinning, loud-laughing Negroes" in a musical rendition of "darky life on the Old Plantation," according to a contemporary playbill, became one of the most popular entertainments in nineteenth-century America.[2]

Ironically, the minstrel show spawned the modern black musical. As early as 1855 the minstrel stage began to accept black performers. By 1870, several troupes of Afro-American minstrels, billed as "real and original," crisscrossed the United States with their version of a white

1. Yvonne Shafer, "Black Actors in the Nineteenth Century American Theatre," *CLA Journal,* XX (March, 1977), 387–400; Herbert Marshall and Mildred Stock, *Ira Aldridge: The Negro Tragedian* (Carbondale, Ill., 1968).

2. See Robert C. Toll, *Blacking Up: The Minstrel Show in Nineteenth-Century America* (New York, 1974).

entertainment. By 1890, most of the 1,490 black actors enumerated by the census were employed in touring minstrel companies. Saddled with the stage conventions of minstrelsy, black entertainers had to wear the same baggy pants, oversized shoes, and occasionally even the burnt cork that whites wore. The minstrel show trained generations of black performers—W. C. Handy, Bert Williams, and Bessie Smith, to name a few—for theatrical and musical careers, but it also forced them to perpetuate the genre's derogatory stereotypes of black life. Since the minstrel show was often the only outlet for black performers, they had no choice.

The minstrel entertainments generally played the second-class burlesque houses, so patrons of the legitimate theatre did not usually frequent these performances. Instead, the newly popular "coon songs" brought minstrel stereotypes in musical form to Broadway audiences. These melodies owed their unusual nickname to the efforts of black performer Ernest ("The Unbleached American") Hogan. Hogan composed a syncopated ditty called "All Coons Look Alike to Me" in 1890, and it succeeded beyond his wildest dreams. Although the tune is actually a love song of a "dusky maiden" forced to choose between two handsome young men, the public ignored the lyric and remembered only the title. It soon became a catchphrase, and the latest ragtime numbers became known as coon songs. Both black and white composers outdid themselves with these tales of the "gastronomical delights of chicken, pork chops, and watermelon." A black critic found these new songs "crude, raucous, bawdy, and obscene," but they nevertheless swept the nation.[3]

The Broadway musical theatre took note of this popular trend, and producers interpolated the new coon songs into their shows. May Irwin became the most famous "coon-shouter" of the stage after the premiere of *The Widow Jones* (1895). The "Bully Song," which told of a "razor-toting nigger," stopped the show:

> I was sandin' down the Mobile Buck just to cut a shine
> Some coon across my smeller swiped a watermelon rin'
> I drawed my steel dat gemmen to fin'
> I riz up like a black cloud and took a look aroun'
> There was dat new bully standin' on the ground.
> I've been lookin' for you nigger and I've got you found.

3. James Weldon Johnson, *Along This Way* (New York, 1968), 153; Benjamin McArthur, *Actors and American Culture, 1880–1920* (Philadelphia, 1984), 51.

Razors 'gun a flyin', niggers 'gun to squawk,
I lit upon that bully just like a sparrow hawk,
And dat nigger was just a dyin' to take a walk.
When I got through with bully, a doctor and a nurse
Wa'nt no good to dat nigger, so they put him in a hearse,
A cyclone couldn't have tore him up much worse.

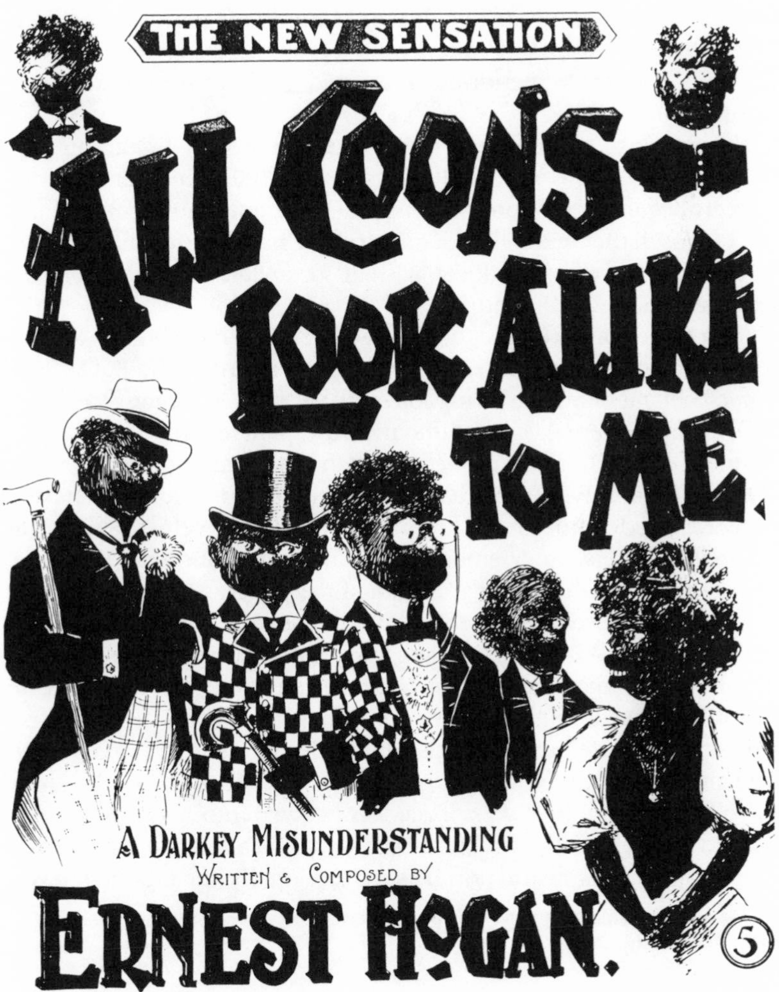

Sheet music of Ernest Hogan's hit song
Courtesy Billy Rose Theatre Collection, New York Public Library

White songwriter Charles Trevathan clearly outdid himself in incorporating predominant stereotypes of black life in this popular song. It was such a success that the blond-haired blue-eyed Miss Irwin demanded that coon songs be added to all her future Broadway musicals.[4]

Although Ernest Hogan's hit tune brought him financial security, its title haunted him to the end of his days. On his deathbed he reportedly wished that he had never written "All Coons Look Alike to Me."[5] Hogan was not alone in this desire. Many black performers had to accept the stereotypes of American popular culture in order to have the opportunity to perform. It seemed a difficult but necessary compromise.

Nevertheless, several black actors began to profess discomfort with the roles they were expected to portray. By 1890, promoters and performers began to envision a new type of black entertainment, one that might loosen the rigid bonds of minstrelsy. Change would be cautious, to be sure, since no producer wished to deviate abruptly from the expectations of the audience.

Sam T. Jack, a burlesque theatre owner and manager, made the first tentative move with *The Creole Show* (1890), starring Sam Lucas, Fred Piper, Billy Jackson, and Irving Jones, all veterans of the minstrel stage. Jack brought a female chorus into the show, whereas minstrel acts had all-male casts. He also dropped the standard plantation background and replaced it with an urban environment. The show did have a minstrel interlocutor for the first act, though, for novelty's sake, it was a female. The ensemble embarked on a lengthy tour from Boston to Chicago (during the World's Fair) and finally to New York City, where it nudged the respectable Broadway theatre zone.[6]

The success of *The Creole Show* caused John W. Isham, an agent for the show, to organize his own Negro production, *The Octoroons,* in 1895. Billed as a musical farce rather than a minstrel show, *The Octoroons* emphasized song, dance, and burlesque sketches. It also utilized the talents of female leads and a female chorus. As the show traveled from city to city *The Octoroons* evolved into "one continuous farce in two acts with a semblance of a story and a constant interjection of specialties and musical numbers." Occasionally, the production was

4. Stanley Appelbaum (ed.), *Show Songs from "The Black Crook" to "The Red Mill"* (New York, 1974), 81.

5. Tom Fletcher, *The Tom Fletcher Story: 100 Years of the Negro in Show Business* (New York, 1954), 139.

6. For a history of these black revues, see James Weldon Johnson, *Black Manhattan* (New York, 1968), Chap. 9.

billed as "The Octoroons" in *A Tenderloin Coon,* a book musical that discussed preparations for war in Act I, and scenes at Camp Black and the New York Armory in Act II. The two stars, Walter Smart and George Williams, inevitably sang their hit song, "No Coon Can Come Too Black for Me," and Stella Wiley (who later married musical comedy writer Bob Cole) also attracted attention as a talented comedienne.[7]

Isham followed *The Octoroons* with a more ambitious effort entitled *Oriental America* (1896). While the earlier show emphasized so-called Negro songs and dances, such as the cakewalk, *Oriental America* demonstrated that blacks could also perform material hitherto reserved for whites. The finale included selections from *Faust, Rigoletto, Carmen,* and *Il Trovatore,* sung by Sidney Woodward, William C. Elkins, and Maggie Scott. *Oriental America* not only abandoned the burlesque houses for its performances, it even had a short run on Broadway at Palmer's Theatre. The show apparently demonstrated that audiences would pay to see black performers away from the minstrel stage.

A second show with an operatic slant followed *Oriental America. Black Patti's Troubadours* (1896) featured Sissieretta Jones, dubbed Black Patti by *Clipper* magazine after the Italian singer Adelina Patti. Jones had studied opera for several years, but made her first splash at the 1892 Jubilee Spectacle and Cakewalk in Madison Square Garden. Shortly afterwards she sang at a White House reception for President Harrison, and then left on a concert tour of Europe. When she returned to the United States, her new managers decided to present her in an all-Negro show. Half "musical farce" and half "operatic kaleidoscope," *Black Patti's Troubadours* played several seasons, once again suggesting that there was an audience for black musical entertainments. The producers of *Troubadours* hired Bob Cole to write the show. While Black Patti's operatic sequences were sacrosanct, Cole began to experiment with short book musicals to fill the remainder of the show. With the help of Billy Johnson and Cole's wife Stella Wiley, a mini-musical, "At Jolly Coon-ey Island," was the finale. Cole portrayed "Willie Wayside, a tramp of the lowly genteel variety," and Johnson portrayed Jim Flimflammer. Cole nightly stopped the show with his rendition of "The Blow Almost Killed Father." This enterprise was later the core of Cole's first full-length musical, *A Trip to Coontown.*[8]

7. "John W. Isham's Octoroons," Providence (R.I.) *Telegram,* n.d., clipping in Scrapbook (Zan J632+, Z c. 1), Book 2, p. 4, JWJP.

8. Henry Henriksen, "Black Patti," *Record Research,* no. 177/8 (November, 1980), 8.

It was in this atmosphere that both Will Marion Cook (1869–1944) and Bob Cole (1868–1911) began to dream of presenting an all-black musical comedy on Broadway.[9] They discussed their ideas and discovered that they had radically different notions of the Negro's proper role in American musical theatre. Cole believed that blacks should strive for excellence in artistic creation and must compete on an equal basis with whites. His musicals therefore had to rival those of white composers and lyricists, and thus demonstrate that the Negro was capable of matching whites in all realms of cultural production. Cook, however, felt that "Negroes should eschew white patterns" and not try to do what "the white artist could always do as well, generally better." Negroes should look to themselves for the wellsprings of creativity, developing artistic endeavors that reflected the soul of black people. This fundamental disagreement soured the relationship between Cook and Cole. Whenever the songwriters entered a room, tensions soon flared and insults flew. Friends tried to keep them apart whenever possible.[10]

Cook and Cole each went his own way in devising a musical comedy based on his philosophy of black culture. And in 1898, Cook's *Clorindy, the Origin of the Cakewalk* and Cole's *A Trip to Coontown* gave birth to black musical comedy.

Will Marion Cook's parents assumed that their son would become a classical violinist or an orchestra conductor instead of a composer for musical theatre. They sent their thirteen-year-old child prodigy to the Oberlin Conservatory to study violin. At age sixteen, Will left Ohio for Berlin, Germany, to study with the renowned violinist Joseph Joachim. On his return to New York City, he attended classes in composition with Antonín Dvorák at the National Conservatory of Music. Cook's mind began to wander during this period, partly as a result of his intense dislike for Dvorák. Dvorák devoted all his attention to his pet pupil, Harry T. Burleigh, who became a noted black classical composer. Cook's fingers grew stiff from lack of practice, and Dvorák finally barred him from class.

9. For a brief discussion of the musical talents of Cook and Cole, see Eileen Southern, *The Music of Black Americans: A History* (New York, 1971), Chap. 10.
10. Johnson, *Along This Way,* 173.

Cook instead turned his attention to the black bohemians of New York City's theatrical world. He was particularly fascinated by the new vaudeville team of Bert Williams and George Walker, who, after their debut in *The Gold Bug* (1896), surprised New Yorkers with their fancy steps and comic patter. During their forty-week run at Koster and Bial's vaudeville theatre, they popularized the cakewalk, a black dance of slave origin. Within weeks it was taken up by high society. As a publicity stunt, Williams and Walker even challenged William Vanderbilt to a cakewalk contest. The winner would receive fifty dollars. Vanderbilt, however, declined.

Will Marion Cook decided to explore the cakewalk craze in his first musical comedy, *Clorindy, the Origin of the Cakewalk,* set in Louisiana of the 1880s. He would thus be able to use Negro themes and music in his stage work. Williams and Walker encouraged the young Cook, who would build his show around the talented comedy team. Habitually short of funds, Cook borrowed ten dollars from Will McConnell, Williams and Walker's manager, in order to return to his parents' home in Washington, D.C., to write *Clorindy.* After he arrived, he asked his friend Paul Laurence Dunbar to write the libretto and lyrics. Dunbar had recently completed three collections of poems—*Oak and Ivy, Majors and Minors,* and *Lyrics of Lowly Life*—and he seemed dubious about shifting his attention to the theatre. After several lengthy arguments, though, Dunbar finally agreed.[11]

Cook and Dunbar barricaded themselves in the basement of a house near Howard University. Equipped with beer, whiskey, a T-bone steak, but no piano, they finished the songs and libretto for *Clorindy* by early the next morning. The libretto underwent several revisions, and Dunbar's original script was never used. The experience so disconcerted Dunbar that he resolved never to work with Cook, who irritated him "beyond endurance."

That morning, however, Cook was jubilant. He entered the parlor and began to play what was to be one of the most popular songs from *Clorindy,* "Who Dat Say Chicken in Dis Crowd?":

11. For the genesis of *Clorindy,* see Will Marion Cook, "Clorindy, the Origin of the Cakewalk," *Theatre Arts* (September, 1947), 61–65. Quotations concerning Cook in ensuing paragraphs are from this source. The libretto of *Clorindy* is in MC/LC. Additional material is available in Edith J. R. Isaacs, *The Negro in the American Theatre* (College Park, Md., 1968).

There was once a great assemblage of the culled population
All the culled swells was there.
They had got themselves together to discuss the situation and the rumors in the air.
There were speakers there from Georgia and some more from Tennessee, who were making feathers fly,
When a roostah in a bahn-ya'd flew up whah those folks could see,
Then those darkies all did cry:

Who dat say chicken in dis crowd?
Speak de word a-gin and speak it loud.
Blame de lan', let the white folks rule it,
I'se a lookin' fu a pullet,
Who dat say chicken in dis crowd?

Will's mother listened from the kitchen and then walked into the parlor with tears in her eyes. She said to her son, "Oh, Will! Will! I've sent you all over the world to study and become a great musician, and you return such a nigger!" She disapproved, since "she thought that a Negro composer should write just like a white man." Cook dismissed his mother's complaints, without realizing how much the latest coon songs had affected his and Dunbar's writing. Cook left for New York in search of a producer for *Clorindy.*

A friend had arranged a one o'clock appointment with Isadore Witmark, a noted music publisher. At three o'clock, Witmark stormed into the room and shouted, "Go ahead! What's you got?" Cook performed the songs from *Clorindy* as Witmark listened impatiently. After forty minutes, Witmark interrupted the recital and told Cook that he was "crazy." Did he really expect a Broadway audience to pay money to hear Negroes sing a Negro opera? Witmark rushed out, leaving a dejected Cook behind. Once again without money, Cook was forced to smuggle his way aboard a Washington-bound train in order to return home.

Several days later, Will received a tip from the head usher at the Casino Theatre Roof Garden that Ed Rice, the manager, was searching for a new show. Cook hurried to Rice's office, which he found crowded with aspiring talents. Ignored by Rice for almost a month, Cook finally heard him tell another act to come to the rehearsal hall the following Monday for an audition. Cook decided to gamble. He gathered his friends together and told them that they were auditioning for Rice in a few days. They rehearsed throughout the weekend.

Cook and his cast arrived at the hall before Rice did. John Braham, the conductor of the Casino orchestra, welcomed him and patiently listened to his credentials. Braham turned to the orchestra and said, "Gentlemen, a new composer." Braham reached for the music, but Cook resisted, claiming that his cast understood only "his gestures and direction." Braham stepped back and announced, "Gentlemen, a new composer and a new conductor."

The cast of twenty-six began singing "Darktown Is Out Tonight" as Ed Rice entered the theatre. He waited a moment and then shouted to Braham, "No nigger can conduct my orchestra on Broadway!" Braham replied, "Ed, go back to your little cubby-hole and keep quiet." Rice finally agreed to present *Clorindy* at the roof garden of the Casino Theatre.

Clorindy underwent several changes before it opened. Since it was to be an after-dinner entertainment, it had to be drastically shortened. Rice decided to eliminate virtually the entire Dunbar libretto, since dialogue on the outside stage had to compete with noise from the street below. Soon only the songs and dances remained from the original conception. Williams and Walker were unable to appear in *Clorindy,* so Ernest Hogan, who had just completed a run in *Black Patti's Troubadours,* joined the cast.

Despite the last-minute changes, *Clorindy* seemed ready for its premiere on Tuesday, June 28, 1898. Slightly before the 11:45 P.M. curtain time, a massive thundershower drenched the cast and the audience. Rice had to delay the premiere until the following Monday.

When opening night finally arrived, Rice introduced Cook, who stepped to the podium and started the first song. After the final note the audience cheered and applauded. Cook was so surprised by the favorable reception that he was unable to continue conducting. Hogan had to step across the footlights and shout, "What's the matter, son? Let's go!" Cook finally regained his composure and began Hogan's hit song:

> Behold the hottes' coon
> Your eyes have lit on!
> Velvet ain't good enough
> For him to sit on.
> When he walks down the street,
> Folks yell like sixty,
> Behold the hottes' coon in Dixie!

Clorindy ended at 12:45 (Hogan had ten encores of "Who Dat Say

Chicken in Dis Crowd?"), and the audience cheered. The cast retreated to a local bar, where Cook drank several glasses of water, thinking he was having wine, and got gloriously drunk. As Cook basked in the praise for the show he commented, "Negroes are at last on Broadway, and here to stay!"

Cook's bravado notwithstanding, *Clorindy* remained a tentative beginning. A musical sketch rather than a full-length musical comedy, it retained many of the stereotypes inherent in the minstrel tradition as the numerous coon songs demonstrated. Cook followed *Clorindy* with *Jes' Lak White Fo'ks,* which was produced at the New York Theatre Roof Garden the following summer. Dunbar once again was persuaded to contribute the lyrics, but Cook wrote the libretto.

Jes' Lak White Fo'ks expressed Cook's personal philosophy in a one-act operetta. Pompous Johnson, the lead character, discovers a pot of gold and decides to use his money "jes' lak white fo'ks" do and enter high society. He contracts a matchmaker to arrange a marriage for his daughter Mandy to an African prince. The prince, a seedy character, turns out to be a phony, and Pompous realizes that "an honest American Negro will . . . make the best living for his daughter." Mandy marries her true love, and Pompous decides to stop acting "jes' lak white fo'ks." The moral is that the Negro should not vainly attempt to imitate the ways of whites, but should instead seek happiness in the culture of his own people.[12]

Jes' Lak White Fo'ks was considerably less successful than was Cook's earlier show. James Weldon Johnson, author of *Black Manhattan* and himself a Broadway lyricist, analyzed its problems some years later: "In *Clorindy,* New York had been given its first demonstration of the possibilities of Negro syncopated music, of what could be done with it in the hands of a competent and original composer. Cook's music, especially his choruses and finales, made Broadway catch its breath. In *Jes' Lak White Fo'ks,* the book and lyrics were not so good, nor was the cast; and naturally, the music was not such a startling novelty."[13] The show's quick demise ended the Cook and Dunbar collaboration, though their names appear on the sheet music for several later Williams and Walker shows. The songs were actually recycled melodies from *Jes' Lak White Fo'ks.*

12. *Jes' Lak White Fo'ks* libretto, in MC/LC. For a Dunbar bibliography, see Virginia Cunningham, *Paul Laurence Dunbar and His Song* (New York, 1969). A description of *Jes' Lak White Fo'ks* is found in New York *Journal,* October 20, 1901, but the show is named *The Cannibal King.*

13. Johnson, *Along This Way,* 175.

Cook's theatrical apprenticeship ended in 1900 when he contributed songs to the Broadway musicals *The Casino Girl* and *The Policy Players*. Thereafter he became known as the resident composer for the Williams and Walker entertainments: *In Dahomey* (1903), *Abyssinia* (1906), and *Bandanna Land* (or *Bandana Land*) (1908).[14] He also wrote Broadway's first interracial musical, *The Southerners* (1904). Many claimed that Broadway was not ready for such an exhibition and prophesied trouble. The critic for the New York *Times* noticed the tense atmosphere on opening night:

> When the chorus of real live coons walked in for the cake[walk] last night at the New York Theatre, mingling with the white members of the cast, there were those in the audience who trembled in their seats, as if expecting an . . . explosion. It was only a year ago that the entire cast of a farce at Madison Square struck because a single gentleman of color was engaged to play the part of a Negro porter, and held out until the gentleman was entirely cast out. And here were scores of blacks and whites mingling. But it presently became evident that the spirit of harmony reigned. The magician was discovered on inquiry to be the Negro composer Will Marion Cook, who all alone had succeeded in harmonizing the racial broth as skillfully as he had harmonized the accompanying score.[15]

Perhaps Cook was correct. Maybe Broadway was now ready to accept blacks as full partners in American musical theatre.

Unlike Will Cook, Bob Cole always dreamed of a stage career. After graduating from Atlanta University, he traveled north, as many had, in search of success in the theatre. Although he had no formal training for the stage, Cole was willing to accept any job. After a short run in *The Creole Show,* he joined Worth's Museum All-Star Stock Company. This small Negro repertory theatre provided training in all aspects of stage production for its fifteen-member company. Cole soon demonstrated his mastery of a variety of skills. He directed, choreographed, and wrote the comic and dramatic sketches that made this company one of the most popular Negro attractions in New York.[16]

14. The spelling of names and of titles of productions is in some cases erratic at best. In fact, some names change over time. I have chosen to use the spelling given in the playbills. Alternatives will be noted in parentheses.

15. New York *Times,* May 24, 1904, p. 9.

16. Johnson, *Black Manhattan,* 101–102.

Voelckel and Nolan, Black Patti's managers, admired Cole's work at Worth's and hired him to write songs and sketches for *Black Patti's Troubadours.* After its success, Cole asked the producers for a raise in salary. When they hesitated, Cole gathered his music and left. Voelckel and Nolan, not accustomed to being challenged in this manner, had Cole arrested and brought to trial. Cole stated in court that "these men have amassed a fortune from the product of my brain, and now they call me a thief; I won't give it [the music] up!" The judge ruled against Cole, who had to surrender his compositions to Voelckel and Nolan.

This was only one of Cole's many disappointing encounters with white theatrical producers. Also in 1896 he managed to arrange an appointment with George Lederer, who had the reputation of being sympathetic to Negro talent. Cole took his first play, which he wrote in the morning hours after his performances at Worth's Museum, to Lederer's office. Lederer invited the cast of the Casino's new musical, *The Lady Slavey* (1896), which featured Marie Dressler and Dan Daley, to attend Cole's dramatic reading. Since most of the rehearsal rooms were in use, the group repaired to the boiler room in the basement of the theatre. When Cole began his reading, a fireman began to stoke the huge furnace. As Cole continued his performance the noise became louder and the room grew hotter. By the middle of the play, Cole's entire audience had disappeared.[17]

Cole decided that it was absurd to depend on white producers for entrée to Broadway, so he established a black production company for his first musical comedy. *A Trip to Coontown,* which opened on April 4, 1898, at the Third Avenue Theatre, has the distinction of being the first full-length musical comedy written, directed, performed, and produced by blacks.

The show's title was strikingly similar to *A Trip to Chinatown* (1891), the musical hit that remained Broadway's long-run champion for almost twenty-five years. *A Trip to Coontown* also offered a visit to one of New York City's ethnic enclaves, but there the similarity ended. Cole's show provided a loosely structured plot concerning Jim Flimflammer (Billy Johnson), a con artist, who tries to bilk Silas Green, "an old Negro," out of his $5,000 pension. At the last moment, Willie Wayside (Bob Cole) saves the gullible old man from Flimflammer's schemes. The plot was ignored throughout most of the evening, since the visit to Coontown allowed the appearance of several specialty acts, such as

17. Pittsburgh *Leader,* May 7, 1909.

The Freeman Sisters (Contortional Dancers), Jim Wilson (Equilibrist), Juvia Roan (The Cuban Nightingale), and Lloyd G. Gibbs (The Greatest Living Black Tenor). Thus *A Trip to Coontown* differed little from earlier black revues, despite the superimposed story line.[18]

Although the show played only briefly on Broadway, Cole and Billy Johnson toured with *A Trip to Coontown* for several weeks. They returned to New York City the following September, playing the Grand Opera House at Eighth Avenue and Twenty-third Street. Now billed as "The Kings of Koon-dom," Cole and Johnson demonstrated that an audience existed for all-Negro productions.

Nevertheless, Cole was dissatisfied. He wished to produce musical comedies that equaled those by white artists. *A Trip to Coontown,* however, was a parochial entertainment not markedly different from the minstrel show. Cole decided to search for new directions for black musical comedy.

18. *A Trip to Coontown* playbill, in Theatre Collection, Museum of the City of New York.

II

THE END OF THE COON SONGS

Bob Cole and the Johnson Brothers

Two brothers from Jacksonville, Florida, came to New York in 1899 with the dream of presenting an original operetta on Broadway. They arrived with only a letter of introduction to the editor of a music trade journal, but within three months they had met the most prominent figures in American musical comedy at the turn of the century. Although *Tolosa or the Royal Document* was never produced, the brothers became part of the hottest song-writing team on Broadway.

John Rosamond Johnson (1873–1954) first became interested in musical comedy while studying piano at the New England Conservatory of Music in Boston. After six years of work, Rosamond jettisoned his career in classical music and toured the United States with the company of *Oriental America.* The vision of success in the theatre entranced Rosamond, and he returned to Jacksonville to persuade his brother James Weldon Johnson to join him in New York City and write lyrics for his melodies. Rosamond won over the hesitant James. Rosamond taught music and James taught mathematics in order to support themselves, and they devoted their spare time to writing a musical comedy. The brothers presented *Tolosa,* a tale of life on a South Sea island after the arrival of the British, for Jacksonville's white musical patrons in 1898. With their support and encouragement, James and Rosamond left for New York City in the summer of 1899.

The Johnsons performed their songs for Isadore Witmark, who had become more receptive to black talent since *Clorindy*'s success. Reginald De Koven and Harry B. Smith, composers of numerous operettas, also listened in. All were impressed. Oscar Hammerstein, the famed theatrical producer, heard of the Johnson brothers and visited them in their small apartment on West Fifty-third Street in order to hear the score of *Tolosa*. Hammerstein liked the songs a great deal, and his name helped open many doors for the song-writing team.

James Weldon Johnson reminisced about his youthful journey to Broadway, acknowledging that it was "an absurd and improbable venture." How could two young and inexperienced black men from Florida have hoped to achieve success on Broadway within one year? James attributed their conquest of the Great White Way both to a youthful naïveté and an "invincible faith in themselves." It also indicated that the rigid color bar between minstrelsy and musical theatre had finally begun to collapse.[1]

It seemed a Cinderella story. Soon the Johnsons were meeting the elite of New York theatrical society. They were impressed with the leaders in black theatre: Williams and Walker, Hogan, Cook, Burleigh, and Cole. The Johnsons became friends with Cole, and they decided to become partners in writing musical comedies. It was a felicitous arrangement, as Cole's perceptive knowledge of the theatrical world would prove useful to the inexperienced Johnsons.[2]

Although coon songs were the rage when Cole and the Johnson brothers began their collaboration, they soon decided they could not write songs that presented such repellent portraits of black life. Instead, their songs would elevate the image of Negroes. The team's first published melody, "Louisiana Lize," avoided the popular stereotypes prevalent in the songs of the era.

Bob Cole performed his new song for famed "coon-shouter" May Irwin in early 1900. Delighted with the melody and lyrics, the musical comedy star purchased the song and inserted it in her new show, *The Belle of Bridgeport* (1900). Cole and the Johnsons received a check for fifty dollars for their maiden effort. Exuberant, they rushed out to cash it. At the Garfield National Bank, the teller was suspicious of the three young men and sent them to the bank on which the check was drawn. After considerable effort, they eventually received their well-deserved money.

The success of "Louisiana Lize" encouraged the team to continue their partnership. The Johnson brothers moved to the Marshall Hotel on West Fifty-third Street, which was the center of black theatrical

1. Johnson, *Along This Way*, Chap. 16. See also Eugene Levy, *James Weldon Johnson: Black Leader, Black Voice* (Chicago, 1973). Copies of *Tolosa* (Item 542–43) and an earlier version, *The Fakir* (Item +204), are available in JWJP.

2. Bob Cole, "The Negro and the Stage," *Colored American Magazine* (1902), 301–307.

activity at the turn of the century. Every Sunday the greatest black musicians of the age attended a special dinner and performed their latest compositions. The group often spent hours discussing the Negro's role in the world of music and the theatre.

Bob Cole, who lived two doors down from the Marshall, found the new living arrangements conducive to writing songs. He met the Johnson brothers every morning for breakfast at the Marshall, and they began their work by noon. They often worked ten-hour days, pausing only for a snack in the late afternoon, and then went out for a midnight supper of lobster or steak. In the early days of their collaboration, this seemed an extravagant end to a long day, but the team felt that a healthy meal was a just reward for their labors.

The three men, gathered around the piano, worked as one. James Weldon Johnson confessed that it was virtually impossible to identify the contribution of any one of them to the completed song. Yet, informal partnerships arose early. Two men wrote the songs, and the third acted as critic or adviser. Each member assumed the critic's role at various times. Since all seemed to contribute equally to the final product, they resolved that all royalties would be split three ways.

The success of *The Belle of Bridgeport* created new opportunities for the song-writing team. They provided music for a play by Peter Dailey, *Champagne Charlie,* and contributed songs to *The Supper Club,* which opened at the Winter Garden Theatre. Bob Cole also helped to stage the latter show and even taught Donald Brian his dance steps. Brian (then known as Brine) later became a matinee idol after his appearance in *The Merry Widow* in 1907.

The famed Broadway producers Klaw and Erlanger heard the trio's early songs and summoned their stage manager, Ben Teal, to find the composers of these delightful tunes. Teal met Bob Cole on Broadway and asked if he could help locate "the two brothers named Johnson." Cole archly answered, "I know just where I can put my hands on them for you." Klaw and Erlanger hired them to provide specialty numbers for their American version of the Drury Lane pantomime *The Sleeping Beauty and the Beast* (1901). This spectacular show displayed some the most dazzling scenic designs and special effects the Broadway stage had ever seen. For example, the entire female chorus portrayed fairies in the second act and flew en masse across the stage. The spectacle almost dwarfed the Cole and Johnson brothers' songs into nonexistence. Although "Tell Me, Dusky Maiden," "Come Out, Dinah, on the Green," and "Nobody's Lookin' but the Owl and the Moon" pleased the critics, music sales were minimal.

Not until "The Maiden with the Dreamy Eyes" appeared in 1901 did the song-writing team begin to earn enough money to live comfortably in New York City. Anna Held performed the song in *The Little Duchess,* and Elsie Janis later adopted the tune. James Weldon Johnson confessed that the trio had deliberately designed this song to be a popular hit. The key to royalties at this time was sheet music sales—people took the melodies home to play on the piano in the parlor. Cole and the Johnsons realized that if they praised a blue-eyed maiden in their lyrics, they would lose the audience of dark-eyed women. So they made the lyrics virtually universal:

There are eyes of blue,
There are brown eyes, too,
There are eyes of every size
And eyes of every hue;
But I surmise
That if you are wise
You'll be careful of the maiden
With the dreamy eyes.[3]

Although "The Maiden with the Dreamy Eyes" became one of the trio's biggest hits, royalties were slow in coming. In January, 1902, the team was $1,300 in debt to their music publishers. So Bob and Rosamond readily accepted $100 to entertain at a private party which Lillian Russell attended. The performance was such a success that Bob and Rosamond decided to form a vaudeville act to tide them over this lean period. James returned to Jacksonville, where, as principal of the Stanton School, he hoped to use part of his salary to help pay off the group's debts. The trio's hard times were short. In June, James received a letter from his brother, explaining that their songs were selling and that the new vaudeville act was a smash hit. Their debt had been erased, and they had earned almost $1,500. James cashed the enclosed money orders, resigned from the Stanton School, and swiftly returned to New York City. The reversal in fortune surprised James on his arrival. He found that Rosamond and Bob had taken additional rooms at the Marshall for their rehearsals and song writing. They also purchased extensive new wardrobes, which made James feel like a "country cousin." Perhaps James's greatest surprise was Bob and Rosamond's vaudeville act.

The act exemplified the trio's contention that the black artist and the

3. "The Maiden with the Dreamy Eyes" lyrics, in MC/NYPL.

Bob Cole and J. Rosamond Johnson perform their vaudeville act
Courtesy Billy Rose Theatre Collection, New York Public Library

white artist were equal. Bob and Rosamond would have nothing to do with minstrel show stereotypes that governed black performances before white audiences. There would be no shuffling, no coon songs, and no condescension. As James sat in the audience he was startled by Bob and Rosamond's audacity, for they presented an act "unlike anything done by Negro performers":

> [The act] was quiet, finished, and artistic to the minutest details. The two entered dressed in evening clothes—they did make a handsome appearance—and talking about the program they had best give in entertaining a party to which they were on their way. Rosamond, seating himself at the piano, suggested that they open with an instrumental number, and proceeded to play Paderewski's *Minuet* which went over well. Rosamond then suggested further that they ought to follow with a little classic song. Bob demurred slightly, but Rosamond went ahead and sang *Still wie die nacht* in German. The singing of this song never failed to gain applause; perhaps for the reason Dr. Johnson assigned for admiration at seeing a dog walk on his hind legs. Bob then expressed the fear that classic music might be what people at the party would least like to hear, and suggested the singing of their own little song, "Mandy." From this point on, the program consisted of original songs, sung one after another, Rosamond playing the accompaniments.[4]

Although James was proud of Rosamond's and Bob's success, he felt a twinge of regret. Before, each had contributed equally. Now James began to feel that he was the lesser member of the trio.

At first James had little time for indecision concerning the group's future, for soon after his return they wrote their most popular song, "Under the Bamboo Tree," which Marie Cahill sang in *Sally in Our Alley* (1902). The idea for the song originated with Bob Cole. He suggested that they revise the spiritual "Nobody Knows the Trouble I've Seen" into a popular song. Rosamond thought the idea was sacrilegious, but Cole reportedly replied, "What kind of musician are you, anyway? Been to the Boston Conservatory and can't change a little old tune around?" Rosamond and James agreed, and "Under the Bamboo Tree" was born.[5]

Although the song eventually achieved hit status, the team's publisher, Joseph Stern Company, was initially reluctant to release it. Stern filed the manuscript in a safe and then professed to have lost it. The music company complained that the song was "too repetitious," with its talk of "If you lak-a me lak I lak-a-you and we-lak-a both the same," and suggested that Cole and the Johnson brothers begin work on some new tunes. Abandoning the song temporarily, Cole and Rosamond continued to perform at parties for the white theatrical elite, hoping for a break. Marie Cahill, the star of *The Wild Rose* (1902), attended one of these soirées and was attracted by the talents of Cole

4. Johnson, *Along This Way,* 187.
5. Louisville *Post,* May 4, 1907.

and Johnson. She asked them if they could write something for her, and Cole replied, "Why, that's awfully funny, Miss Cahill, here's a little song we wrote just last night, 'Under the Bamboo Tree.' " Johnson tried to hide his surprise at his partner's quick thinking.

Cahill adored the song and insisted that it be interpolated into her latest show, *Sally in Our Alley.* Nevertheless, the producers of the show hated it and refused. Cahill threatened to quit, and they finally relented. Most producers were not as pliant, but Cahill had proven her talent for picking songs in *The Wild Rose.* Complaining about the lackluster quality of the score, she insisted that Clifton Crawford's "Nancy Brown" should be included. Her hunch was correct—the song became the hit of the show. On opening night it received six encores. The producers gave in, hoping that "Under the Bamboo Tree" would produce a similar magic in *Sally in Our Alley.*[6]

The critics and public staunchly agreed with Cahill's choice. One critic found it "the best musical number": "With the stage all to herself, but assisted by a hidden chorus and a string orchestra, Miss Cahill sang this pretty coon ballad in a manner both charming and captivating. The audience could have listened to this melody all evening without growing tired of it."[7]

"Under the Bamboo Tree" became the runaway hit of the show, but it still had not been formally published. Stern ransacked his office, but was unable to discover the original copy. Cole and Johnson, in the meantime, were performing in Colorado, so Stern sent agents to meet them in order to obtain another copy of the song.[8] Within one year the song sold over 400,000 copies for Stern, making it one of the company's top hits to date.

Cahill became the champion of the songs of Cole and the Johnsons. When she appeared in *Nancy Brown* (the title derives from Crawford's hit song) in February, 1903, no one questioned the addition of their "On the Congo" (or "Congo Love Song"). The New York *Evening Star* found it "another instance of Cole and Johnson to the rescue." The *Herald* added: "She [Cahill] sang a song with an African motive. It was as original as a banana peel—nevertheless we all slipped into the refrain. It may be hummed from the housetops today. . . . While 'On the Congo' has, even more than its predecessor, that particular unmis-

6. Gerald Bordman, *American Musical Theatre* (New York, 1978), 181, 184.

7. Unidentified review in Johnson, Theatre Scrapbooks (Zan J 632 +ZC 2.1, 1–3), 9, JWJP.

8. *Vanity Fair* (January, 1926), 56.

takable lilt, which, once heard, is heard for all time." By this point, several other stars were vying for the opportunity of introducing Cole and Johnson songs and appearing with them on the sheet music covers. May Irwin, Lillian Russell, Irene Franklin, George Walker, Lew Dockstader, and Fay Templeton joined the line forming behind Cahill.[9]

Not everyone, however, was willing to work with the black musical comedy team. Harry B. Smith hired them to provide songs for *The Girl From Dixie* (1903), but composer A. E. Aarons found this objectionable. Smith explained that he wanted several composers to do the work, "to give the melodies varied color, you know, sort of a musical rainbow." Aarons replied, "With whom will I have the honor of associating?" Smith answered, "There will be quite a few. . . . Among others I have arranged with Will Cook, Cole and Johnson—." "That will be about all," responded Aarons. "You can take my name off the list. . . . Oh, you won't need me. I think you have enough color in your music without me. You may consider this incident closed."[10]

Aarons, however, was the exception. Abraham Erlanger called the trio after he heard "Under the Bamboo Tree" and offered them an unprecedented three-year contract. Cole and the Johnson brothers would write exclusively for Klaw and Erlanger productions. In return, the three would receive a monthly salary, a flat sum for each ensemble number, and royalties for each song. Shortly after the ink was dry, interviewers flocked to the new composing team, asking them to explain the secret of their success: "What we aim to do . . . is evolve a type of music that will have all that is distinct in the old Negro music and yet which shall be sophisticated enough to appeal to the cultured musician. We want the Negro spirit—its warmth and originality—to color our music; we want to retain its marked rhythms, but we are trying to get away from that minor strain that used to dominate it. I think that the Negro music of the future will be something akin to the Spanish, but not so vigorous. Something of a more languid music." Rosamond disagreed, and Cole qualified his remarks. "What I meant is that it would be as distinctively rhythmic as Spanish music is, so that no matter where you hear it, you will recognize it as Negro music." Cole said he intended to include such a song in the forthcoming Klaw and Erlanger show, *Mother Goose* (1903). He foresaw an "Evolution of the Negro Song" number (later called "The Evolution of Ragtime")

9. Reviews in Theatre Scrapbooks, 24, 39; *Vanity Fair* (January, 1926), 56.
10. New York *Telegraph*, June 16, 1903.

that "would take a simple melody—a regular jungle song with its boom-boom accompaniment like the pounding of log drums and trace it up through all the stages of Negro development." For Cole, the stages were the Jim Crow style; the Stephen Foster manner; the march song; "the cakewalk with its exuberance"; and the modern Negro song.[11]

The trio began work on *Humpty Dumpty* (1904), another Drury Lane pantomime. During rehearsals, they earned the trust and respect of Erlanger, who was easily one of the age's most irascible theatre producers. Rosamond had spent considerable time coaching the female lead. She performed acceptably in private, but at rehearsal she was unnerved by Erlanger's pacing and muttering at the back of the theatre. Her voice cracked and she often missed the proper notes. Erlanger commented caustically and raucously on every error. Finally he ran down the aisle, shouting, "Rossmore [Erlanger's erroneous name for Rosamond], we'll have to take that woman out and get somebody who can sing the part." Rosamond immediately retorted, "How in the world can you expect her to sing when you keep yelling at her?" A hush fell over the theatre: someone had, apparently for the first time, spoken back to Erlanger. After the incident, Erlanger treated the songwriters gingerly.[12]

The years with Klaw and Erlanger were generally prosperous, with the exception of the musical *In Newport* (1904). Erlanger pronounced the show "rotten," and Cole and the Johnsons readily agreed. The show closed at the end of the first week, and Erlanger brought in *Little Johnny Jones,* which had been enjoying a lengthy tour. This new musical brought George M. Cohan to Broadway with his two song hits, "I'm a Yankee Doodle Dandy" and "Give My Regards to Broadway." Thus Cole and the Johnsons' one failure paved the way for Cohan's eventual success.

By the time the Erlanger contract expired, Cole and the Johnsons were earning more than $25,000 each year in royalties from "Oh, Didn't He Ramble," "My Castle on the Nile," "Congo Love Song," "The Old Flag Never Touched the Ground," and "Tell Me, Dusky Maiden." Bob and Rosamond decided to resume their vaudeville act, since they had no immediate song-writing obligations on Broadway. They traveled throughout the United States and Europe. James accompanied them, and he especially enjoyed visiting Paris. Yet, once again, he was disturbed by his decreasing importance in the collaboration. When

11. Cleveland *Plain Dealer,* n.d., clipping in Theatre Scrapbooks, 2.
12. Johnson, *Along This Way,* 197–98.

Bob and Rosamond agreed to write a musical comedy in which they would also perform, James realized that the time for the break had come. James worked on the lyrics and libretto for *The Shoo-Fly Regiment* only halfheartedly, for he had set his sights elsewhere. He went to Washington, D.C., and took an exam for the consular service. With the help of a political ally, Charles W. Anderson, James was appointed American consul at Puerto Cabello, Venezuela. The split was amicable and allowed James to consider a new direction for his life. Within a short time, he would become a noted novelist, poet, and black political leader.

Cole and Johnson emerged from behind the scenes with *The Shoo-Fly Regiment* in 1907.[13] They not only wrote the libretto and songs for the musical, but they also starred in it. It was also their first show performed by an all-black cast. The plot centers on Hunter Wilson (Cole), a young graduate of Tuskegee Institute who is about to become a teacher. But the Spanish-American War erupts, and Hunter decides to defend his country. His patriotic zeal pleases his friends and neighbors, but his sweetheart, Rose Maxwell (Fannie Wise), feels that Hunter should remain at home. In the final scene of the first act, Rose returns Hunter's engagement ring.

Hunter is sent to the Philippines, where he leads an attack on an enemy fortress. The charge was carried out successfully every evening but opening night, when recalcitrant scenery refused to tumble after the cannon's volley. After some hasty adlibs to explain this incongruity, Hunter becomes a hero. He returns triumphantly to his Alabama home, and Rose finally agrees to marry him.

Although the plot may seem hackneyed by modern standards, it represented a major advance over other black musicals. First of all, the male leads were brave, educated, and patriotic, a far cry from the shuffling stereotypes of minstrel origin. Second, *The Shoo-Fly Regiment* included scenes of romance. While perfectly acceptable in white musical comedies, love scenes were taboo in black shows, since it was assumed that romancing would offend white audiences. Hence, a love duet in a black musical had to be done in a burlesque fashion, so the audience would not take it seriously. Cole and the Johnsons attempted to destroy this outrageous notion with the serious and tender love scenes between Hunter and Rose. Despite this effort to revise stereotypic notions of black behavior, the lovemaking taboo lingered into

13. "Cole and Johnson" File, TC/NYPL.

the 1920s on the Broadway stage. Noble Sissle recalled his fear as cast members of *Shuffle Along* sang the tender duet "Love Will Find a Way" in 1921. He expected the audience to pelt the performers with rotten eggs afterwards. He was greatly relieved and surprised when the audience instead demanded several encores.[14]

The critics greeted the new musical with rhapsodic notices, praising virtually every aspect of the production. Cole and Johnson won plaudits for their performances as well as for their "jingling catchy songs." The New York *Dramatic News* singled out "There's Always Something Wrong," "If Adam Hadn't Seen the Apple Tree," and "Won't You Be My Little Brown Bear?" as probable hits.[15]

Only one sour note marred the initial reaction to *The Shoo-Fly Regiment.* The critic for *Theatre* voiced a complaint that surfaced whenever a black musical refused to utilize the stereotypes that had evolved on the American stage: "[The colored authors] have much to learn before they can instruct or entertain our public. They may reach a certain standard, but, for the present, such performances are futile. If they are to advance, they must advance in a direction of their own. In the direction of imitation they will accomplish nothing, or nothing that is worth while, and by means of which they can attain to any dignity of their own."[16] *Theatre* dismissed the Cole and Johnson play because it was too imitative of white works. Blacks should therefore continue to write shows of a minstrel nature and leave modern musicals to white authors.

Cole and Johnson began to write their next musical while they were performing in *The Shoo-Fly Regiment. The Red Moon,* which opened on Broadway in 1909, was billed as "a sensation in red and black." The folklore of two of America's minorities—blacks and Indians—was the basis of this new musical comedy. Cole claimed that they decided to do the show while traveling through the western United States with their vaudeville act. Cole and Johnson performed on an Apache reservation, and they discussed Indian music and folklore with their hosts. Rosamond eventually integrated Indian-style melodies into his score for *The Red Moon.*[17]

The red moon of the title was an omen of bad luck to the blacks

14. Robert Kimball and William Bolcom, *Reminiscing with Sissle and Blake* (New York, 1973), 93.

15. New York *Dramatic News,* [1907], clipping in "Cole and Johnson" File, TC/NYPL.

16. *Theatre* (September, 1907), n.p., *ibid.*

17. *The Red Moon* libretto, in Howard University Library; score, in MC/LC.

Blue Book cartoon of Cole and Johnson in *The Red Moon*
Courtesy Billy Rose Theatre Collection, New York Public Library

Cole (Slim Brown) and Johnson (Plunk Green) in *The Red Moon*
Courtesy Philadelphia Free Library Theatre Collection

in the cast and a call to war to the Indians. Needless to say, this dual meaning led to several plot complications. Minnehaha (Abbie Mitchell), half-Indian and half-black, lives with her mother on a Virginia farm. Her delinquent father, Chief Lowdog (Arthur Talbot), decides that he misses his long-lost daughter, so he kidnaps her and takes her to his reservation. Slim Brown (Cole) and Plunk Green (Johnson), Minnehaha's boyfriend, try to rescue her from her father's clutches. Brown and Green disguise themselves as Indians and depart for the West. After several war dances in the second act, Plunk rescues Minnehaha, and the chief and his wife are reconciled.

The New York *Dramatic News* called *The Red Moon* "brilliant," and the *Mirror* found it "well worth seeing." The only complaint that the latter critic could find to mention was that "the colored young women should be taught to put on their make-up properly." Johnson's score was praised as "ambitious," especially the songs with Indian motifs—"Land of the Setting Sun," "Big Red Shawl," and "I Want to Be an Indian."[18] The show was such a success that Cole and Johnson toured with *The Red Moon* for almost a year. Once again they had produced a black musical that avoided the derogatory stereotypes that had afflicted other such ventures. The audiences, mostly white, but with a few blacks in the balcony, rarely objected to this new style of black musical.

Bob Cole's health began to deteriorate during the lengthy tour of *The Red Moon.* His personal physician thought he had had a nervous breakdown, and advised him to take a rest cure. Cole packed his bags with the pills and powders the doctor recommended, and sought out a small boardinghouse in the Catskills. The landlady and the cook welcomed the New York celebrity and promised that they would do everything in their power to nurse Cole back to health.

With few distractions, Cole slept the nights and days away. He confided to his landlady that he finally enjoyed his first full night's sleep in months. When Cole was not sleeping, he was eating the hearty meals prepared by the friendly cook. Although the doctor had prescribed a light diet, the cook overruled him. She prepared roast chicken, cream of tomato soup, roast beef, and mountain trout in her attempt to put some flesh on the bones of her thin lodger. The cook's regimen seemed to be helping. After a two-week period of nothing but eating and

18. New York *Dramatic News,* May 15, 1909, New York *Mirror,* May 15, 1909, clippings in "Cole and Johnson" File, TC/NYPL.

sleeping, Cole began to exercise at the cook's insistence. He chopped wood for the kitchen fire and began working in the nearby fields. Soon he grew stronger, but callouses, warts, and bunions continued to nag him.

Although Cole was feeling remarkably better, one fact began to disturb him. After his fourth week in the country, his body seemed to be puffing up. His clothes, which always hung loosely on his lanky frame, now no longer buttoned. He called the local doctor, who was bewildered by Cole's condition. A specialist was summoned from New York City to analyze this supposedly grave condition. The physician calmed Cole and explained that he had been overeating and merely gaining weight. The phenomenon had appeared to be a disease to Cole, since he had never before experienced flabbiness.

The long rest had restored Cole's health, and he returned to New York City to undertake a variety of projects. Cole and Johnson began to talk of ambitious new shows that would broaden the horizons of musical comedy. Johnson suggested to Oscar Hammerstein that they do an operatic version of *Uncle Tom's Cabin.* He envisioned it as a "one-act opera, beginning lightly, showing the sports of the slave quarters, the slave auction, and ending with the separation of Uncle Tom and his wife." At the same time Cole began work on a "Negro operetta" called *Sambo's Dream.* He first thought of the show after a conversation with his adopted son, who had a fondness for fairy tales and fantastic stories. Cole's libretto concerned "a little Sambo dreaming of a mystic land, where he encountered the spectre who takes care of bad boys and the cheerful fellow who has the care of good boys." In addition to writing the libretto and lyrics, Cole intended to direct and choreograph.[19]

As Cole and Johnson planned the successors to *The Shoo-Fly Regiment* and *The Red Moon,* they inaugurated a new vaudeville act. Their twenty-three-minute act featured their newest songs ("Prophylactic Pluto Lee" and "Ring Dem Bells") as well as their old standards ("Under the Bamboo Tree" and "Congo Love Song"), which were usually reserved for encores. Cole also had a new specialty monologue that threaded the titles of current hit Broadway shows into a humorous story. In the middle of one of his songs, a gong would sound and Cole would step forward and recite: " 'Tis *The Witching Hour.* I will call up *The Girl Behind the Counter,* make a compact with *The Servant in the*

19. New York *Telegraph,* October 9, 1910.

House of the famous *Warrens of Virginia,* who are entertaining *The Yankee Prince* on *The Merry-Go-Round,* steal into the house like *The Thief,* outwit *Father and the Boys,* . . . while the *Girls* are asleep, I'll sustain *The Honor of the Family* by implanting *The Soul Kiss* on the ruby lips of *The Merry Widow* and in *Three Weeks,* I know I'll be *Paid in Full.*"[20] Contemporary audiences delighted in Cole's skillful tale, often laughing and applauding at great length.

Cole and Johnson traveled from city to city and theatre to theatre with their successful vaudeville routine. At the same time they continued work on theatrical projects. The pressure became too much for Cole, and after an engagement at Keith and Proctor's Fifth Avenue Theatre, he appeared to be on the verge of collapse. Cole's father and mother attempted to take him to Bellevue Hospital in a cab, but Cole managed to get away.

The next day, a former member of the Cole and Johnson vaudeville company saw Bob on Ninety-eighth Street near Columbus Avenue, where he was singing incoherently and tap dancing. She called the police, and they convinced Cole to come to the station to give a performance. Meanwhile, they called an ambulance from J. Hood Wright Hospital. Cole fought the attendants, but they overpowered him. After a brief examination, Cole was sent to Bellevue.

Doctors first diagnosed Cole's malady as general paresis, a disease of the brain caused by syphilis, and announced that there was no cure. They explained that "his death may occur at any moment, although it is one of the vagaries of the disease that, while it disposes quickly of some victims, it lingers on indefinitely with others." A premature obituary in the New York *Review* (which abandoned all hope for Cole's getting well) explained that Cole "was one of the cleverest men of his race upon the stage."[21]

Specialists revised the pessimistic assessment. They decided that the diagnosis was erroneous and attributed Cole's condition to a nervous breakdown. Cole was shifted from one private hospital to another, until he slowly began to improve in the spring of 1911. He decided to return to the Catskills, site of his first recovery, and join his mother at the family's summer vacation retreat. Cole seemed in fine spirits, and he often performed his songs for guests at the lodge. One Saturday morning, while walking with friends near a stream, Cole excused

20. *Ibid.*, May 3, 1908.
21. New York *Review,* November 12, 1910.

himself and slowly waded into the water. He swam for a few minutes and then abruptly stopped. He allowed himself to sink to the bottom without uttering a word. His friends finally realized that Cole had disappeared, and they rushed to save him, but it was too late. Cole died at the age of forty-three.

Cole's illness and death placed J. Rosamond Johnson's career in limbo. While Cole had remained in various hospitals, Rosamond performed only occasionally, whenever money was needed for his partner's medical treatment. After Cole's suicide, Johnson temporarily stopped performing. In early 1912, he began searching for a new partner. Fate supplied a likely candidate in Charles Hart. Hart's partner, Dan Avery, died suddenly after a performance at the Fifth Avenue Theatre, the site of Cole and Johnson's last booking.

Hart was the exact opposite of Bob Cole. Cole always remained the gentleman; Hart was the buffoon. Cole was noted for his verbal humor; Hart specialized in the pratfall. For example, Hart devoted several minutes of the act to a pantomime of his sitting on a hot stove and fanning his backside. *Variety* urged that this tired shtick be eliminated.[22]

Not everyone compared Hart unfavorably with Bob Cole. The critic for the New York *Telegraph* noted: "Bob Cole was undeniably a clever man, but a little too legitimate in his methods to be accepted as a colored comedian. The public is inclined to accept a colored comedian only if he is grotesque, this applying in a degree even to that wonderful humorist, Bert Williams, to whom Charles Hart is often likened." It is ironic that "grotesque" became a compliment in describing a "colored comedian" near the turn of the century. Cole's genius lay in his ability to fracture the minstrel stereotypes. Hart's depiction of the "lazy, slouchy and shuffling smoke," as the *Telegraph* called it, negated Cole's attempts to eliminate black stereotypes on the musical stage.[23]

Despite favorable reviews for the new team, Johnson dropped Hart and turned to other pursuits. Oscar Hammerstein appointed Johnson musical director of his Grand Opera House in London. While there, Johnson married his childhood sweetheart, Nora Floyd. The couple returned to New York City, where Rosamond established the Music School Settlement for Colored People, which trained several generations of students. During this period, Rosamond seemed to lose interest in the musical comedy stage, which had brought him fame. He began

22. *Variety,* June 8, 1912.
23. New York *Telegraph,* June 4, 1912.

to research black music in America and, with his brother James, wrote *The Book of American Negro Spirituals* (1925). Although Rosamond was lured back to the Broadway stage as an actor in the 1930s and 1940s (*Porgy and Bess, Mamba's Daughters,* and *Cabin in the Sky*), he never returned to writing musical comedies. Bob Cole's death ended the career of one of the most promising musical comedy teams yet seen on Broadway. As both writers and performers, the pair dazzled audiences throughout the nation. The Toledo *Blade* noted that when the "Negro made his first appearance on the stage as a musical comedy entertainer, the public looked askance at him." Now, "white producers should take a lesson" from Cole and Johnson, since the black team was raising the quality of musical comedy.[24]

24. Toledo *Blade,* n.d., clipping in "Cole and Johnson" File, TC/NYPL.

III

THE BACK-TO-AFRICA MUSICALS

Bert Williams and George Walker

At the turn of the century a modern minstrel appeared on the musical stage. He wore shabby clothes, ankle-length pants, oversized shoes, an old top-hat, and a heavy layer of burnt cork on his face. This comic figure, "a shambling, shuffling, darky," as James Weldon Johnson called Bert Williams, masked a tall, handsome gentleman who became one of the leading performers in black musicals in the first decade of this century. Williams and his partner George Walker proved to theatre managers that white audiences would attend black shows in the city's most elegant theatres. Williams and Walker legitimized the role of the black performer in the Broadway musical, just as Bob Cole and the Johnson brothers proved that black songwriters could write successfully for the musical stage. The new team appeared in a string of all-Negro shows, effectively opening Broadway's musical comedies to black performers, writers, and directors.[1]

Williams and Walker never dreamed of such success when they were young. Current wisdom suggested that the black man could never be more than a mere minstrel on the musical stage. George Walker began his career with a troupe of black minstrels in his hometown, Lawrence, Kansas. Walker visited the farthest corners of the state with this show, but he realized that he had to strike out on his own if he was to become a success. He traveled slowly west, taking odd jobs to support his improbable quest. Usually Walker would arrive in a town and seek out a medicine show. The quack doctors found that Walker's ability to "sing and dance, beat the tambourine, and rattle the

1. For biographical information, see Ann Charters, *Nobody: The Story of Bert Williams* (New York, 1970). Also of interest is Sandra Richards, "Bert Williams: His Stage Career and Influence on the American Theatre" (Ph.D. dissertation, Stanford University, 1973).

bones" attracted large crowds of willing customers for the patent medicine. As soon as Walker earned enough money in one place, he moved on. When Walker finally reached San Francisco, he abandoned medicine shows and began to search for theatrical employment. Walker had little luck until he spotted a "gaunt fellow over six feet, of orange hue, and about eighteen years of age, leaning on a banjo, haggling with a manager." This striking fellow was Egbert Austin Williams, a West Indian whose family had migrated to Los Angeles by way of Panama. He told Walker that his friends called him Bert and that he, too, wanted a stage career.[2]

Williams, unlike Walker, had not always dreamed of appearing in the theatre. During his high school years in southern California, Williams hoped to attend Stanford University. However, three white friends persuaded him to join their theatrical troupe. They traveled through California by bus and entertained people living in small towns. The tour was a disaster, for Williams had his first contacts with race prejudice. Often Williams' partners would get rooms at a local hotel, but the innkeeper would say to Bert, "I know you, Williams, and I like you, and I would like nothing better than to have you stay here, but, you see, we have Southern gentlemen in the house and they would object." After their long tour, the quartet reached San Francisco. All they had were their clothes, which were so ridden with lice that they had to be burned. Williams parted company with his friends and took to the road as a solo act.

Williams and Walker joined forces and found a job as a vaudeville act for fourteen dollars a week. They spent as much time working as not, and they devoted their free evenings to visiting other performances in search of a gimmick that would help their struggling act. Williams and Walker found the local "coon" (minstrel) shows fascinating, as white actors donned black makeup in order to imitate the singing and dancing of Negro performers. They thought these presentations absurdly unnatural, and they reasoned that black entertainers could present these routines in a more interesting and enjoyable fashion.

Williams and Walker billed themselves as the "Two Real Coons," but the light-skinned Williams felt compelled to adhere to current stage conventions and wear burnt cork, despite personal misgivings.

2. George W. Walker, "The Real 'Coon' on the American Stage," *Theatre Magazine* (August, 1906), 224.

Williams at first played the straight man and Walker the stooge, but they discovered that they were better suited for the opposite roles. Walker became the fast-talking dandy, and Williams the slow-moving, poorly dressed clown. They assumed these roles during their entire career, but with each year these mere outlines grew. Williams added a unique sense of pathos to his comic persona, and Walker's dress and rhetoric dazzled the critics and the public alike.[3]

The novelty of the new act attracted the attention of local managers, and the team was booked into San Francisco's Midway Theatre. After a successful run on the West Coast, the Two Real Coons embarked on a road tour that would end in New York City. George Lederer, a Broadway theatre manager and producer, claimed credit for bringing the Williams and Walker duo to New York City. In 1896, Lederer was producing *The Gold Bug,* an early effort by Victor Herbert and Glen MacDonough. Although Herbert later became America's most renowned composer of operettas, he had already written two Broadway failures, *Prince Ananias* (1894) and *The Wizard of the Nile* (1895), and *The Gold Bug* looked like another disaster. Lederer thought the show could be saved if the comic elements were emphasized. He had heard of a new comedy team, Williams and Walker, then performing in Indiana, whose routines might be able to save *The Gold Bug.* Lederer wired them that "if they could get to New York by September 14th they could have an engagement in *The Gold Bug.*" Williams read the telegram and shouted, "If we could get there! As if we wouldn't have crawled there on our knees!"[4]

The comic duo hurried to New York City, and Lederer asked them to perform for a group of friends. The show business audience greeted the Two Real Coons coldly, and several individuals advised Lederer not to use them in *The Gold Bug.* Some argued that Williams and Walker's material was mediocre; other said that their color would limit their chances for success on the Broadway stage.

Lederer accepted the opinions of his cohorts. *The Gold Bug* opened without Williams and Walker—and received the disastrous reviews everyone had expected. In a last-ditch effort to save the show, Lederer asked Williams and Walker to appear in the second night's performance. At an early rehearsal, the team distributed their music to the orchestra. Their ragtime melodies offered a sharp contrast to Herbert's

3. Bert Williams, "The Comic Side of Trouble," *American Magazine* (January, 1918), 33–35.

4. *Variety,* March 17, 1922, p. 14.

operetta-style score. In fact, many members of the orchestra claimed that they were unable to play the newfangled music.

After a long day of rehearsals, Williams and Walker managed to interpolate their act into *The Gold Bug*. Although the rest of the show remained as mediocre as the night before, the audience loved the new comedy team. Lederer commented: "It was the first time I had seen a musical moke team stop a show." Although *The Gold Bug* quickly closed, Williams and Walker had made a name for themselves on Broadway. They were immediately booked for a New York vaudeville stand and an East Coast tour. In 1900 the team returned to Broadway in their own show, *The Policy Players,* a vaudeville farce with music.

Within three years, Williams and Walker had risen from a second-rate vaudeville act to Broadway stardom. Yet, during this period, they remained the Two Real Coons of their earlier days. Essentially they had borrowed white images of black performers from the minstrel show. Although these roles were popular with white audiences, they tended to perpetuate archaic stereotypes of black behavior. Williams and Walker began to envision a new direction for their act.

The Sons of Ham (1900) marked the first major change in their stage relationship. While Williams was appearing in this show, he and Alex Rogers wrote a new song that humanized Williams' shuffling minstrel image—the pathetic figure managed to be funny and tragic at the same time. This new characterization allowed audiences to laugh at as well as with Bert Williams. "I'm a Jonah Man" provided the key to the new persona:

> My luck started when I was born,
> Leas' so the old folks say.
> Dat same hard luck's been my bes' frien'
> To dis very day.
> When I was young, Mamma's friends—to find a name they tried,
> They named me after Pappa—and de same day Pappa died, Fo' . . .
>
> *Chorus:*
> I'm a Jonah. I'm a Jonah man,
> My family for many years would look at me and den shed tears.
> Why I am dis Jonah
> I sho' can't understand,
> But I'm a good substantial, full-fledged, real, first-class Jonah man.
>
> A frien' of mine gave me a six month's meal ticket one day.
> He said, "It won't do me no good, I got to go away."

I thanked him as my heart with joy and gratitude did bound,
But when I reached the restaurant, the place had just burned down.

Delivered in a slow and deliberate fashion, the song expressed Williams' bewilderment at the predicaments fate had in store for him. As a Jonah man, he became a person who waited for disaster to happen to him.

As Williams solidified his stage identity, Walker also began to search for new directions for the team's work. Although *The Policy Players* and *The Sons of Ham* were full-length plays, both were essentially improvised. Working from a plot outline, Williams and Walker changed routines nightly, keeping the bits and pieces that seemed to work. The script, if indeed there was one, often evolved after the fact. Walker envisioned a more formal structure for their next show. It would be a musical comedy rather than a collection of vaudeville routines.

In Dahomey (1903) first revealed Williams and Walker's fascination with African themes and characters.[5] Walker believed that shifting the focus of their work might help them lose the remnants of minstrel characterizations that still remained in their routines. The choice of Dahomey stemmed from an adventure in the early days of their collaboration. In 1893, several natives of Dahomey were imported to San Francisco to be part of an exhibit at the Midwinter Fair. Unfortunately, the ship was delayed, so the promoters hired American blacks as substitutes. Desperate for money, Williams and Walker donned loincloths and feathers in order to impersonate the absent Africans. When the ship arrived shortly thereafter, Williams and Walker were relieved of their jobs. Nevertheless, the team remained to observe the Dahomeans. It was there that the team decided that "if we ever reached the point of having a show of our own, we would delineate and feature native African characters."[6]

Despite lofty motives, *In Dahomey* spent only a short time in Africa. Rareback Pinkerton (Walker) and Shylock Homestead (Williams) search for a "silver casket with a cat drawed on the outside," which was stolen from Mr. Cicero Lightfoot of Gatorville, Florida. Unable to find the valuable box, Pinkerton and Homestead decide to go to Florida and con Lightfoot out of the $500 reward. With their newfound wealth Rareback and Shylock hope to escape to Dahomey with the African Colonization Society. Rareback paints an image of the golden

5. *In Dahomey* libretto, in MC/LC.
6. Walker, "The Real 'Coon,'" 224.

The cast of *In Dahomey:* Hattie McIntosh, George Walker, Ada Overton Walker, Bert Williams, and Lottie Williams
Courtesy Billy Rose Theatre Collection, New York Public Library

future awaiting them: "Stick to me and after we're in Dahomey for six months, if you like it, I'll buy it for you and I'll tell the king over there that I'm a surveyor and you're a contractor. If he asks for a recommendation I'll tell him to go to New York and take a look at Broadway. It's the best job the firm ever did, and, if he don't mind, we'll build him a Broadway in the jungle." Rareback and Shylock then explain the glories of their firm's work in "On Broadway in Dahomey":

> If we went to Dahomey, suppose the king would say,
> We want a Broadway built for us, we want it right away.
> We'd get a bunch of natives—say ten thousand or more,
> Wid banyan trees build a big department store—
> We'd sell big Georgia possums—some watermelons too—
> To get the coin for the other things we'd like to do—
> If we couldn't have real horse cars we'd use zebras for awhile,
> On the face of the Broadway clock—use a Crock-o-(dial).

Cicero Lightfoot finds a pot of gold in Act II, which allows everyone in the cast to visit Dahomey in Act III, where the plot's loose ends become resolved. The silver casket is found, and Lightfoot, disgusted with Dahomey, announces his intention to return to America. Shylock and Pinkerton, however, decide to remain, since they have become the new rulers of Dahomey:

> Evah dahkey is a King,
> Royalty is jes' de ting.
> Ef yo' social life is a bungle,
> Jes' you go back to yo' jungle,
> An' remember dat you daddy was a king.
>
> White fo'ks what's got dahkey servants,
> Try and get dem everything.
> You must never speak insulting
> You may be talking to a king.

In Dahomey became the first all-black show to play a major Broadway theatre. As a result, the social implications of the theatrical event received greater press coverage than did the play itself. Once the New York *Times* reviewer discovered that rumors of a race war on opening night had proved unfounded, he began to survey the show's audience. He noted that the footlights drew a "sharp color line" in the theatre—the only blacks on the main floor of the house were James Vaughn, the conductor, and the ushers. Onstage, however, was a "rhapsody of

Williams and Walker in *In Dahomey*
Courtesy Philadelphia Free Library Theatre Collection

color": "The actors were dark, medium, and light. Some of them were so light that they might have passed for white, except that the flare of a nostril, the weight of an eyelid, or the delicate fullness of a lip betrayed them to minute inspection. One of the chorus girls clearly had blonde hair that was not peroxide."[7]

Once the novelty of the spectacle had worn off, the press turned its attention to the stars and the show. *Theatre Magazine* lavishly praised Williams and Walker's latest effort, calling it an "unquestionable success." The review singled out Bert Williams: "He is spontaneously and genuinely funny. Nature has endowed him with a comic mask, and he succeeds in obtaining with voice and gesture ludicrous effects that are irresistible." *In Dahomey* was such a success in New York that it was booked into the Shaftesbury Theatre in London. Williams and Walker were somewhat apprehensive, since they had appeared in England during their vaudeville days and the British were unable to understand their particular brand of humor. The show was a modest success at first, but a command performance at Buckingham Palace generated substantial interest and publicity that turned *In Dahomey* into a hit. There were some worries about performing "Evah Dahkey Is a King" before the royal family, but Edward VII seemed to enjoy the show immensely.[8] After a tour of the provinces, *In Dahomey* reopened in New York City in 1904 prior to an American tour. The show returned a 400 percent profit to producers Hurtig and Seamon, which seemed to finally quash the notion that all-Negro shows inevitably lost money.

Despite the lofty expectations of George Walker, *In Dahomey* did little to enlighten audiences about African culture. Indeed, some critics thought that Williams and Walker had gratuitously put their old vaudeville routine into an African setting without the slightest thought. Albert Ross, a black professor of business at a midwestern university, wrote to the team shortly after the close of *In Dahomey,* complaining that they "held the old plantation Negro, the ludicrous darkey, and the scheming grafter up to entertain people." He suggested that the duo write of prominent Negroes, such as "Locke, the Negro Rhodes scholar at Oxford," so the "young Negro mind would imitate and emulate these heroes."

Williams and Walker replied in an open letter printed in *Variety* in

7. New York *Times,* February 19, 1903.

8. *Theatre Magazine* (April, 1906), xiv. See R. C. Simmons, "Europe's Reception to Negro Talent," *Colored American Magazine* (1905), 635–42; and Jeffrey P. Green, "*In Dahomey* in London in 1903," *Black Perspective in Music,* xi (Spring, 1983), 22–40.

SHAFTESBURY THEATRE
SHAFTESBURY AVENUE, W.
Proprietors ... ... Representatives of the late JOHN LANCASTER
Sole Lessee ... ... Mr. GEO. MUSGROVE

Every Evening at 8.15, Matinee Wednesday and Saturday at 2.15,
Messrs. HURTIG & SEAMON present
WILLIAMS & WALKER
IN THEIR RECENT SUCCESS,
"IN DAHOMEY,"

A Musical Comedy in Two Acts, Preceded by a Prologue, Written and Staged by JESSE A. SHIPP.
Lyrics by PAUL LAWRENCE DUNBAR and ALEX ROGERS. Music Composed by WILL MARION COOK.

PROLOGUE.
TIME—Three months before beginning of Play. PLACE—DAHOMEY.
CHARACTERS.
Je-Je, a caboceer ... CHAS. MOORE
Menuki, Messenger of the King ... WM. ELKINS
Mose Lightfoot, Agent of Dahomey Colonization Society ... WM. BARKER
Soldiers, Natives, etc.

Cast of Characters.
Shylock Homestead, called "Shy" by his friends ... BERT A. WILLIAMS
Rareback Pinkerton, "Shy's" personal friend and adviser ... GEO. W. WALKER
Hamilton Lightfoot, president of a colonization Society ... PETE HAMPTON
Dr. Straight (in name only), street fakir ... FRED DOUGLAS
Mose Lightfoot, brother of Hamilton, thinks Dahomey a land of great promise ... WM. BARKER
George Reeder, proprietor of an intelligence office ... ALEX ROGERS
Henry Stampfield, letter carrier, with an argument against immigration WALTER RICHARDSON
Me Sing, a Chinese cook ... GEO. CATLIN
Hustling Charley, promoter of Get-the-Coin Syndicate ... J. A. SHIPP
Leather, a bootblack ... RICHARD CONNORS
Officer Still ... J. LEUBRIE HILL
White Wash Man ... GREEN TAPLEY
Messenger Rush, but not often ... THEODORE PANKEY
Cecilia Lightfoot, Hamilton's wife ... Mrs. HATTIE McINTOSH
Mrs. Stringer, dealer in forsaken patterns, also editor of fashion-notes in "Beanville Agitator" ... Miss DAISY TAPLEY
Rosetta Lightfoot, a troublesome young thing ... AIDA OVERTON WALKER
Colonists, Natives, etc.

SYNOPSIS.
PROLOGUE: Scene—Garden of the Caboceer (Governor of a Province)
ACT I., ... Public Square, Boston
ACT II., Scene 1, Exterior of Lightfoot's Home, Gatorville, Florida
Scene 2 ... Road, one-and-a-half miles from Gatorville
Scene 3 ... Interior of Lightfoot's Home

SPECIAL.—At Finale of last Act will be presented a Grand Spectacular CAKE WALK.
The Management accord a Prize to the couple who have, by the verdict of the audience as shown by their applause, best deserved the Cake.

MUSICAL NUMBERS.
PROLOGUE.
Dahomian Queen Mattie Edwardes, Morris Smith & Company
"Caboceers Choral" ... Company
ACT I.
Overture...
Opening Chorus "Swing Along" ...
"Mollie Green" ... Henry Troy and Chorus
"My Castle on the River Nile" (interpolated) ... Geo. W. Walker and Chorus
"Broadway in Dahomey" (interpolated) ... Williams, Walker and Company
ACT II.
"A Actor Lady" ... Aida Overton Walker and Misses Maggie Davis, Nettie Glinn, Odessa Warren, Rein Norris, Jessie Ellis, Katie Jones, Ida Day, Lavinia Gaston, Laura Bowman, Pauline Freeman
"Brown Skin Baby Mine" ... Ada Guignesse and Chorus
"Society" Pete Hampton, Hattie McIntosh, Lloyd Gibbs, Richard Connors and Company
(Soprano Solo by Ella Anderson).
"The Jonah Man" (interpolated) ... Bert Williams
Minuet, "Al'Africaine," Aida Overton Walker & Male Chorus
"The Czar," with Dreams of Spanish Royalty, &c., George Walker assisted by Aida Overton Walker and Company
"Emancipation Day" ... Williams, Walker and Company
Emancipation Day March and Cake Walk Finale.
The Statue in this scene is done by Mr. Walter Richardson.

The Orchestra under the Direction of Mr. James Vaughan.
JAMES LENT, America's Best Orchestral Drummer.
Lyrics of "Broadway in Dahomey," "Jonah Man" and "The Czar," by ALEX ROGERS. "Dahomian Queen" written by F. B. WILLIAMS and J. LEUBRIE HILL.

Music published by Messrs. KEITH, PROWSE & Co., Ltd., 48, Cheapside, E.C.

Manager ... (for Messrs. Hurtig & Seamon) ... Mr. GEO. H. HARRIS
Personal Representative ... (for Williams & Walker) ... Mr. CHAS. L. MOORE
Acting Manager ... Mr. L. A. GROTH

PRICES OF ADMISSION.—Private Boxes, £3 3s., £1 11s. 6d. and £1 1s. Stalls, 10s. 6d. Balcony Stalls (First Four Rows), 7s. 6d. Other Rows, 6s. Upper Circle, 4s. Pit, 2s. 6d. Amphitheatre, 1s. 6d. Gallery, 1s. Box Office (Mr. J. WATTS) Open All Day.

Extract from the Rules made by the Lord Chamberlain.
(1). The name of the actual and responsible Manager of the Theatre must be printed on every play bill. (2). The Public can leave the Theatre at the end of the performance by all exit and entrance doors, which must open outwards. (3). Where there is a fire-proof screen to the proscenium opening, it must be lowered at least once during every performance to ensure its being in proper working order. (4). Smoking is not permitted in the Auditorium. (5). All gangways, passages and staircases must be kept free from chairs or any other obstructions, whether permanent or temporary.

G. HARMSWORTH & Co., Printers, 42, Floral Street, Covent Garden, W.C. Telephone 664 Central.

In Dahomey program from London opening
Courtesy Billy Rose Theatre Collection, New York Public Library

1907. Their answer revealed the strictures that governed the black performer on Broadway then. The team cautioned the professor to remember that they were entirely dependent on white audiences and critics for their livelihood. Therefore, black artists had to keep in mind the expectations of those audiences. Williams and Walker acknowledged that they often conformed to whites' stereotypes of Negroes, but they were still proud that their shows were written and staged by blacks. Thus they performed an important task in bringing black creative artists such as Alex Rogers, Jesse Shipp, and J. Leubrie Hill to the Broadway stage. They also provided employment for numerous black actors and actresses. Elevating the black image in the American mind remained a task for future generations.[9]

Abyssinia (1906), the Williams and Walker musical that followed *In Dahomey,* fulfilled the team's promise. The view of Africa does not seem terribly dated even at the present time. Indeed, several of the scenes foreshadow *Timbuktu!* (1978), Geoffrey Holder's reworking of *Kismet.* The Africans of *Abyssinia* were depicted as representatives of an ancient and praiseworthy culture, and Americans were the targets of humor.[10]

Rastus Johnson (Walker) enters riding a mule, and Jasper Jenkins (Williams) follows on foot. Rastus recently won $15,000 in a lottery, so he decided to take his relatives and his friend Jasper on a tour of Europe. However, an unfortunate incident forced them to flee from the Parisian police and continue their tour in faraway Abyssinia:

> From London I just thought I'd take a run to dear old Paris gay,
> To buy more wine and see more sights and throw more coin away.
> But to tell you the truth folks, Paris ain't no hit with me,
> 'Cause all you get on every hand's, "Wee-wee, Monsieur, wee-wee."
> A man once said to me, says he, you'se Coon African.
> I fairly screamed, screamed I, no sir, I'll have you understand.
>
> I'm just plain Rastus Johnson from the U.S.A.
> Now I think, sir, that you are simply poking fun at me,
> To add insult to injury, the man just grinned and said, "Wee-wee."
> Assault and batt'ry, Rastus Johnson U.S.A.

This was certainly a far cry from the "coon songs" at the turn of the century; it was one of the first black songs to show any dissatisfaction with the term.

Menelik, the Grand Emperor of Abyssinia, invites Ras to a feast (*ras* means "prince" in the Abyssinian tongue). Ras takes advantage of the confusion and courts a young princess named Miram. Miram listens to Ras's tales of his Kansas homeland, but is unable to understand the strange customs of that distant country: "Americans are so strange. Men with income of $10,000 a year are always in debt, and, in conse-

9. *Variety,* December 14, 1907.
10. *Abyssinia* libretto, in MC/LC; playbill information, in TC/PFL.

Bert Williams and Lottie Williams in *Abyssinia*
Courtesy Billy Rose Theatre Collection, New York Public Library

quence, lead miserable lives, while others raise a family of ten children on ten dollars a week and all are happy."

Ras and Jas attend the feast, but Ras is mistaken for a rebel chief. He flees from the feast and is cornered in the market. Jas grabs a vase from a market stall to defend his friend, and he is charged with theft. The penalty for thievery is the loss of the offending hand. Jas looks at the vase and then at his hand, and, in a bewildered state of mind, he sings another Jonah man song, "Here It Comes Again":

> I b'lieve I'm about to find myself where I started from.
> They say that money does bad things, well, I've been handling some.
> And yet I know bad luck would come, it's as plain as ABC
> 'Cause something's buzzing in my ear and whispering it to me.
>
> Here it comes again—plague take it, here it comes again,
> But when the feeling comes a-stealing, it's no use to complain.
> I thought that Jonah spell had passed, but I was figuring it too fast.
> My dream, it was too good to last, Dog bite it, here it comes again.
>
> I had brain fever one time and had fierce pains in my head.
> And now I know exactly what Doc Smith meant when he said,
> "If any time insanity should stare you in the face,
> You'll find an awful funny strange sensation taking place."
>
> Here it comes again, good gracious, here it comes again.
> But when that feeling comes a-stealing, it's no use to complain,
> The doctor says it is a fact, that I'm some kind of a maniac,
> My upper story is cracked, I feel it, here it comes again.

Miram intercedes with Menelik and explains the misunderstanding. Ras and Jas are freed, and they decide to leave immediately for home:

> Good-bye, good-bye Ethiopia, we may come back some day,
> You have been good to us, your land would do for us,
> But we can no longer stay.
> Good luck, good luck to our new found friends,
> To keep your friendship we will try,
> We all wish you success, may you ever progress,
> Ethiopia, good-bye.

The reviews of *Abyssinia* were generally favorable, and all reviewers praised the costumes and the spectacular scenery. Only *Theatre Magazine* offered a sour note, as it criticized Williams and Walker for their excessive ambition. By attempting to leave stereotypes of Africa be-

Ernest Hogan and Carita Day in *The Oyster Man*
Courtesy Billy Rose Theatre Collection, New York Public Library

hind, Williams and Walker created "a white man's show acted by colored men, whereas to be entirely successful it should have been a colored men's show acted by themselves." This criticism would be heard repeatedly until the 1930s whenever black authors and performers attempted to shatter the common stereotypes that were engraved in the white mind. A "separate, but equal" rule began to exist in the world of musical comedy: black shows and white shows assumed rigid characteristics in the opinion of major critics. If a black musical abandoned the stereotypes that survived from the minstrel era, it was often criticized for lacking the genre's standard conventions (as defined by white critics).[11]

This irony reveals the difficulty of using reviews for reconstructing the history of black theatre. White critics for the major newspapers determined in most cases the success or failure of each new show. As ambition was often discouraged among black creative artists, success often meant producing a musical or a drama that would satisfy the preconceptions or stereotypes held by the major reviewers—a practice that certainly stifled innovation. Hence, more adventurous shows might receive the worst reviews, and conventional ones might have a successful run. Only in the 1920s would the dominance of white theatrical opinion be slightly lessened as black drama critics presented their views in such journals as the *Messenger* and *Opportunity* as well as in the Harlem press. While alternative views of new plays would appear, the major New York City dailies continued to determine the fate of most theatrical presentations.

Bandanna Land (1908) was the most highly praised of the Williams and Walker shows. The New York *Dramatic Mirror* explained that it was "one of the rare plays that one feels like witnessing a second time."[12] This musical abandoned the African locale and switched to a topic closer to home. *Bandanna Land* involved the attempts of Bud Jenkins (Walker) to swindle a railway company in a land speculation deal. At the same time, Jenkins hopes to relieve Skunkton Bowser (Williams) of his fortune. Jenkins successfully tricks the railway firm, but, at the last moment, Bowser realizes Jenkins' foul intentions and outwits him. Critics praised every aspect of the show—the songs, the performances, and the staging. It seemed to be the most joyful Williams and Walker effort. Unfortunately, it was the last.

11. *Theatre Magazine* (April, 1906), xiv.

12. New York *Dramatic Mirror,* February 3, 1908. For an interview with Walker following a performance of *Bandanna Land* (or *Bandana Land*), see "Over the Color Line," unidentified article, February 24, 1908, in "Bert Williams" File, SCCF/NYPL.

George Walker and Ada Overton Walker in *Bandanna Land*
Courtesy Billy Rose Theatre Collection, New York Public Library

Early in the run of *Bandanna Land,* Walker began to exhibit symptoms of general paresis. He lisped, stuttered, and forgot his lines. He continued his role until February, 1909, but the disease had progressed too far. *Bandanna Land* was Walker's last stage appearance, and he died in 1911. During the final weeks of the show's run, Walker's wife, Ada (Aida) Overton Walker, donned his costume and substituted for him.

Bert Williams appeared as a single for the first time in sixteen years in *Mr. Lode of Koal* (1909). Despite the presence of veterans from the previous Williams and Walker shows, he felt apprehensive appearing without his partner. His nerves calmed soon after he arrived onstage and heard the laughter of the audience. Nevertheless, it shortly became apparent that audiences and critics missed the presence of George Walker, whose flash and wit offered a sharp contrast to the slow and occasionally dour Williams persona. As a result, *Mr. Lode of Koal* failed to duplicate the success of the team's earlier vehicles.[13]

Flo Ziegfeld noted Williams' problems and offered him a role in the *Follies of 1910.* Such an opportunity was unprecedented, since the black and the white worlds of musical comedy had tended to remain separate. Williams accepted the offer, though several cast members of the Ziegfeld show expressed their discontent, many threatening to quit. Ziegfeld called their bluff, telling them, "Go ahead, quit!" Faced with the loss of their jobs, the disgruntled actors muffled their complaints and remained with the show. Williams himself also seemed somewhat dubious about the transition to the *Follies.* He had been a star, and now he would be one of many performers. If he were sick during the run of *Abyssinia,* the show would be cancelled; in the *Follies,* the show would continue without him. Nevertheless, Ziegfeld's persuasive powers and his attitude toward race led Williams to join the *Follies.*[14]

Despite Williams' initial misgivings, the *Ziegfeld Follies* gave a new boost to his career. His debut allowed him three solo numbers, which rivaled those of the other *Follies* newcomer, Fanny Brice, for critical attention. Williams continued with Ziegfeld until 1919, and during this period he was a major Broadway attraction. It was not until 1920 that Williams finally left the *Follies* (along with another stalwart, Eddie Cantor) for a leading role in *Broadway Brevities of 1920.* It became Williams' last role; he died suddenly at age forty-nine in 1922.

13. New York *Dramatic Mirror,* November 13, 1909.
14. Johnson, *Black Manhattan,* 108.

Bert Williams proved to be a valuable addition to the *Follies.* However, his move to the white world of musical comedy was a staggering loss to the fledgling world of the black musical, which was facing a major crisis. By 1911 it seemed that this novel and promising theatrical genre was about to disappear from Broadway.

IV

THE TERM OF EXILE, 1910–1917

James Weldon Johnson dubbed the period from 1910 to 1917 the "term of exile" in his classic study of black theatrical life, *Black Manhattan.*[1] The all-black shows that had flourished on Broadway during the first decade of this century seemed to vanish. The primary reason was that by 1911 the major stars had all but disappeared. Ernest Hogan, Bob Cole, and George Walker were dead. Will Marion Cook, James Weldon Johnson, and J. Rosamond Johnson had pursued new interests or careers. And the giant of them all, Bert Williams, had moved to the *Ziegfeld Follies.* As a result, the new black musicals were suddenly leaderless.

From the vantage point of Broadway, the second decade of the century seemed barren of black theatrical accomplishments. Yet, the supposed exile tended to mask other opportunities. Black theatre abandoned Broadway for advantages elsewhere, as black stage productions flourished in Harlem and in major cities throughout the United States. Instead of a period of exile, what actually occurred was an extended road show or tryout, allowing black theatre to develop without the presence of white audiences and critics, which had so often determined its course.

The boom in black musical comedy from 1898 to 1910 obscured the fact that these entertainments were primarily intended for white audiences. The word *black* in "black musicals" referred to the people onstage, not necessarily the people in the audience. Developments in black musical theatre were often constrained by the expectations of white audiences and critics.

1. Johnson, *Black Manhattan,* 170.

At the turn of the century, only a few black patrons were able to attend the black shows that enjoyed Broadway runs. If blacks purchased tickets, they usually had to sit in the upper reaches of the balcony. This seating arrangement was not based on preference or lack of money, but was simply a form of *de facto* segregation. Such a policy was prohibited by New York's State Penal Code (Section 514), which declared it a "misdemeanor for any person to exclude from full enjoyment of an inn, tavern, restaurant, public conveyance, theatre or other place of amusement a citizen by reason of race or color." Nevertheless, New York City theatre owners continued the practice because the assumption was that white audiences would not enjoy the presence of Negro theatregoers in the orchestra. The separation of races was often maintained by ticket agents who would inform black patrons that orchestra seats were unavailable for the desired performance.[2]

Thus, while black writers and actors could appear onstage or provide music and lyrics for a show, it was not easy for them to sit in the orchestra section at a performance. James Weldon Johnson recalled that as the rehearsals for a Klaw and Erlanger show progressed he found the seats littered with pamphlets from the "Southern Society," which discussed the evils of integrating the main floors of Broadway theatres. Johnson protested to Erlanger, insisting that the pamphlets be removed.[3] Although Erlanger agreed and had the racist material taken away, old customs prevailed in most theatres.

Johnson experienced the humiliation of this practice when he took his wife and a good friend to see one of the latest Broadway hits. His party passed the ticket collector without incident, but when they entered the orchestra all the ushers seemed busy, and they had to find their own seats. Despite signals to the ushers, no one brought them a program. A kind gentleman seated next to Johnson finally loaned him one. As the lights dimmed, someone tapped Johnson on the shoulder. It was a man from the box office. Johnson later recalled the exchange:

> "Have you the coupons for these seats?" he asked.
>
> "Yes," I replied.
>
> "May I see them?"
>
> "Certainly." I held the coupons up to him, displaying the numbers, but kept them tightly gripped between my thumb and forefinger.
>
> "I'd like to look at them."

2. New York *Times*, April 20, 1910, p. 9.
3. Johnson, *Along This Way*, 200.

> "You're looking at them."
>
> "You don't think I want to steal them?"
>
> "I don't intend to give you the chance." He went away. Had I handed him the coupons he would have rushed off with them to the box office, then come back and told us there had been a mistake made about the tickets and that we would have to give up our seats. I was determined not to undergo the injustice and humiliation, so held fast to my coupons. But I was so blind with anger and resentment that I did not see the first act.[4]

There were occasional protests against this policy. In 1910, James Davis, a black, cleverly sent a white messenger to pick up his tickets at the Victoria Theatre. When Davis arrived at the performance, the head usher refused to admit him to the orchestra and suggested that he accept seats in the balcony. Davis refused, and the usher escorted him from the theatre. Davis complained to the police, and the usher (also a black man), who was following theatre policy, was arrested for a few days.[5]

Little had changed by 1912, when F. Baldwin, a black real estate broker, was summoned from his orchestra seats by the manager, who calmly informed him that Negroes were not admitted to the first floor of the theatre. Baldwin decided to protest and brought the case to court with the assistance of the NAACP. The situation attracted the attention of the editors of the New York *Times,* who sympathized with the manager. They argued that "theatres would admit Negroes to orchestra seats as readily as white persons if it were found profitable. It is a matter of business with them, not prejudice. If compelled to admit Negroes, they would find that the prejudice of white patrons would deprive them of profit." The judge found some slight merit in Baldwin's case, and fined the theatre manager $50, the minimum punishment required by law. W. E. B. Du Bois, angered because the judge did not apply the maximum penalty of $500 and one year in jail, wrote a harsh letter to the New York *Times*: "I do not think that any decent man objects to sitting in a theatre beside another decent man simply because that man has a darker skin; and if some do object, is it good public policy to let such persons have their way and make me suffer because of their whims?"[6]

Most of the white critics for the major papers tended to ignore

4. *Ibid.*, 200–201.
5. New York *Times,* April 20, 1910, p. 9, April 21, 1910, p. 10.
6. *Ibid.*, April 21, 1910, p. 10, January 24, 1912, p. 10, February 10, 1912, p. 10.

segregation in the theaters except for passing reference to isolated applause from the balconies at black-performed plays or musicals. Only Robert Benchley, critic for *Life* magazine, condemned the practice. He noticed that Claude McKay, the Jamaican-born poet and current backup drama critic for the *Liberator,* and his friend, artist William Gropper, were stopped by the usher in the lobby prior to a performance of *He Who Gets Slapped* (1922). The usher returned with the manager, who confiscated the tickets, stammering, "The—the wrong date." He then took the orchestra seats and came back from the box office with balcony seats. McKay recalled: "Suddenly the realization came to me. I had come here as a dramatic critic, a lover of the theatre, and a free soul. But—I was abruptly reminded—those things did not matter. The important fact, with which I was suddenly slapped in the face, was my color. I am Negro—*He, the One Who Gets Slapped.*" Benchley later rebuked the theatrical community (and other New Yorkers as well) in his weekly column:

> This is, of course, New York's customary treatment of Negroes. It is nothing new. In the South they are at least frank about their discrimination. There is no pretense. In New York, which claims to being a modern community, such hypocrisy makes things worse. And for the Theatre Guild, which above all producing bodies in this city snaps a delicate finger at commercialism in the name of the universality of art, even to condone the shunting of a writer of beautiful verse into the balcony of the theatre because he happens to be colored, would be comic if it were not so terribly tragic.[7]

Despite such isolated protests, blacks tended to be relegated to the balcony until 1921, when *Shuffle Along,* one of the most popular black shows of the 1920s, began to tinker with that pattern of segregation.

One of the ironic benefits of the term of exile was that blacks were able to perform primarily for black audiences and develop new skills, techniques, and theatrical styles without the constraints of white audiences and critics. If the exile is viewed in this fashion, the popularity of black musicals in the 1920s is not such a sudden or surprising development. Rather, the evolution of black theatre from 1910 to 1920

7. Robert Benchley, *Benchley at the Theatre: Dramatic Criticism, 1920–1940,* ed. Charles Getchell (Ipswich, Mass., 1985), 14–15. McKay had earned considerable praise for his early poetry collections, *Songs of Jamaica* and *Constab Ballads* (1912), and *Spring in New Hampshire and Other Poems* (1920). For McKay's recounting of the event, see *A Long Way From Home* (New York, 1969), 140–45.

was mostly away from Broadway, and thus outside the view of most white observers.

The primary locale of these developments was Harlem, where black theatre flourished in the prewar years. The Lincoln Theatre (first located at West 135th Street) and Lafayette Theatre (at 132nd Street and Second Avenue) became the new Broadway for black theatrical performers. Due to the efforts of Anita Bush, a stock company for black actors was formed at the Lincoln (which was showing films to minute audiences while waiting for a vaudeville revival). The theatre opened in 1915 with a production of *The Girl at the Fort,* which received favorable reviews. After a policy disagreement with the Lincoln's management, Bush moved her company to the rival Lafayette, where it prospered for many years as the Lafayette Players. Lester Walton, a black drama critic and co-manager of the Lafayette Theatre, supplied favorable press commentary for the new group, and it quickly prospered. The troupe, which was not bound by Broadway conventions, appeared in a wide variety of plays and musicals during the latter part of the decade. Minstrel formulas, which had lingered in the Broadway musicals at the turn of the century, were banished. Black performers endeavored to assert their ability to perform every style of drama and musical.[8]

The Lafayette nurtured black actors during the lean Broadway years. Here, talented black veterans of the Williams and Walker shows or the Cole and Johnson shows performed with talented newcomers who wanted to learn the tricks of the trade. When Broadway once again sought black talent in the 1920s, a large and skilled pool was available. When James Weldon Johnson listed the most notable performers at the Lincoln and the Lafayette theatres, it was no surprise that those same individuals became the major figures in the black dramatic and musical revival on Broadway in the 1920s. These performers who distinguished themselves in the Harlem theatres during this period included Inez Clough, Abbie Mitchell, Ida Anderson, Evelyn Ellis, Lottie Grady, Laura Bowman, Susie Sutton, Cleo Desmond, Edna Thomas, Charles Gilpin, Frank Wilson, Tom Brown, Charles Moore, Sidney Kirkpatrick, Lionel Monagas, A. B. Comathiere, Walter Thompson, "Babe" Townsend, Charles Olden, Andrew Bishop, Clarence Muse, and Jack Carter.[9]

8. See Sister M. Francesca Thompson, O.S.F., "The Lafayette Players, 1917–1932," in Errol Hill (ed.), *The Theater of Black Americans* (2 vols.; Englewood Cliffs, N.J., 1980), II, 13–32.

9. Johnson, *Black Manhattan,* 173.

Another major center of black theatrical development was the Pekin Theatre in Chicago, which specialized in musicals and warmhearted comedies. The Pekin Stock Company developed its own talent, but also welcomed New York stage veterans into its ranks. Will Marion Cook, for example, contributed music to several Pekin shows. Perhaps the most notable graduates were Flournoy Miller and Aubrey Lyles. In such popular shows as *The Mayor of Dixie* they developed the comic personae that would become the focus of *Shuffle Along*.

Black actors, writers, and composers also had "the road" as a training arena. An ample number of black touring companies traveled throughout the United States, bypassing the major legitimate theatres and playing to black audiences. From Boston to St. Louis, the black musical continued its evolution without the goal of eventually running on Broadway. Such shows could make a reasonable profit on the road, but they would be hard pressed to compete with the expensive Broadway or touring shows. With extremely low production values, the shows of S. H. Dudley or Salem Tutt Whitney and partner J. Homer Tutt thrived during the term of exile.[10]

Occasionally, these touring shows briefly nudged the respectable Broadway theatre district during their lengthy runs. S. H. Dudley, who later became a noted booking agent for black talent, had two shows reach Broadway during this period. *His Honor the Barber* enjoyed a brief run at the Majestic Theatre in May, 1911. This Smart Set Company presentation featured a barber named Raspberry Snow (Dudley), who has two dreams in life—to shave the president of the United States and to marry the beautiful Lily White (Elizabeth Hart). Snow's wishes come true in Act II, but Act III reveals that he has been dreaming. Several critics heartily approved the enterprise, praising both Dudley and his able partner, Ada Overton Walker (the widow of George Walker). The New York *Dramatic Mirror* led the chorus of raves: "Dudley and . . . Walker lead the contingent with much assurance and allow no dull moments while they hold the stage. Dudley is a quiet comedian of much resourcefulness, while Miss Walker, as is well known, is the best Negro comedienne of today. Her tomboy number, her Spanish song and dance, and her impersonation of a Negro 'chappie,' the last of which is the real hit of the play, are minutely favorable creations. With such material as Dudley and Miss Walker have, they do wonders." Both black and white customers enjoyed the opening per-

10. For biographies of Dudley, Whitney, and Tutt, see *Messenger*, VII (1926), 46–47, 50, 62.

formance, though the theatre was only one-quarter filled. The biggest surprise at the opening of *His Honor the Barber,* however, was that blacks were not relegated to the balcony. Instead, blacks and whites had seats in alternate sections throughout the theatre. Although segregation remained, its structure within the theatre audience was beginning to change.[11]

The Smart Set returned the following year for a brief engagement at Hurtig and Seamon's Music Hall. Dudley led the company in *Dr. Beans From Boston.* One critic briefly dismissed the show: "There's not much of a plot. It revolves around the adage that a 'n——r will always steal.' The scene is laid at Buckroe Beach, a summer resort for Negroes in Virginia. The story hinges on the purchase of a drug store with borrowed money, raised from the sale of a mule. Having no knowledge of drugs, Dr. Beans undertakes to get by on his nerves, but he gets so disgusted that he loses his drugstore in a crap game." Dudley's company enjoyed a brief New York run and then returned to such high spots of the tour as Pittsburgh and Cincinnati.[12]

The theatrical enterprises of black companies in New York City attracted notice in the major newspapers and began to lure white audiences to Harlem. The musical shows proved most popular, and *Darktown Follies of 1914* (by Williams and Walker veteran J. Leubrie Hill) the major hit of the year. Flo Ziegfeld was so impressed that he optioned portions of the show for his own *Follies.* The big musical hit downtown was the "After the Ball" number, though Hill received no credit in the *Follies* program. Ziegfeld even had to call on *Darktown* cast member Ethel Williams to teach the dance routines to the *Follies* cast. But he did not hire her to appear in the show.[13]

Darktown Follies of 1914 also attempted to move downtown in its entirety in order to invade Broadway. After a brief run at the Hammerstein Roof Garden, the producers sought a legitimate theatre in order to capitalize on the show's surprising success. The Bijou, a former movie house at Broadway and Twenty-ninth Street, proved available, and it was reopened as "a theatre for colored people" under the aegis of J. Leubrie Hill (who also starred in the show). Hill explained to reporters that "all the employees of the Bijou will be colored persons

11. New York *Dramatic Mirror,* May 8, 1911; *Variety,* May 13, 1911.

12. Cincinnati *Herald,* February 19, 1912. See also "*Darktown Follies* in a Negro Theatre Is New York's Newest Stage Success," New York *World,* November 9, 1913.

13. Johnson, *Black Manhattan,* 174. For an account of the evolution of *Darktown Follies,* see Marshall Stearns and Jean Stearns, *Jazz Dance: The Story of American Vernacular Dance* (New York, 1968), Chap. 17. *Ziegfeld Follies* (1914) program, in TC/NYPL.

from the man in the box office to the ushers and water boys. The orchestra will also be made up of colored musicians." Hill hoped to hold the price of the best seats to just one dollar, so black patrons could sit in the orchestra for the first time. He also expressed his intention to have "professional matinees, so white chorus men and women of other Broadway shows would be invited to come and hear some real singing and dancing."[14] On opening night the theatre was only half-filled, though blacks and whites attended the performance in equal proportion. The Bijou's effort to bring black theatre to Broadway (from distant Twenty-ninth Street) failed. The theatre was razed in 1915.

For James Weldon Johnson, the term of exile ended on April 5, 1917, when the Coloured Players premiered a collection of three plays by white author Ridgely Torrence at the Garden Theatre. Johnson proclaimed that on that evening "the stereotyped traditions regarding the Negro's histrionic limitations were smashed. It was the first time anywhere in the United States for Negro actors in dramatic theatre to command the serious attention of the critics and of the general press and public."[15] The three plays, *The Rider of Dreams, Granny Maumee,* and *Simon the Cyrenian,* provided opportunities for fine comic and dramatic acting for several veterans of the Williams and Walker shows and the Lafayette Players. Many white critics agreed with Johnson's bold assessment of the significance of this event. In addition, George Jean Nathan singled out Inez Clough and Opal Cooper in his year-end listing of the best theatrical performances.[16]

Despite James Weldon Johnson's exaltation after seeing the production by the Coloured Players, black shows continued to be a rarity on Broadway. Not until the premiere of *Shuffle Along* in 1921 would black writers and performers be both welcomed and acclaimed on Broadway.

14. New York *Times,* June 8, 1914, p.7.

15. Johnson, *Black Manhattan,* 175–79. The *Theatre Magazine* critic noted: "What would seem the most remarkable incident of the performance was the self-possession of the performers and the fact that they were, for the most part, letter perfect. Marie Jackson-Stuart had several speeches of a length that would tax any memory. Sincerity was in their work, refinement of art was lacking; the exhibitions of naturalness were interesting, crude but not ineffective" (*Theatre Magazine,* XXV [1917], 280). For a summary of the play, see *ibid.*, 350–51. (The organization is also given as Colored Players in several contemporary articles and reviews.)

16. "To my mind this [the three plays by Ridgely Torrence] was one of the most important things that has happened in the history of the American stage" (Louis Sherwin, "The Beginnings of the Negro Theatre and the Recent Success of the Colored Players in New York," *Vanity Fair* [June, 1917], 96).

V

SHUFFLE ALONG

The Broadway season drew to a close at the beginning of May in 1921. This was somewhat unusual, since shows normally opened until the first heat wave in mid-June. This year the weather seemed satisfactory, but New York City's financial condition was not. In April and May several major department stores retrenched, firing employees by the hundreds. As a result, theatre owners foresaw a long bleak summer. Only *Sally* appeared a strong candidate among the new musicals: with a Flo Ziegfeld production, a Jerome Kern score, and sparkling performances by Marilyn Miller and Leon Errol, it seemed a sure bet for a long run.[1]

As both old and new shows shuttered throughout May, no one seemed to be paying attention to the announced opening of an all-Negro show at the 63rd Street Theatre. *Shuffle Along* seemed an unlikely candidate for a run. Broadway had not seen a successful all-black show in years, and theatre managers argued that ticket buyers would stay away in droves. The composers and cast were virtual unknowns, and the theatre, on the fringes of Broadway, was somewhat dilapidated and not prepared to handle a major musical. Word from the road was also bleak, as the *Shuffle Along* company left a well-marked trail of unpaid bills as it moved from city to city. It arrived in New York City in 1921 almost $18,000 in debt.

Shuffle Along nevertheless became a surprise hit. It not only lasted the summer, but its 504-performance run was surpassed only by *Sally* of all the season's shows. Composer Eubie Blake and lyricist Noble Sissle produced a score that delighted critics and audiences with its

1. *Variety,* May 6, 1921.

Shuffle Along songwriters Noble Sissle and Eubie Blake
Courtesy Philadelphia Free Library Theatre Collection

modern tempos. The cast of unknowns was catapulted to stardom. Leads Flournoy Miller and Aubrey Lyles, who also wrote *Shuffle Along*'s libretto, appeared on Broadway almost every season throughout the 1920s. Even members of the replacement cast (Florence Mills) and the chorus (Josephine Baker, Paul Robeson, and Adelaide Hall) found *Shuffle Along* the first step to international stardom.

Shuffle Along also legitimized the black musical. It proved to producers and theatre managers that audiences would pay to see black talent on Broadway. As a result, *Shuffle Along* spawned a series of imitators, and black musicals became a Broadway staple. The effects of its gargantuan success were not limited to Broadway alone. Langston Hughes, who claimed that he chose to attend Columbia University so he could see *Shuffle Along,* credited the show with giving a "scintillating send-off to that Negro vogue in Manhattan" known as the Harlem Renaissance: "For nearly two years it was always packed. It gave the proper push—a pre-Charleston kick—to the vogue that spread to books, African sculpture, music, and dancing."[2]

The creators of *Shuffle Along* were talented, but generally unknown, newcomers. Miller and Lyles had become partners while they were students at Fisk University. Miller claimed that they learned to be comedians because "they couldn't make money any other way." From the first, they found it necessary to "black up." They discovered that jobs were easier to get if the theatre managers and the audiences assumed they were white men wearing burnt cork makeup. This early adaptation to the demands of the audience became their trademark (as it did with Bert Williams), and they retained their comic masks throughout the 1920s.[3]

Miller and Lyles drifted throughout the United States, spending considerable time with the Pekin Stock Company, where they developed several of their routines. Their humor was both verbal and physical. Their favorite skits, which combined a healthy dose of malapropisms and some acrobatic dancing, often burlesqued southern life in small towns. "The Mayor of Dixie," an early comedy routine, seemed appropriate for expansion into a musical comedy. James Reese Europe, the composer and bandleader, suggested to Miller that he talk

2. Langston Hughes, *The Big Sea* (New York, 1940), 223–24; Hughes, "When Harlem Was in Vogue," *Town and Country* (July, 1940), 64.

3. Robert Cogswell, "Miller, Flournoy E., and Aubrey Lyles," in Allen Woll, *Dictionary of the Black Theatre: Broadway, Off-Broadway, and Selected Harlem Theatre* (Westport, Conn., 1983), 232–34.

to Noble Sissle and Eubie Blake about contributing songs to such a show.

Sissle and Blake met at a Baltimore party in 1915. Blake needed a lyricist; Sissle, a composer. They shook hands and immediately joined forces. Both had had considerable musical experience. Sissle, born in Indianapolis in 1889, first exercised his singing talents in his high school glee club. After graduation he toured with the Thomas Jubilee Singers in order to earn money for college. Sissle's college career was brief—the lure of singing jobs with dance bands proved too great. In 1916, Sissle joined James Reese Europe's Society Orchestra.[4]

James Hubert Blake, a native of Baltimore, was born in 1883. Blake claimed that he began reading music and playing the piano at the age of six. By 1899, he wrote "The Charleston Rag" and other ragtime melodies, much to the distress of his mother, who refused to have the devil's music in the house. He polished his performing style in Atlantic City, where he met such ragtime greats as Willie ("The Lion") Smith and James P. Johnson.[5]

Sissle and Blake's initial partnership was brief but successful. Sophie Tucker sang their first song, "It's All Your Fault." World War I interrupted the collaboration—Sissle joined James Europe in overseas duty. After the war, Sissle and Blake, now "The Dixie Duo," performed their latest compositions in a promising vaudeville act. During this period, Miller and Lyles approached them with a unique proposition—the creation of a musical comedy for Broadway audiences.

The obstacles at first appeared insurmountable. The money for such an enterprise seemed unobtainable, since no one believed that Broadway audiences would attend an all-Negro show. Al Mayer, Miller and Lyles's booking agent, arranged a meeting with Harry Cort, son of theatrical producer John Cort. He in turn persuaded his father to listen to their proposals. John Cort eventually agreed to give *Shuffle Along* a trial run. The four writers assembled a cast of talented unknowns: Miller and Lyles recruited some friends from the Pekin Stock Company, and Sissle and Blake called on several cabaret performers from San Francisco, New Orleans, and Memphis. After a brief rehearsal period in Harlem, the company began a lengthy period of short runs and one-night stands. Cort visited the show during the tryout period with fellow producer Abraham Erlanger. Sissle recalled that they

4. *Amsterdam News*, n.d., in Clipping File, TC/NYPL.

5. For the best survey, see Kimball and Bolcom, *Reminiscing with Sissle and Blake*. See also Al Rose, *Eubie Blake* (New York, 1979).

"laughed themselves sick." Yet after the show, Cort "pointed out that we had a colored audience and that a white audience wouldn't enjoy it." Nevertheless, Cort was persuaded to continue the tour for an additional three weeks.[6]

Money was continually tight, if not nonexistent, on the tour. Since few hotels would accept black patrons, cast members often stayed in private homes, paying for their meals and lodging with passes to the show. Yet, the *Shuffle Along* company rarely starved. Miller recalled: "You learn a lot of tricks on the road. Sissle and I would visit people who were boarding some members of the cast—always at mealtime—and I would take a bite of everything on the table and insist that Sissle taste it too, because it was so delicious. Then we'd go to another house and do the same thing—we usually had plenty to eat."[7]

After a rocky tryout tour, *Shuffle Along* arrived at the 63rd Street Theatre, which John Cort had just acquired. It was woefully inadequate for a musical comedy production. Slightly off the beaten track, it was used primarily for recitals and lectures. As a result, the theatre had virtually no stage depth. Carpenters soon extended the stage, devouring the first boxes in the process. The orchestra then took what had been rows A to C, and a makeshift curtain was also added. Work on the theatre continued throughout the run. Miller remembered that he often heard hammering during the performances.[8]

It was not quite Broadway, but it was close enough. Eubie Blake explained: "It was really off-Broadway, but we caused it to be Broadway. . . . It was the price of the ticket that mattered. Our tickets cost the same as any Broadway show. That made it Broadway!" *Shuffle Along,* which had charged $1.00 on the road, upped its admission to $2.00 for half the orchestra seats. The rest of the orchestra was priced at $1.50.[9]

Shuffle Along had two premieres. On May 22, 1921, a Sunday evening, the management invited songwriters and theatre performers to a special preview. Response from the theatrical crowd was good, and *Variety* noted that "wiseacres predicted that some of the big shows downtown would receive a suggestion or two." The official opening night for the public on Monday evening also was a success. Blake recalled: "The proudest day of my life was when *Shuffle Along* opened.

6. Stearns and Stearns, *Jazz Dance,* 135.
7. *Ibid.,* 136.
8. *Variety,* May 27, 1921.
9. *Ibid.*

Shuffle Along orchestra
Courtesy Billy Rose Theatre Collection, New York Public Library

Shuffle Along chorus members

Courtesy Billy Rose Theatre Collection, New York Public Library

At the intermission all those white people kept saying: 'I would like to touch him, the man who wrote the music.' Well, you got to feel that. It made me feel like, well, at last, I'm a human being."[10]

Critics responded warmly to the comedy, music, and performances of *Shuffle Along*. Miller and Lyles drew their stock characters Steve Jenkins and Sam Peck from their vaudeville act and placed them in the midst of a hotly contested mayoral campaign in the southern city of Jimtown. The main contenders are party-backed candidate Steve Jenkins ("We stand for everything that we can get / Our man is for the country going wet"), Sam Peck, and Harry Walton (Roger Matthews), the reform candidate. Walton's major problem is that he has discovered that the only way to obtain votes in Jimtown is to buy them at five dollars a head, but he will have nothing to do with such practices. Walton wishes not only to bring reform to Jimtown but to marry Jessie Williams (Lottie Gee), the daughter of the richest man in town. Unfortunately, her father (Paul Floyd) will not give his permission unless Harry wins the election.

Sam and Steve, however, discover that the best way to win votes is to "borrow" money from the cash register of their jointly owned grocery store. Nevertheless, traditional politics come to the fore as election day nears, and both candidates take to the streets to explain their positions to the voters:

Sam: Let's hear it for the candidate!

Steve: (in pompous fashion) Ladies, gentlemenses, peopleses, and folkses . . .

Sam: Well, you ain't left out nobody, I'm give you praise for that.

Steve: Now, don't be corruptin' me there, pal. As I stand before you gazing into each and every one of you eyes, the question that raises in my mind is what do you think of me?

Sam: Don't tell him!

Steve: I told you to quit corruptin' me there now. I may not be bedecked with jewels and diamonds rare; I may not wear watches and chains, but I have worn . . .

Sam: Ball and chains!. . . .

Steve: We will pay no more attention to my reponent. We will talk of much more matters of heap much more reportance. Look at the re-

10. *Ibid.*; New York *Post*, July 3, 1975; "Eubie Blake" File, TC/NYPL.

Politics in Jimtown. Chief of Police Aubrey Lyles and Mayor Flournoy Miller in *Shuffle Along*
Courtesy Billy Rose Theatre Collection, New York Public Library

dition of your city today. . . . We have no 'lectric lights here. Statistics will show you that there ain't been no electric lights in Jimtown in . . . since . . . before . . .

Sam: Oh, there ain't never been none here.

Steve: And there wasn't none here before dem neither.

Sam: And dere ain't gwine be none here after dis.

Steve: What we need is electric lights. Look how dark it is here all de time. (repeat)

Sam: What are you looking at me for?

Steve: It's so dark here at night that if you light a match, you got to light another one to see if the first one is lit or not. If I get elected mayor, I'll see the whole town is lit up!

Sam: And if you vote for him, you all ought to be electrocuted![11]

Both Mrs. Peck (Mattie Wilks) and Tom Sharper (Sissle), Steve Jenkins' campaign manager, discover that the candidates are stealing money from the grocery store, so they independently send for "Keen-eye, that great colored detective" to catch their rival with the illicit funds. In the interim, Sam and Steve begin to realize the merits of cooperation, and they agree that the winner in the upcoming election will appoint the loser the chief of police. Thus they will obtain complete power over the town, no matter who wins. After they shake hands, Tom arrives with the news that Steve has won. As they leave the stage triumphantly, Mr. Williams tells his daughter that she may not marry Harry, who has lost the election. But, as the curtain falls, Harry and Jessie sing "Love Will Find a Way."

Act II begins, and Jessie explains that she's "just wild about Harry, and Harry's wild about her," a fitting introduction to the show's best-known song. Nevertheless, Steve begins to consolidate his power. He walks down Main Street, cancelling all his campaign promises. He even tells Sam, "If you ain't got no better sense den to pay any attention to dem election promises, you ain't got enough sense to be no Chief of Police." This statement infuriates Sam, and in the "Jimtown's Fisticuffs" sequence, they have a wildly choreographed twenty-minute comic fight. A triumphant Sam manages to resurrect the preelection

11. *Okeh Records,* 1921. This transcription is of the recording of "Election Day in Jimtown." It differs slightly from a script dated November 18, 1922, of *Shuffle Along* in MC/LC. All other quotation and the plot summary are from the script. The recording reflects the improvisational flair of the performance with greater accuracy than does the typescript of the dialogue.

Miller and Lyles in their classic "Fisticuffs" routine
Courtesy Billy Rose Theatre Collection, New York Public Library

promise and becomes the most diligent chief of police ever in Jimtown. After all, Sam explains, he receives fifty cents for each person he arrests. Soon, the town's jails are filled to capacity. The new mayor also begins his reign with a vengeance—taxpayers finance his new limousine, his chauffeur, six beautiful stenographers (who unfortunately cannot take shorthand), and his magnificent office furnishings.

Finally the New York detective assembles proof that Sam and Steve did steal from the grocery store and presents the crooks and the town council with the evidence. The crooks are told to return to their store and run it honestly, and Harry becomes the town's new mayor. At last Mr. Williams allows his daughter to marry the newly respectable Mr. Walton.

The libretto and songs were clearly not integrated in the modern sense of the term. The two creative teams used the plot to display the talents that had earned them praise in vaudeville. Miller and Lyles once again fractured the English language during their political speeches in Act I, and they brought their "Jimtown's Fisticuffs" routine to the second act. Blake wrote few new songs for the show: "I used to tell people I only wrote three songs for *Shuffle Along,*" he claimed. "That's because I had been writing songs all along. I sent them out, but the people on Broadway said they were no good. I took all the numbers Broadway said were no good and I put them in *Shuffle Along.*" In the second act, the show ground to a halt for "a few minutes with Sissle and Blake." The team revived their vaudeville routine, often featuring "Serenade Blues" and "Ain't You Comin' Back Mary Ann to Maryland," but the tunes could change nightly. This practice was not unusual (Al Jolson often did it—announced or unannounced), but it may have lent credence to the oft-repeated myth that *Shuffle Along* was a revue rather than a book musical.[12]

The score for *Shuffle Along* was one of the most highly praised of the 1920s. When James Weldon Johnson reviewed the musicals of the decade, he found it difficult to remember a show with as many song hits. Blake explained the reasons for the score's success in a 1921 interview. The reporter asked how a hit song was written, and the master replied: "The successful song writer of today must be something more than a mere juggler of harmonious sounds. He must be a student of what the public wants—a sort of a psychologist. The mushy, sobby, sentimental love songs of twenty or more years ago would not

12. *New Yorker,* December 25, 1978, pp. 25–26.

be at all popular today. Nor would the semi-martial music of songs popular during the United States' participation in the war make a hit now. What the public wants today are lively, jazzy songs, not too jazzy, with love interest, but without the sickly sentimentality in vogue a generation ago." Blake's response was not mere hyperbole. It accurately described why the score was popular. *Shuffle Along* reflected the rhythms and spirit of the age, but other Broadway shows tended to remain mired in the past, which bound the musical to its European antecedents.[13]

Critics praised Sissle and Blake's fertile and vibrant score, giving special attention to "Love Will Find a Way," "I'm Craving for That Kind of Love" (especially in Gertrude Saunders' rendition), "Shuffle Along," and "In Honeysuckle Time." The song that has endured the longest is "I'm Just Wild About Harry," which was originally written as a waltz. When ingenue Lottie Gee complained that she was unable to sing the verse in waltz time, Blake rewrote the song for her. She also argued that "colored shows didn't have waltzes in them." Blake, who had enjoyed the great black musicals of the turn of the century, recalled that Williams and Walker's *Abyssinia* had a waltz, but still complied with Gee's wishes.[14]

Miller, Lyles, Sissle, and Blake garnered the most press attention, but the rest of the company was not ignored. Alan Dale, writing for the New York *American*, lavished great praise on the cast's singing ability: "Some of the voices were excellent in quality and in cultivation. Miss Lottie Gee, for instance, has a singularly pure soprano and knows how to use it. Downtown, where they don't want voices and rarely suffer from them, Miss Gee would be quite a novelty. . . . She sings with taste, discretion, and distinction. . . . The same may be said for Roger Matthews, who also boasts a voice that musical comedy managers would say was too good for business. But they are not ashamed of their voices, and the damsels of the chorus are almost equally disposed to warble." Eubie Blake credited Dale's review with attracting audiences to the show. Crowds eventually came in such droves that New York City had to make Sixty-third Street one way in order to handle the traffic. Dale's comments best conveyed the infectious enthusiasm of the *Shuffle Along* crew:

13. Johnson, *Black Manhattan*, 186–87; Kimball and Bolcom, *Reminiscing with Sissle and Blake*, 108.

14. New York *Times*, December 1, 1978, C-2.

> Act, and the audience acts with you. This seemed to be the motto of the "troupe" at the Sixty-Third. How they enjoyed themselves! How they jigged and pranced and cavorted, and wriggled and laughed. It was an infection of amusement. It was impossible to resist a jollity that the company itself appeared to experience down to the very marrow. Talk of your pep! These people made pep seem something different to the tame thing we know further downtown. Every sinew in their bodies danced; every tendon in their frames responded to their extreme energy. The women were wreathed in smiles that did not suggest the "property" brand; the men simply exuded good nature.[15]

The critics generally agreed on one major flaw: the show looked more cheaply produced than did the shows downtown. *Variety* noted that the costumes looked like hand-me-downs from another Cort show. The reviewer was quite observant—the costumes had been used in *Roly-Boly Eyes* (1919) and included piles of kimonos and minstrel garb. The inventive duo improvised and added "Oriental Blues" and "Bandana Days" to the *Shuffle Along* score in order to use their inherited costumes. The *Variety* critic hoped that "some day Sissle and Blake would be tendered a real production."[16]

Some critics delayed the trek to Sixty-third Street, but none as long as Percy Hammond did. He did not file his review until March 31, 1922. Perhaps it was just as well. He wrote: "*Shuffle Along,* with all its imposing renown, is merely an indifferent troupe of colored persons, imitating with self-satisfied precision a mediocre musical comedy as it would be done by mediocre white performers."[17]

Despite the generally favorable notices, ticket sales were initially slow. The location of the theatre and the impending dog days of summer seemed to be working against the show's success. During the third week, the management added a midnight show on Wednesday in place of the matinee. The late show drew crowds from theatrical circles. By the seventh week, both matinees were eliminated in favor of midnight shows, and receipts began to hover at a respectable $8,000 each week, with a break-even figure of $7,500. By the eleventh week, *Variety* suggested that *Shuffle Along* might even run into the fall season.

Receipts improved dramatically in September—the $9,500 weekly gross was remarkable in the face of new competition. In November,

15. New York *American,* May 22, 1922.
16. *Variety,* May 27, 1921.
17. New York *Tribune,* March 31, 1922.

the management was assured of *Shuffle Along*'s success and pushed the top admission price to $3.00. Gross receipts hit the $13,000 mark. Its 504-performance run silenced the skeptics who argued that New Yorkers would never pay to see an all-Negro show.[18]

Who attended *Shuffle Along* during its lengthy run? *Variety* assumed that the show would attract a black audience: "A few blocks westward is a Negro section known as San Juan Hill. The Lenox Avenue colored section is 20 minutes away on the subway, so that *Shuffle Along* ought to get all the colored support there is along with which patrons who like that sort of entertainment." Yet, when *Variety* sampled the audience in November, 1921 (after the price hike), the reviewer found the clientele almost 90 percent white.[19]

What is surprising about the *Shuffle Along* audience is not the absolute number of black patrons but their placement in the theatre. James Weldon Johnson credited *Shuffle Along* with breaking the rigid barriers of segregation in New York City's legitimate theatres that restricted blacks to the balcony. *Variety*'s critic noted on opening night that "colored patrons were noticed as far front as the fifth row," as though he were surprised by such a sight. While the show brought black customers into the orchestra, it did not end segregation entirely. Two-thirds of the orchestra was reserved for whites, and blacks were seated in the remaining third. Once again, the box office controlled the seating patterns. *Variety* calmed its readers by noting that "the two races are rarely intermingled."[20]

Thus, despite some slight change, the balcony of the Broadway theatre remained a "Nigger Heaven." Carl Van Vechten, noted author and a patron of the Harlem Renaissance, later used this metaphor as a symbol for Harlem's relationship to Manhattan (and white America): "Nigger Heaven! That's what Harlem is. We sit in our places in the gallery of this New York theatre and watch the white world sitting down below in the good seats in the orchestra. Occasionally, they turn their faces up towards us, their hard cruel faces, to laugh or sneer, but they never beckon. It never seems to occur to them that Nigger Heaven is crowded, that there isn't another seat, that something has to be done."[21]

18. *Variety,* November 25, 1921.
19. *Variety,* May 27, November 25, 1921.
20. *Variety,* May 27, December 9, 1921.
21. Carl Van Vechten, *Nigger Heaven* (New York, 1926), 149. For an excellent discussion of the controversy surrounding Van Vechten's work, see Jervis Anderson, "Some

Alexander Woollcott, critic for the New York *Times,* was one of the few to cast a glance at the black audience seated in the balcony. After a performance of *Taboo* (1922), a play about black myths and superstition by white dramatist Mary Hoyt Wiborg, he archly noted:

> There sat whole rows of matinee ladies, who had detrained from the Social Register, formed a hollow square and advanced on the play. They surveyed through lorgnettes the Negro antics and agonies of which the play was wrought. It would have been an interesting experiment for someone to have risen from his seat and inquired loudly by what coincidence or what device the negroes who had ventured to come to see this piece about themselves had all been shunted up into the balcony. Such an interruption would have been mischievous and grossly irrelevant. As a gesture it would scarcely have risen above the plane of disorderly conduct. Yet it might have given vent to a vague and indefinable disquiet which Tuesday's enterprise must have bred in more minds than one.[22]

Nevertheless, *Shuffle Along* marked the beginning of the end of segregation in New York City's legitimate theatres. With each succeeding black show produced during the 1920s, seating restrictions gradually disappeared. James Weldon Johnson was finally able to write in 1930: "At the present time the sight of colored people in the orchestras of Broadway theatres is not regarded a cause for immediate action or utter astonishment."[23]

New York City had finally welcomed *Shuffle Along,* but other cities seemed a trifle hesitant. John Cort eventually persuaded a Boston producer to open his theatre for the show in July, 1922. It was hardly a major risk, since the theatre was vacant at the time because of the summer's heat. Initially set for a two-week run, *Shuffle Along* attracted audiences in surprising numbers. As the run stretched into three months, a Shakespearean troupe found its engagement continually delayed. Finally, after the threat of a lawsuit, *Shuffle Along* had to vacate the theatre.

Writers," in his *This Was Harlem: A Cultural Portrait, 1900–1950* (New York, 1981). A fine study that emphasizes the social context of the Harlem Renaissance is David Levering Lewis, *When Harlem Was in Vogue* (New York, 1979).

22. New York *Times,* April 9, 1922, Sec. VIII, p. 1. Despite Woollcott's caustic dismissal of the audience in his Sunday commentary, he failed to comment on a fresh young actor by the name of Paul Robeson. Wiborg's play closed after three performances, so only the first-night critics and a small audience noted his presence.

23. Johnson, *Along This Way,* 201.

The Boston engagement still failed to convince theatre managers that *Shuffle Along* would succeed. Chicago was the closest city that would accept the company, and even then it was a struggle. Blake recalled: "We had to jump all the way to Chicago—nobody else would take us. At the last minute we were let in by a lady who owned the Olympic, a rundown burlesque house. The audience was peeking around a lot of posts to see the show." The resistance to *Shuffle Along* began to fade after a Milwaukee run, and the show continued on a tour of major American cities.[24]

Virtually every cast member's career received a boost from the *Shuffle Along* mania. Lottie Gee, Gertrude Saunders, Ina Duncan, and others formed a talent pool for the plethora of black dramas and musicals that emerged in the 1920s. Yet, the true success story concerns unknown members of the chorus and the replacement cast: Florence Mills, Paul Robeson, Josephine Baker, and Adelaide Hall.

Florence Mills replaced Gertrude Saunders when the latter left for nightclub work. Mills's rendition of "I'm Craving for That Kind of Love" stopped the show every night, erasing all memory of Saunders' performance. Her rise was meteoric, and Lew Leslie gave her *Plantation Revue* (1922) as a starring vehicle. She toured European capitals in a new Leslie show *(From Dover to Dixie)* and returned to New York City for *Dixie to Broadway* in 1924. During this show she performed the song that became her trademark, "I'm a Little Blackbird Looking for a Blue Bird."[25]

Paul Robeson also began his work in the theatre with *Shuffle Along*. Eubie Blake recalled: "Why I'm the direct cause of his being onstage. We lost the bass singer of the Four Harmony Kings and we needed someone fast." Robeson, the Rutgers football star, seemed dubious at first, as did Noble Sissle. "I told them all, " said Blake. "He doesn't have to dance with the girls onstage; all he has to do is sing. And he did just fine!" Within a short time Robeson became the premier black actor on Broadway. During the 1920s, he appeared in *Taboo* (1922), Eugene O'Neill's *All God's Chillun Got Wings* (1924) and *The Emperor Jones* (1925), and *Black Boy* (1926) and then embarked on an international stage and screen career.[26]

24. Stearns and Stearns, *Jazz Dance*, 138.

25. Donald Bogle, *Brown Sugar* (New York, 1980), 41–42.

26. *Playbill* (November, 1978), clipping in "Eubie Blake" File, TC/NYPL. For additional information on Robeson's lengthy and controversial career, see Dorothy Butler Gilliam, *Paul Robeson, All-American* (Washington, D.C., 1976); Virginia Hamilton, *Paul Robeson: The Life and Times of a Free Black Man* (New York, 1974); and Susan Robeson, *The Whole World in His Hands* (Secaucus, N.J., 1981).

Josephine Baker emerged from the chorus line by embellishing her tiny role. Every night she rolled her eyes, purposely got out of step, and mugged to the audience. The crowds loved her, and by the Philadelphia run she was billed as the "Comedy Chorus Girl." Sissle and Blake gave her a leading role in their next black show, *The Chocolate Dandies* (1924), and she attracted the attention that propelled her to international stardom.

Adelaide Hall was one of the original Jazz Jasmines of the *Shuffle Along* chorus. Miller and Lyles chose her for a prominent role in *Runnin' Wild* (1923), and she starred in *My Magnolia* (1926), *Blackbirds of 1928*, and *Brown Buddies* (1930). She interrupted her Broadway career for nightclub work in France, Great Britain, and the United States.

Shuffle Along not only boosted the career of virtually everyone involved, it also legitimized black musical comedy on Broadway. In just three years, New Yorkers saw nine musicals written by and starring black performers: *Put and Take* (1921); *Strut Miss Lizzie, Plantation Revue, Oh Joy!*, and *Liza* (1922); *How Come?* and *Runnin' Wild* (1923); *The Chocolate Dandies* and *Dixie to Broadway* (1924). Black composers also wrote melodies for three shows with white casts in 1923: C. Luckeyeth Roberts' *Go-Go* and *Sharlee*, and Sissle and Blake's *Elsie* (with additional songs by Monte Carlo and Alma Sanders).[27] *Shuffle Along* was a milestone in the development of the black musical, and it became the model by which all black musicals were judged until well into the 1930s.

27. However, black composers wrote songs for white shows as early as the turn of the century—for example, Will Marion Cook's *The Southerners* (1904). Indeed, even Sissle and Blake's successful *Shuffle Along* was preceded by *Three Showers* on April 5, 1920, written by black composers Henry Creamer and Turner Layton.

VI

"IT'S GETTING DARK ON OLD BROADWAY"

On the evening of June 5, 1922, Gilda Gray, one of the stars of the *Ziegfeld Follies of 1922*, immortalized Broadway's newest phenomenon in song. She strode to center stage and sang "It's Getting Dark on Old Broadway." This fox-trot melody revealed to critics and audiences how quickly habits of theatregoing had changed during the past year:

We used to brag about the Broadway white lights,
The very famous dazzling White-Way night lights.
They used to glare and glimmer,
But they are growing dimmer;
Perhaps you've noticed the night cafes now,
If you go out for a lark,
Just take a tip from me,
Take a trip and you will see,
Broadway is getting quite dark.

Refrain:
It's getting very dark on Old Broadway,
You see the change in ev'ry cabaret;
Just like an eclipse on the moon,
Ev'ry cafe now has the dancing coon.
Pretty choc'late babies
Shake and shimmie ev'rywhere
Real dark-town entertainers hold the stage,
You must black up to be the latest rage.

Yes, the great white way is white no more,
It's just like a street on the Swanee shore.
It's getting very dark on old Broadway.[1]

1. "It's Getting Dark on Old Broadway" sheet music, in MC/NYPL.

From "ev'ry cabaret" to Shubert Alley, the success of *Shuffle Along* provided countless opportunities for black talent in midtown. Nevertheless, the change was not immediate. Even during *Shuffle Along*'s profitable run, black shows still seemed to pose a major financial risk. As a result, theatre owners often gave these new entertainments the lowest priority for Broadway showcases. Some shows chose out-of-the-way or dilapidated Broadway theatres; others opened during the dog days (prior to air conditioning), when new shows actively avoided premieres and marginal shows quickly shuttered. Black musicals, therefore, initially served the function of filling theatres in periods of low use. Rather than leave a theatre empty, managers would occasionally be willing to take a chance on a new black musical or revue. Thus opening night for these new shows often occurred between May and August. *Liza* (1922) was the first of the *Shuffle Along* sequels to open at the height of the season (November 27), but it remained berthed in the distant Daly's Theatre. Not until 1924 would black musicals be considered a worthy risk for a major theatre during the most profitable months.

Put and Take (1921), the first black revue to follow *Shuffle Along*, secured the Town Hall for its performances. The show had been in preparation for well over a year and had already toured the nation for thirty weeks as *Broadway Rastus*. Its route included Newark, Philadelphia, Chester, Wilmington, Baltimore, Washington, D.C., Richmond, Lynchburg, Newport News, Roanoke, Winston-Salem, Memphis, Atlanta, Chicago, Houston, Dallas, and Kansas City. *Put and Take* was therefore not hastily designed to pick up a few dollars from the latest Broadway trend. Nonetheless, *Put and Take*'s being showcased so near Broadway does remain a tribute to the change in thought that *Shuffle Along* caused.

In other matters, *Put and Take* had no direct theatrical link to the earlier show. Authors Irvin Miller (Flournoy Miller's brother), Spencer Williams, Tim Brymm, and Perry Bradford provided a revue rather than a book musical. They also avoided the southern slant of *Shuffle Along* and fashioned an urban and northern-oriented musical. Most links to the minstrel era of comedy were broken—the show assumed a contemporary tone. On one level, this move may be seen as an adventurous one. But the major critics failed to recognize it as such. The critic for *Variety* was particularly harsh:

> There is too much effort to be dressed up and dignified. . . . Colored performers cannot vie with white ones, and colored producers cannot

> play within an apple's throw of Ziegfeld and try to compete with him. . . . And here the colored folks seemed to have set out to show the whites they're just as good as anybody. They may be as good, but they're different and, in their entertainment, at any rate, they should remain different, distinct, and indigenous. . . . A quartet hacked away in dress suits when it should have been a success in plantation jumpers. The girls' wardrobe ran to tawdry gowns when they should have been fancifully dressed as picks, Zulus, cannibals, or cotton pickers.[2]

Comments such as these were familiar, particularly from the early days of black musicals. Reviewers often criticized black writers, composers, and performers for what might be considered "ambition," any effort to break or alter the white conventions that governed black theatre on Broadway.

Shuffle Along encouraged black theatre in a variety of ways, but also strangely limited it. This show broke several barriers (the love taboo, for instance), but its links to the minstrel stage were strong. Its comedy of malapropisms and black chicanery tended to reinforce existing stereotypes rather than change them. Thus, as *Shuffle Along* became the model for all black musicals of the 1920s, it also set certain boundaries as well. Any show that followed the characteristics of *Shuffle Along* could usually be assured of favorable reviews or at least a modest audience response. Yet, if a show strayed from what had become the standard formula for the black musical, disastrous reviews became almost inevitable. *Put and Take* was the first musical revue of the 1920s to suffer this fate; others would follow. The result of this critical stranglehold on the black musical was that *Shuffle Along* imitators swiftly became commonplace in the 1920s, as black authors and composers prepared shows within extremely narrow constraints.

Put and Take initially weathered several bad reviews, perhaps because it was the only new black musical in midtown. With a $2.00 top admission, the show grossed almost $8,000 per week, a profitable sum for the Town Hall. Nevertheless, *Put and Take* stayed there only briefly. Unnamed opposition suggested that offering a musical show ran counter to the goals of the Town Hall, which, the committee claimed, was conceived with "civic purposes in mind." They urged that the show be terminated. This was the first such complaint, since the Town Hall had been showing films during recent months in order to fill the empty theatre. Even *Variety* suggested that it was the presence of a "colored

2. *Variety,* August 26, 1921, p. 17.

company" that led to the complaints.[3] *Put and Take* had to vacate the Town Hall on September 23, though it was still making a profit. No other theatre was available, so it retreated to the road, which had generally proved more hospitable.

No black musical show followed *Put and Take* during the regular 1921–1922 season. However, as summer arrived and weak shows withered away, new prospects for black musicals appeared. *Strut Miss Lizzie,* by Henry Creamer and Turner Layton, took advantage of a vacancy at the Times Square Theatre and opened the "black musical season" on June 19, 1922. *Variety's* critic noted the reason for its presence: "Had the show come in at any other time but the end of the season, the chances are that it would not have secured a house in the theatrical zone. Uptown managers figure any profit at this period is gravy, although one manager refused the lease of his house for the colored attraction." Despite the difficulties in finding a booking for *Strut Miss Lizzie,* the authors seemed to realize that their show heralded an important trend—as the opening scene revealed:

> He: Well, well, well. Here I am again in my dear old homeland! And there, as I live, is my dear old mammy!
>
> She: If it isn't little Josephus! Come to you mammy's arms! Have you come home to stay?
>
> He: No, rather I have come to take you back up No'th with me, mammy. This is a colored year on Broadway.

Billed as "Glorifying the Creole Beauty," *Strut Miss Lizzie* suggested the Ziegfeld revues, which "glorified the American Girl," but there the similarity ended. Actually the show retained the spirit of *Shuffle Along,* without the constraints of a libretto. Percy Hammond, critic for the New York *Tribune,* found the show "a regulation near-Negro vaudeville and revue. Many dark comedians shuffle in and out with the familiar gait of Bert Williams, and as many yaller prima donnas sing slow, anecdotal ballads containing numerous, too numerous stanzas."[4]

The best part of the new show, according to several of the critics, was Creamer and Layton's performing some of their greatest hits. Like Sissle and Blake before them, Creamer and Layton interrupted the show for a short concert. They sang such songs as "Dear Old South-

3. *Ibid.,* September 16, 1921, p. 17.
4. *Ibid.,* June 23, 1922, p. 15; New York *Tribune,* June 20, 1922.

land" and " 'Way Down Yonder in New Orleans," which they billed as "a southern song without a mammy, a mule, or a moon."[5]

Despite praise for several lively songs, *Strut Miss Lizzie* survived for only thirty-two performances. Such a run often connotes a box office disaster, but the show did rather well in some ways. Box office action was healthy, but financial difficulties kept the show's creators from paying off their debts. *Shuffle Along* and *Put and Take* had slipped into town on a shoestring without reasonable hopes of success. But *Strut Miss Lizzie* appeared when white producers and managers were beginning to realize the financial potential of these new black musicals. As a result, Henry Creamer's Creole Producing Company faced stiff demands from theatre owners. In order to meet these costs and eventually present *Strut Miss Lizzie* on Broadway, Creamer ultimately lost financial control of the show.

Creamer originally hoped to produce *Strut Miss Lizzie* on the basis of a hefty royalty check that he had received for writing a song for the *Ziegfeld Follies,* but all too soon the money dwindled away. He then reached a rental agreement with William Minsky, who managed the Times Square Theatre, for $2,500 of each week's gross. Minsky, however, was extremely slow in providing a statement (or money). Creamer also borrowed $1,600 from Jack Mills, who published his songs, to defray the preliminary expenses of the opening. With no money arriving from Minsky, Creamer was forced to borrow $1,500 from Arthur Lyons, a vaudeville agent with ties to Minsky, in order to pay the first week's salaries. Lyons in turn would receive the royalties from ten of Creamer's hit songs, until the loan was repaid.

Additional funds were soon needed. Both Minsky and Lyons agreed to advance money to Creamer in exchange for 75 percent (37.5 percent each) control of the show's profits. Neither would be responsible for any losses *Lizzie* incurred. By the middle of the second week, Minsky and Lyons took over the production chores from the Creole Producing Company and in return offered 25 percent of the stock to Creamer. The certificates, however, were not delivered to him. The show grossed a healthy $8,600 during the first week, but Minsky repaid most of his own loans from that sum. While he profited, no cast member received a salary check. Instead, all performers received an IOU from him, along with a warning that salaries would be reduced during the second week of the run as well. Creamer received a check

5. Playbill, in "*Strut Miss Lizzie* File," TC/NYPL.

from Minsky for $141, which was immediately garnished by the tax collector for unpaid taxes on an earlier (uptown) version of *Strut Miss Lizzie.* After the second week, the remnants of the Creole Producing Company decided to move the show to another theatre in hopes of improved profits. Interestingly, the Times Square Theatre had an immediate occupant to fill the vacancy, as *Sue, Dear* (1922) swiftly filled the bill. Thus, Minsky's onerous treatment of the Creamer company may have been designed as a way to remove a minor musical and provide a long-run occupant for his theatre. If so, the strategy failed—*Sue, Dear* closed in early September.

In the meantime, *Strut Miss Lizzie* lingered on bravely. The show moved to the Earl Carroll Theatre, but the management demanded a much higher rent ($3,400). The show faltered during its third week and posted a tentative closing notice. The cast, having received almost no salary, nevertheless attempted to form a cooperative that would continue to run the show. The Carroll management agreed to reduce the rent to $2,500, and the cast split a $900 profit at the end of the third week. Box office receipts declined during the fourth week, and the cast owed the theatre management $159. Complicating matters during the fourth week was a suit by Arthur Lyons against Carroll for stealing his show. The cast countersued Lyons for payment of back salaries. Both suits became moot: marshals arrived with warrants for the seizure of props and costumes for nonpayment of debt.[6]

Creamer's lengthy tale of woe was hardly unusual in the early days of the black musicals. After *Shuffle Along* the financial potential of these new shows became evident, and white producers and theatre managers hoped to cash in on the new trend. As a result, it became increasingly difficult to mount new black musicals without the support of the traditional financial methods for Broadway shows. One consequence of black artists losing financial control would be the loss of creative control.

This became apparent as soon as a month after the premiere of *Strut Miss Lizzie.* Broadway's latest black musical, *Plantation Revue,* opened July 17, 1922, at the 48th Street Theatre, which "had a couple of weeks to spare at a rental, and opened to get the gravy."[7] Much of the behind-the-scenes talent was white. Lew Leslie, who was to become the patron of the black musical revue in the 1920s, produced the show.

6. *Variety,* July 28, 1922, p. 12, August 4, 1922, p. 13.
7. *Ibid.*, July 21, 1922.

Roy Turk and Russell Robinson wrote the score, despite the presence in the cast of talented black songwriter Shelton Brooks ("Some of These Days" and "Darktown Strutters' Ball") and orchestra leader Will Vodery, who had also contributed songs to Broadway scores in earlier years.

Some critics complained that *Plantation Revue* was just a cabaret performance that had migrated from uptown, but others admitted that it was quite a show. Shelton Brooks, as the master of ceremonies, introduced a wide variety of acts that included Edith Wilson, Chappy Chapelle, and Juanita Stinette. The stage setting was modest, though grotesque. Suspended over the center of the stage was a large imitation half of watermelon that emitted beams of light at varying intervals. The New York *Globe* heartily approved of the setting, which "added to the conviviality of the atmosphere."[8]

The success of all Leslie's shows during the 1920s and 1930s was based on his ability to select magnificent talent that often carried lackluster or average productions. His casting coup for *Plantation Revue* was the selection of Florence Mills for a major role. As the replacement for Gertrude Saunders in *Shuffle Along,* Mills had been a showstopper. Leslie began to build her into one of the top international stars of the age. Within a short time, she would be billed as "the world's greatest colored entertainer."

Oh Joy! finished the 1922 summer season when it opened at the corner of Fifty-seventh Street and Eighth Avenue on August 3, 1922. Unfortunately, no theatre existed there at the time. Producer Lewis Rogers and authors J. Homer Tutt and Salem Tutt Whitney had a show that had been a hit in Boston, even weathering the competition of the touring version of *Shuffle Along.* When no theatre was available, they decided to convert the former Van-Kelton tennis stadium. They rented a tent for $1,000, built a stage for $2,000, and placed cushions on the tennis benches. *Voilà,* New York City had its newest theatre, the Bamboo Isle.[9]

Although *Oh Joy!* finally obtained a theatre, it ultimately lost its star. Ethel Waters was earning $125 per week in the Boston version of the show, when Whitney and Tutt asked her to appear in New York. Waters recalled: "But when I went downtown I found out that the show was opening there all right—but in a tent set up in an empty lot. 'Here in

8. New York *Globe,* July 18, 1922.
9. *Variety,* August 11, 1922, p. 13.

New York,' I was told, 'a tent show will be a novelty.' 'It ain't no novelty to me,' I said. 'The days when I worked in a tent are over forever. I have slept with horses for the last time, I trust.' "[10]

Waters also hesitated to continue her association with the *Oh Joy!* company because of difficulty in obtaining her generous salary. In her autobiography, *His Eye Is on the Sparrow,* Waters explained the many ways in which she and the cast did not get paid. One method was the "we can pay you, but we can't pay the rest of the cast" routine. Therefore, the management explained, the show would have to close, and the entire cast would be walking the street. Waters had to accept a greatly reduced salary. The converse of this excuse was then given to the cast members, as they learned that the star (Waters) demanded her entire salary, and so they could not be paid. As might be expected, the relationship between the star and her fellow performers declined rapidly.

The producers also tried gathering the cast together to explain their economic difficulties. They then added that old refrain, "If you can only hang on a little longer, we'll pass the danger point and have a hit." On other occasions they spread the rumor that "the Shuberts were going to take over the show, and Mr. Shubert was catching the show that very evening!" A "Mr. Shubert" did invariably appear in a private box that evening, but cast members discovered that the producers had hired a bum, dressed him up in a tuxedo, and had him portray the impresario.[11] Waters' catalog of producers' excuses echoed throughout the world of the black musical in the 1920s. Unless the show was a marked success, producers often siphoned money from the black actors and composers. While this practice was typically accepted as normal (indeed, Waters in her autobiography laughs off these instances) in the early 1920s, actors eventually responded to these repeated excuses from producers. By 1923, in many cases, the new rule was "No salary, no show."

Liza followed *Oh Joy!* on Broadway, but it opened during the regular season (November 27, 1922). It had enjoyed a lengthy tryout in Harlem during the previous months as *Bon Bon Buddy, Jr.* Its 169-performance run made it the most successful black musical of the 1922–1923 season. Part of the reason was its willingness to copy *Shuffle Along.* Both shows had the same director, and both plots con-

10. Ethel Waters, with Charles Samuels, *His Eye Is on the Sparrow* (New York, 1978), 153–54.

11. *Ibid.,* 152–53.

cerned political machinations in the mythical southern city of Jimtown. Irvin Miller's libretto concerns Jimtown's attempt to construct a monument to the previous mayor (Steve Peck from *Shuffle Along*?). Squire Norris (Alonzo Fenderson) directs these efforts with the help of his daughter Liza, who is "simply full of jazz." Dandy (Thaddeus Drayton) falls in love with Liza (Margaret Simms), but he realizes that the Squire will never accept him as a son-in-law. He disguises himself as the new schoolteacher, who has yet to arrive in town, and assumes dignified airs. The townspeople witness the courtship and begin to suspect the ersatz schoolteacher. In particular they worry that he is using Liza in order to embezzle money from the statue fund. True identities are revealed during the final scene, the Squire gives his blessing to the marriage, and everyone is ecstatic. The play concludes with several specialty dance numbers, one of which, "The Charleston Dancy" (the most popular dance of the Roaring Twenties), received its Broadway premiere during this sequence.[12]

How Come? finished the Broadway season with a whimper. This musical, which opened on April 16, 1923, starred Eddie Hunter. It received harsh treatment from the critics, especially from the New York *Sun* reviewer: "It's getting dark on Broadway. But not very dark, as the young people who make up the personnel of *How Come?* have hardly the shade of darkness. Many of them are light chocolate, but the predominating complexion is white. . . . *How Come?*'s chief defect is an unsuccessful attempt to imitate Broadway musical comedy." Eddie Hunter's libretto told of the Mobile Chicken Trust, whose members had been robbed of a great deal of money by their former treasurer. In order to repay the group, he sets up a bootleg liquor operation with a shoeshine parlor as a front. Customers would ask for white shoes if they wanted gin or tan shoes if they wanted whiskey. This tale of gambling and assorted chicanery imitated the plot of *Shuffle Along*, but had only a brief run on Broadway. Critics, however, did take note of a smashing new dance number, "Charleston Cut-Out," which temporarily enlivened the proceedings.[13]

Each black musical that followed *Shuffle Along* was moderately successful at best, a failure at worst. None seemed able to attract the enthusiastic audiences of the Sissle and Blake hit. George White, the

12. *Liza* script, in MC/LC.

13. New York *Sun*, April 17, 1923; New York *Mail*, April 17, 1923. For an interview with Eddie Hunter, see Loften Mitchell, *Voices of the Black Theatre* (Clifton, N.J., 1975), 35–57.

young Broadway producer of the famed *Scandals* revues, decided to capitalize on the apparent but unfulfilled interest in black musical shows and assemble a worthy successor to *Shuffle Along.* He signed contracts with Flournoy Miller and Aubrey Lyles for a new musical with the tentative title of *Shuffle Along of 1923.* The comedy team would receive $2,000 weekly, a hefty increase over their *Shuffle Along* salary.

The sudden defection of Miller and Lyles shocked and dismayed Sissle and Blake, who had been planning a new road edition of *Shuffle Along.* The *Shuffle Along* company sued White and successfully blocked his use of the show's title. Miller and Lyles, however, were legally free to join White's production.[14]

The suit fractured the unity of the *Shuffle Along* crew. Miller and Lyles brought several members of the original company to join them in their new venture: Paul C. Floyd, Arthur Porter, C. Wesley Hill, Ina Duncan, and Tommy Woods. Also plucked from the Jazz Jasmines chorus was Adelaide Hall, who received critical raves for her leading role in the new show. This remarkable debut began a thirty-five-year career in the American and British musical theatre.

James P. Johnson and Cecil Mack were hired to write the score. Each had some experience in the theatre, but this was their first Broadway effort. Born in New Brunswick, New Jersey, in 1891, Johnson began his career as a pianist in small clubs where his unique style soon attracted considerable attention. He turned to song writing with Will Farrell in 1914, and the team composed "Mama's and Papa's Blues" and "Stop It, Joe." Johnson also contributed songs to J. Leubrie Hill's *Darktown Follies,* the popular Harlem entertainment (1913–1916). Mack, born Richard C. McPherson in 1883, began writing songs in 1901. He also provided special material for Williams and Walker in *In Dahomey* and *Bandanna Land.* As founder of the Gotham-Attucks Music Publishing Company, Mack was instrumental in the promotion of the songs of black artists during the first decades of this century. The Johnson and Mack partnership proved to be a remarkable collaboration.[15]

Although plans for the new show proceeded apace, the proper name for the enterprise seemed to elude its creators. *George White's Black Scandals* was an early suggestion, but White discarded it since he feared confusion with his annual *George White's Scandals. Miller and Lyles'*

14. *Variety,* August 9, 1923, p. 11.

15. Roger D. Kinkle, *The Complete Encyclopedia of Popular Music and Jazz, 1900–1950* (4 vols.; New Rochelle, N.Y., 1974), II, 1184, 1358.

Cakewalkers was also dismissed in favor of the shorter and snappier *Runnin' Wild*.

The show opened at the Howard Theatre in Washington, D.C., on August 23, 1923, for its tryout run. Although the critics lavished praise on Miller and Lyles and Adelaide Hall, ticket sales languished. After a losing first week, White threatened to close the show unless the eighty-two-member cast agreed to work without salary. The company, in an unusual show of solidarity, refused and called White's bluff. Miller and Lyles negotiated a compromise and sacrificed their weekly $2,000 in order to pay the ensemble partial salaries. This seeming violation of "The show must go on" was a realistic reaction. Black performers were learning that producers continually *claimed* poverty during the tryout period and early run of a show and, consequently, demanded salary cuts. The truth of the matter was often in dispute.[16]

Once this crisis was resolved, business began to improve. Increased advertising brought in whites who had rarely attended the Howard Theatre. Often, noted *Variety*'s critic, the house was almost three-fourths white. Special midnight performances were added to attract black audiences. This innovation, initiated by *Shuffle Along*, brought out a hidden black audience that was unable to attend matinee or early evening performances because of job commitments.

In September, *Runnin' Wild* moved to Boston, where it was greeted warmly. On opening night, some musical numbers received as many as six encores. According to the critics, the obvious hit was "Old Fashioned Love," performed by Ina Duncan, Adelaide Hall, and Arthur Porter. No one seemed to notice the rendition by Elisabeth Welch (Elizabeth Welsh) of "Charston," a song that came to symbolize the Roaring Twenties as "The Charleston." *Runnin' Wild* lasted eight weeks in Boston, which provided a healthy financial cushion for the show's New York opening. Once again, the best-attended performances were at midnight.

Runnin' Wild premiered at the Colonial Theatre, a former vaudeville house, in New York City on October 29, 1923. The reviews were favorable, and many critics said that *Runnin' Wild* was the equal of *Shuffle Along* in quality. A few even suggested that it was better because its pace was faster and its scenery more lavish.

George White gave Miller and Lyles above-title billing and dubbed them "America's Foremost Colored Comedians," a notion that most

16. *Variety*, August 30, 1923, p. 13.

"Forty Below." Flournoy Miller and Aubrey Lyles in *Runnin' Wild*
Courtesy Billy Rose Theatre Collection, New York Public Library

critics clearly supported. James P. Sinnott of the *Telegraph* found the team equal to Williams and Walker, and the *Herald* followed suit: "[The show relied on] the comedy of Miller and Lyles, who are individually much more enjoyable than Bert Williams because they don't agonize so much over a point. Their humor seems utterly spontaneous and unstudied, and it is as racially true as their complexion. They are McIntyre and Heath [a blackface comedy team] without the makeup, but their comedy lines, fashioned by themselves, rarely smack of the minstrel show, seeming rather to be characteristic Negro 'back talk.' "[17]

Miller and Lyles crafted a libretto that allowed them to display their classic vaudeville routines once again. The thin plot concerned Steve Jenkins (Miller) and Sam Peck (Lyles), who flee Jimtown when insurance investigators discover a clever plan to bilk their company of thousands of dollars. Jenkins and Peck go to distant St. Paul, where they almost freeze to death:

Steve: Man, it sure is cold out here.

Sam: Oh boy! It certainly is—must be about forty below zero.

Steve: Forty below—it's lower than that!

Sam: Man, I ain't never seen so much cold weather.

Steve: You know one thing, Sam. . . . We got to either change clothes or climate.

Sam: Let's not stand out here in the cold arguing about it. The best thing to do is take that last quarter we got there to buy two bowls of hot soup.

Steve: But I done spent dat quarter.

Sam: You ain't bought nothin' to eat with it.

Steve: I didn't say I did.

Sam: You ain't paid no room rent with it.

Steve: I know I ain't.

Sam: Well what could you find to spend that last quarter on in all this cold?

Steve: I bought a thermometer, that's what I bought. . . . .

Sam: Why you don't even know what a thermometer is, do you? . . . You see this thing here. You see the figures on the side here. You see this red strip in the middle. This here is a thermometer. Now, when this little red thing here gets down here to [minus]20 that means to get an overcoat; when it gets to [minus]30, that means to button up the

17. New York *Telegraph*, October 30, 1923; New York *Herald*, October 30, 1923.

overcoat; but, boy, when it gets to [minus]50, you need a woolen overcoat when it gets there, I'll tell you right now!

Steve: Is there a number on there that tells you how to get a overcoat?[18]

They eventually return home, disguised as "spiritualistic mediums," in their continuous attempt to evade their pursuers.

The *Runnin' Wild* libretto also provided ample opportunities for the Johnson and Mack songs, which received considerable praise. *Variety*'s critic noted: " 'Old Fashioned Love' is the theme song and will undoubtedly be one of the big sellers of the coming season. Others that should bring big returns are 'Open Your Heart,' sung by Revella Hughes and George Stephens; 'Gingerbrown,' with Adelaide Hall and Bob Lee doing a strutting bit that was one of the best of this sort of thing that this reviewer has seen; and 'Charston,' sung by Elisabeth Welch." Despite this favorable comment, "The Charleston" generally escaped the critics' notice when they evaluated the entire score. Not until the following year, when *Runnin' Wild* began its Philadelphia run, did critics finally take note of the song. Soon the rhythmic "Charleston" captured the imagination and spirit of the Roaring Twenties.[19]

Although the song was new, the dance itself evolved much earlier. LeRoi Jones has suggested that the dance had African origins, and Noble Sissle recalled learning it in Savannah, Georgia, in 1905. James P. Johnson first saw the new dance step while playing piano at the Jungles Casino in New York City in 1913. The Jungles was not the fanciest night spot, but it did provide a job for the budding pianist: "It was just a cellar without fixings. The furnace, coal, and ashes were still there behind a partition. The coal bin was handy for guests to stash their liquor in case the cops dropped in."[20]

Johnson described the origin of "The Charleston" to Tom Davin in a 1959 interview in the *Jazz Review*:

The people who came to The Jungles Casino were mostly from around Charleston, South Carolina, and other places in the South. Most of them worked for the Ward Line as longshoremen or on ships that called at Southern ports. . . .

They picked their partners with care to show off their best steps and put sets, cotillions, and cakewalks that would give them a chance to get off.

18. Transcription of "Forty Below," Okeh Records, 40273 (1923).

19. *Variety*, November 1, 1923. See also LeRoi Jones, *Blues People: Negro Music in White America* (New York, 1963), 17.

20. Stearns and Stearns, *Jazz Dance*, 112; Tom Davin, "Conversations with James P. Johnson," *Jazz Review* (July, 1959), 12.

> The Charleston, which became a popular dance step on its own, was just a regulation cotillion step without a name. It had many variations—all danced to the rhythm that everyone knows now. One regular at the Casino, named Dan White, was the best dancer in the crowd and he introduced the Charleston step as we know it. But there were dozens of other steps used, too.
>
> It was while playing for these southern dancers that I composed a number of Charlestons—eight in all—all with the damn rhythm. One of these later became my famous "Charleston" when it hit Broadway.[21]

Unfortunately, George White claimed to hate the new dance and kept complaining. Flournoy Miller recalled that White "brought his friends around to show them—in front of us—that the Charleston was nothing, and he tried everything but cutting the dance, which would have made us quit." Miller later discovered that the real reason for White's supposed hatred of this dance was that he wanted to premiere it in his own *Scandals* revue.[22]

Runnin' Wild was not the first Broadway musical to feature the new dance. Maceo Pinkard composed "The Charleston Dancy" for *Liza,* and *How Come?* presented "Charleston Cut-Out" and "Charleston Finale." Nevertheless, James Weldon Johnson recalled that *Runnin' Wild* "started the dance on its world-encircling course": "When Miller and Lyles introduced the dance in their show, they did not depend wholly upon their extraordinarily good jazz band for the accompaniment; they went straight back to primitive Negro music and had the major part of the chorus supplement the band by beating out the time with hand-clapping and foot-patting. The effect was electrical. Such a demonstration of beating out complex rhythms had never before been seen on a stage in New York."[23]

Runnin' Wild became an immediate success, and business ran three times stronger than it had been during the initial weeks of *Shuffle Along.* With a $5.00 top, *Runnin' Wild* grossed $19,000 its first week. Business was good throughout the year and hit new highs during the holidays. *Runnin' Wild* finished a successful 27-week, 213-performance run in the spring of 1924 and embarked on a successful road tour.

Who attended *Runnin' Wild*? George White liked to brag that "Cha-

21. Davin, "Conversations with James P. Johnson," 10–14.
22. Stearns and Stearns, *Jazz Dance,* 146.
23. Johnson, *Black Manhattan,* 190.

liapin and a number of opera singers, actors, and socially prominent people" visited the show, but critics noted that many patrons were blacks. A New York *Herald* reporter sent to cover the box office trade commented: "These [customers] contained a sprinkling of colored patrons, for *Runnin' Wild* is a revue with a cast entirely composed of Negro performers, and their own race has been rallying to their support, some of the dusky theatregoers attending as often as three times and knowing just the right place to keel over in a paroxysm of joy."[24]

While *Runnin' Wild* swiftly became Broadway's biggest black musical hit, a new musical by the team that created *Shuffle Along* suffered major setbacks. Perhaps the most severe crisis for *The Chocolate Dandies* (1924) was that major talent defected to the *Runnin' Wild* company. Second, the new show was vastly more expensive than Sissle and Blake's earlier effort had been. Critics lauded the gorgeous costumes and the elaborate stage settings, which included a horse race with three live horses on a treadmill. But the show had difficulties paying the bills. Salaries alone were almost twice those of *Shuffle Along*. Exacerbating the situation was the fact that black shows tended to charge lower prices than did white Broadway shows. *The Chocolate Dandies* had the lowest top price on Broadway—$2.50 for orchestra seats. By comparison, the *Ziegfeld Follies* charged the highest price ($5.50). The average ranged from $3.85 to $4.40, with that tale of singing Mounties, *Rose Marie*, at the upper end of the scale.[25]

Perhaps the major problem that *The Chocolate Dandies* faced was that it was condemned by the white critics for "ambition," always a dirty word when they considered a black show. Sissle and Blake had endeavored to escape the strict limitations governing the black musical and were punished for it. Ironically, they had helped perpetuate those very limitations in *Shuffle Along*. Several critics mentioned this problem, but *Variety*'s man in Chicago had the most stinging comments:

> They have some funny moments . . . but they haven't enough to carry the show, and neither dances. The absence of spirited stepping, except by a lively group of eight chorus girls, looks as though it were deliberate in a plan to make the whole piece "high toned." It is that, but the results are achieved at the expense of a genuine negro spirit. The leading woman (Lottie Gee) in action and manner might be a Dillingham prima donna. Ivan H. Browning has all the posing tricks of a soulful tenor in a Winter

24. New York *Herald*, January 20, 1924.
25. *Variety*, September 24, 1924, p. 12.

> Garden musical comedy and Noble Sissle is a dapper straight man. . . . In short it is a negro piece for the most part uninspired by the native spirit. . . . The whole business is "white folks" material of which there is plenty and then some in the show world, and not good darky entertainment, of which there is little enough of the best.

The review ended, "The rest of the score is melodious in an ambitious way, but distinctly away from the style of colored minstrelsy."[26]

Ironically, Sissle and Blake received similar notices from black reviewers. Eric Walrond, writing in *Opportunity,* noted:

> Setting out (it is obvious) to cater to the jaded desires of white comedy lovers [Sissle and Blake had created something] that didn't seem like a colored show at all. . . . The life of the Negro as is sketchily presented in a show like this is false. All those elements of vital spiritual and emotional content that distinguish it from that of other racial groups are taken out. A feeble half-white misanthrope is substituted. Anyone who is familiar with the vaudeville shows given at the Lafayette or the Lincoln in Harlem, knows that there is a reservoir of talent and of material up there lying waste that, if properly commandeered and utilized in a production like *The Chocolate Dandies,* would create a distinct sensation.[27]

Not all black critics agreed with Walrond, however. Theophilus Lewis commented: "*The Chocolate Dandies* is the aristocrat of colored musical shows. On second thought I have decided to strike out the word 'colored,' for there is no more urbane revue or musical show that can compare with *The Chocolate Dandies* in color, speed, and fun, and not one can boast of such blue blooded jazz." He proceeded to enumerate everything favorable about the show. Achieving his ultimate listing was the fact that "there is no ghost in *The Chocolate Dandies.*"[28]

The harsh reviews condemned *The Chocolate Dandies* to a ninety-six-performance run. The message was clear. Despite the success of *Shuffle Along,* only certain types of black musicals would be accepted on Broadway in the 1920s. Those that adhered to the formula had a chance for success; those that deviated would be condemned to failure. Alain Locke, a patron of the Harlem Renaissance and the editor of *The New Negro* (1925), noted this problem as early as 1926 after he witnessed a deluge of virtually identical black musical comedies and

26. *Ibid.,* April 2, 1924, p. 16.
27. *Opportunity* (November, 1924), 345.
28. *Messenger,* VI (1924), 323.

revues: "Negro dramatic art must not only be liberated from the handicaps of external disparagement, but from its self-imposed limitations. It must more and more have the courage to be original, to break with established dramatic convention of all sorts. It must have the courage to develop its own idiom, to pour itself into new moulds; in short, to be experimental."[29] Yet, the formulas established by *Shuffle Along* and, later, by Lew Leslie's *Blackbirds* revues became the norm by which major critics would judge black musicals. In this context, experimentation in the world of the 1920s black musicals was often tantamount to failure. Thus, while many authors claim that *Shuffle Along* opened new doors for black musicals on Broadway, it actually opened them only a crack.[30]

29. Alain Locke, "The Negro and the American Stage," *Theatre Arts Monthly* (February, 1926), 116. Locke writes of this problem again in "Broadway and the Negro Drama," *Theatre Arts* (October, 1941), 745–50. Here his concern is how white images of black characters have limited the freedom of black artists on the stage. Donald Bogle later offers a similar argument for black images in film (*Toms, Coons, Mulattoes, Mammies, and Bucks* [New York, 1973]).

30. For example, see Nathan Irvin Huggins, *Harlem Renaissance* (New York, 1971), 290.

VII

DIXIE TO BROADWAY

Lew Leslie and the Black Revues

Shuffle Along's successors slowly abandoned that most troublesome commodity, the libretto. Critics praised the songs, the choreography, and the performances of the new black musicals, but the libretto often came under intense, and frequently harsh, scrutiny. Perhaps inevitably, each new black musical gave less and less importance to the book and focused more attention on the musical elements of the show. Sissle and Blake's *The Chocolate Dandies,* which retained a standard musical comedy format, suffered for it. Those shows that shelved the book seemed to have a greater chance for success.

This move was in no way limited to black musical theatre. Between 1910 and 1929, book musicals and revues coexisted peaceably. The *Follies* and the *Scandals* presented their blend of musical merriment, sophisticated comedy, and visual dash; Kern and Gershwin tended to provide their melodies for shows with plot. Nevertheless, the revue format offered several advantages for the black musical show in the early 1920s. First of all, it capitalized on the most popular elements of the black musical show and, logically, jettisoned those that major reviewers had criticized. Second, it blurred the line between nightclub and theatre for the audience. Customers who had made the trek to Harlem to see the newest black singing sensations could now attend nearby theatres. Perhaps the Broadway version was an even cheaper alternative. Theophilus Lewis suggested that producers catered to "the large number of white people who would like to enjoy the thrills of the black and tan cabarets, only they can't afford the stiff cover charge and don't like the idea of paying fifty cents for a bottle of beer that they can buy for eight cents at the delicatessen store."[1]

1. Lewis A. Erenberg, *Steppin' Out: New York Nightlife and the Transformation of American Culture, 1890–1930.* (Westport, Conn., 1981), 254–57; *Messenger,* VIII (September, 1926), 278.

The similarity between nightclub revue and Broadway revue also allowed for less expensive tryout performances. No longer would new shows have to travel to various cities of the Midwest and the South. They could use a variety of midtown and Harlem night spots prior to their Broadway premieres. During these tryout runs, changes could be made in the shows and tested before reliable New York audiences. This was a marked advantage, as out-of-town viewers tended to disagree with Broadway taste-setters.

The focus of these new revues was often the talent, rather than the dazzling costumes or exotic scenery of the *Ziegfeld Follies*. Hence, when critics commented that the new black revues looked "cheap" (a common riposte), the comparison was to Ziegfeld's shows or George White's shows. Often, however, the scenery became secondary when the leading roles were filled by, say, Florence Mills, Ethel Waters, or Adelaide Hall. The critical love letters to these stars often masked the comments on the physical aspects of the production, which usually appeared in the last paragraphs of the review.

Put and Take, Strut Miss Lizzie, Plantation Revue, and *Oh Joy!* had varying degrees of success with the revue format after *Shuffle Along*'s conquest. With the opening of *Dixie to Broadway* on October 29, 1924, it seemed that the revue had triumphed. With a "new high for a colored attraction" ($3.30), Lew Leslie's revue immediately attracted ticket buyers.[2] Interestingly, most of the ticket purchases for the show were carried out by brokers. Prior to this date, most of the tickets for black shows were purchased at the box office, as ticket agents believed that those tickets would not be salable commodities to their traditional customers:

> The impressive success of Florence Mills and her company shatters some deep-rooted theories heretofore existing relative to colored musical companies. "No colored musical show can be a financial and artistic success on Broadway," has been a saying for years and regarded as uncontroversial. The line of argument advanced by the theatrical powers was that white amusement seekers would not patronize a colored show as a legitimate theatre proposition, but desired to regard Negro entertainment merely as a lure for slumming parties; that to create the proper atmosphere it was necessary to house a colored attraction in a theatre off Broadway on the fringe of the theatrical district.[3]

2. *Variety,* November 5, 1924, p. 18.
3. "A Dream Come True," unidentifed article, in "Florence Mills" File, TC/PFL.

No doubt the generally glowing reviews accorded hit status to *Dixie to Broadway,* but the appearance of a shining new star, Florence Mills, also excited audience interest.

Mills's rise to prominence on Broadway was meteoric. Born in Washington, D.C., in 1895, she appeared on the stage at an early age as Baby Florence Mills. She later formed a sister act with Olivia and Maude (the Mills Sisters), and they traveled coast to coast as a vaudeville team. In the 1920s she joined her new husband U.S. ("Slow Kid") Thompson, a noted dancer, on the Keith Circuit. She first attracted notice, however, as a replacement cast member in *Shuffle Along.* Gertrude Saunders, who performed "I'm Craving for That Kind of Love," left the cast, and young Florence filled in admirably. By all accounts, her rendition of the hit song overshadowed Saunders' interpretation and consequently launched her career. Unfortunately, though there is a recording of Saunders' version, no disk remains of the Mills performance. As a result, only eyewitness accounts attest to her sexy rendition of this number. Lew Leslie was one of the many audience members impressed by her performance.[4]

Leslie, a young and relatively inexperienced Broadway producer at this time, signed Mills to appear in *Plantation Revue,* which served to further her reputation. One critic wrote: "In that season not to have seen and heard Florence Mills was to be quite out of the know on Broadway. She established a tremendous vogue and the resort was crowded nightly by the connoisseurs of the town who welcomed a talent so new, so rich, so provocative in its tropical appeal, so saturated with emotion, and yet fastidious in its refinement. Right away managers began bidding for her to appear in their revues." Even Ziegfeld offered her a role in the *Follies* (as he had done years earlier for Bert Williams), but she decided to remain with Leslie. He promised to star her in an all-black revue dubbed *From Dover to Dixie* for its overseas premiere:

> I felt [said Miss Mills] that since Williams established the Colored performer in association with a well-known revue [the *Ziegfeld Follies*], that I could best serve the Colored actor by accepting Mr. Leslie's offer, since he had promised to make his revue as sumptuous and gorgeous in production and costume as Ziegfeld's "Follies," George White's "Scandals," or the "Greenwich Village Follies," at the same time using an all-colored

4. For a brief biography of Mills, see Bogle, *Brown Sugar,* 40–43; and Johnson, *Black Manhattan,* 196–201.

cast. I felt that if this revue turned out successfully, a permanent institution would have been created for the Colored artists and an opportunity created for the glorification of the American High-Browns.[5]

Leslie took the show to London and Paris, where Mills made a smashing impression. One London critic wrote: "The success acquired by Miss Florence Mills, the American coloured girl playing in *From Dover to Dixie* is something unequalled by any American playing here in the last decade. She is by far the most artistic person London has had the good fortune to see."[6] Mills toured in *From Dover to Dixie* throughout England, but only half of the show later reached New York as *Dixie to Broadway.* The "Dover" section, which featured white British and American talent, was jettisoned in transatlantic revisions.

The white acting talent may have disappeared for the American premiere of *Dixie to Broadway,* but Leslie continued a trend that first became evident with *Plantation Revue.* Virtually all the behind-the-scenes creative talents were white. Leslie produced and directed the show; Walter De Leon, Tom Howard, Sidney Lazarus, and Leslie wrote the skits; and George W. Meyer, Arthur Johnston, Grant Clark, and Roy Turk supplied the music and lyrics. This soon became a trademark of a Leslie revue: "They [white men] understand the colored man better than he does himself. Colored composers excel at spirituals, but their other songs are just 'what' [white] songs with Negro words. The two greatest Negro songs now sung were written by white men—'Ol' Man River' and 'That's Why Darkies Were Born.' " Leslie relented on occasion (Eubie Blake prepared songs for his *Blackbirds of 1930*) and even admitted in an interview that "there's a charm about Negro songs—even those written by white men and sung by them—that is irresistible."[7]

The fact that Lew Leslie was white was a continuing surprise even to Broadway insiders. The prevalence of the adjective "Caucasian" in gossip columns describing Leslie was surpassed only by similar descriptions of his wife Irene. One interviewer emphasized that she had the "reddest hair in the world, and a skin that gets an exotic greenish pallor when she is tired. She has a cameo profile, and wears bright red lipstick to harmonize with her hair." Yet Leslie's identification with the

5. "Florence Mills—Artiste," unidentified article (publicity release), in "Florence Mills" File, TC/PFL.

6. Johnson, *Black Manhattan,* 198.

7. "Prefers to Stage All-Negro Shows. Lew Leslie Declares No White Girls Work So Hard as Do the Harlem Belles," unidentified article, in "Lew Leslie" File, TC/PFL.

new black revues (from *Plantation Revue* to *Dixie to Broadway*) caused one columnist to express "distinct shock" when he discovered that Leslie was white.[8]

The air of surprise about Leslie's race reflected his Johnny-come-lately status as a producer. Born Lewis Lessinsky in 1886 in Orangeburg, New York, Leslie began his theatrical career as an impressionist, wowing audiences with renditions of David Warfield, Sam Bernard, and other talents of the day. His greatest strength, he felt, was that no one in the audience had seen these stars in person before. He added songs and patter to his act. For a time, he and Belle Baker had a doubles act. He later claimed to be bored with performing and abandoned the stage in favor of discovering new comic and musical talent. Ben Bernie, Frank Fay, Phil Baker, and Bee Palmer were among Leslie's first finds. He brought Palmer and Baker together in a revue that appeared at Broadway's Café de Paris. During the Palmer and Baker run, Leslie conceived a new idea for the nightclub. He decided to change the Café de Paris into a "plantation" and feature an all-black revue. The first *Plantation Revue* proved a success at the club. Leslie, searching for new talent, discovered Florence Mills in the cast of the popular *Shuffle Along* and hired her to appear in the second edition of his nightclub revue. The overwhelming success of the new version of the show convinced Leslie that he should move it to Broadway. *Plantation Revue* enjoyed a modest but highly praised run and then a European tour.[9]

The key to Leslie's success in the 1920s was his ability to discover and exploit new black talent. From Florence Mills to Lena Horne, Leslie managed to build his black revues around one or more dynamic performers, who could carry a modest show to success. Leslie claimed that his ability to discover such talent reflected continual hard work:

> Colored revues . . . are in themselves novelties and therefore expert judgment must be used in the casting. . . . Unlike the usual extravaganza, where names well known to the theatre-goers can be thrown into the breach, the producer of colored shows, because names, except in rare instances, carry little weight with the audiences, is forced to resort to fine-combing the field in an effort to get the best talent available. . . . This is no

8. "Paradox Is Presented in Career of Producer," unidentified article, *ibid.*

9. Stanley Green, *Encyclopaedia of the Musical Theatre* (New York, 1976), 248. For a description of the Plantation Club, see *Smart Set,* LXXI (June, 1923), 87–89.

> easy task, and often a producer has to spend months preparing talented Negro actors for their debut on the legitimate stage. Then, too, there aren't as many stellar actors in the Negro ranks as naturally prevail in the Caucasian theatre because the opportunities for colored artists aren't as great. This, of course, limits the selection, with the result that the Broadway entrepreneur of colored revues has, in most cases, to develop his own talent.[10]

Once the performers for *Dixie to Broadway* were selected, Leslie was also active in writing the show. One critic noted that "he lives for the theatre alone and shuns the spotlight. He begins planning a show six or eight months in advance of the rehearsal and virtually closets himself in a room with his authors until he works out in full his entertainment pattern." Once the show was written, Leslie remained with the cast during rehearsal. He even conducted the orchestra if the tempo were not brisk enough. Quickness was a Leslie trademark. One reviewer noted that "Fast Pace Is Essential Requisite of Negro Musical Success," a dictum Leslie traditionally followed:

> It is one of the anomalies of the theatre that the Negro, who is so slow moving and lackadaisical in life should be expected to turn into a whirling dervish on the stage, but audiences have been educated to this point of expectancy and to slow up now is nothing short of fatal. How to keep the colored artist on the constant que vive is one of the problems that Lew Leslie has satisfactorily solved. There is an ever recurring tendency on the part of the Negro stage entertainer to slow up and Leslie has discovered the one certain method of bridging the gap, and that is through constant rehearsal. It is doubtful if any group of white actors and actresses are rehearsed as much as Negro players are, not only before the show takes to the boards, but after it has been settled down to a long Broadway engagement. Leslie . . . has followed this practice from the very beginning. Of course, it means a great deal of work for him since he supervises all the rehearsals, but tempo is so important that he is ready and willing to sacrifice hours that ordinarily could be turned into other channels.[11]

Although no script for *Dixie to Broadway* remains, it is possible to reconstruct the show's basic structure from the program, newspaper

10. Unidentified article, in "Lew Leslie" File, TC/PFL.

11. "Fast Pace Is Essential Requisite of Negro Musical Success," unidentified article, *ibid.*

Broadhurst Theatre
44th STREET, WEST OF BROADWAY
GEORGE BROADHURST .... DIRECTOR
THOMAS W. BROADHURST .... MANAGER
MRS. TRIMBLE BRADLEY .... GENERAL STAGE DIRECTOR

NOTICE: This Theatre, with every seat occupied, can be emptied in less than three minutes. Choose NOW the Exit nearest to your seat, and in case of fire walk (do not run) to that Exit.
THOMAS J. DRENNAN, Fire Commissioner.

WEEK BEGINNING MONDAY EVENING, NOVEMBER 24, 1924
Matinees Thursday and Saturday
Midnight Tuesday

LEW LESLIE
Presents
Florence Mills
The Sensation of Two Continents
—in—
Dixie To Broadway
—with—
SHELTON BROOKS, HAMTREE HARRINGTON, CORA GREEN
—and—
WILL VODERY'S PLANTATION ORCHESTRA
With JOHNNIE DUNN
Music by George W. Meyer and Arthur Johnston
Lyrics by Grant Clarke and Roy Turk
Book by Walter De Leon, Tom Howard, Lew Leslie and Sidney Lazarus
Arrangements and Orchestrations by Will Vodery
Entire Production Staged and Conceived by
LEW LESLIE

PROGRAM CONTINUED ON SECOND PAGE FOLLOWING

THE BROADHURST THEATRE 11

PROGRAM CONTINUED

ACT I.
Scene 1—Prologue—Evolution of the Colored Race
Scene 2—"Put Your Old Bandanna On"
Danny Small, Maud Russell, the Plantation Chocolate Drops and the Plantation Steppers
Scene 3—"Dixie Dreams"
FLORENCE MILLS and Company
Scene 4—"A Few Steps in Front of the Curtain"
The Plantation Steppers
Scene 5—"Treasure Castle"
By Tom Howard
SAM .... HAMTREE HARRINGTON
SLIM .... SHELTON BROOKS
CHARLIE .... DANNY SMALL
SVENGALI .... WILLIAM DE MOTT
Scene 6—"He Only Comes to See Me Once in a While"
CORA GREEN
Scene 7—"Jungle Nights in Dixieland"
FLORENCE MILLS and the Plantation Chocolate Drops
Scene 8—"Prisoners Up-To-Date"
Byron Jones, Lew Keene, Johnny Nit
Scene 9—"The Right of Way"
By Walter De Leon and Lew Leslie
THE COP .... WALTER CRUMBLEY
THE VICTIM .... HAMTREE HARRINGTON
MR. AND MRS. .... SHELTON BROOKS and MAUD RUSSELL
MISS HIGH HAT .... CORA GREEN
Oldsmobile used in this scene from the New York Oldsmobile Co.

PROGRAM CONTINUED ON NEXT PAGE

Dixie to Broadway program
Courtesy Billy Rose Theatre Collection, New York Public Library

interviews, critical reviews, sheet music, publicity releases, and theatre photographs.[12] This is important since the show eventually served as the model for most of the black revues in the 1920s. Ironically, *Dixie to Broadway,* and its predecessor *Plantation Revue,* perhaps played a

12. The reconstruction of *Dixie to Broadway* draws upon a variety of sources. First, the theatre program (in TC/NYPL) lists songs, scenes, and performers. Newspaper interviews (mainly in TC/PFL and TC/NYPL) with major cast members and Leslie provide comments on rehearsals, stage directions, and performances. Most of the critical commentary was published on October 30, 1924. Major excerpts from reviews are footnoted; excerpts of a sentence or two are not. Lyrics from sheet music (unless otherwise noted) are from MC/NYPL. Cast photographs are also available from the George White Collection, TC/NYPL. They provide most of the information on costumes and sets. Publicity releases (also available at TC/PFL), many of which found their way into print, were also of some help. Although some of the anecdotes tended toward the apocryphal, some biographical data were helpful. Also, despite the utter fallaciousness of some material in the publicity releases, certain statements revealed prevalent attitudes and perceptions of the times.

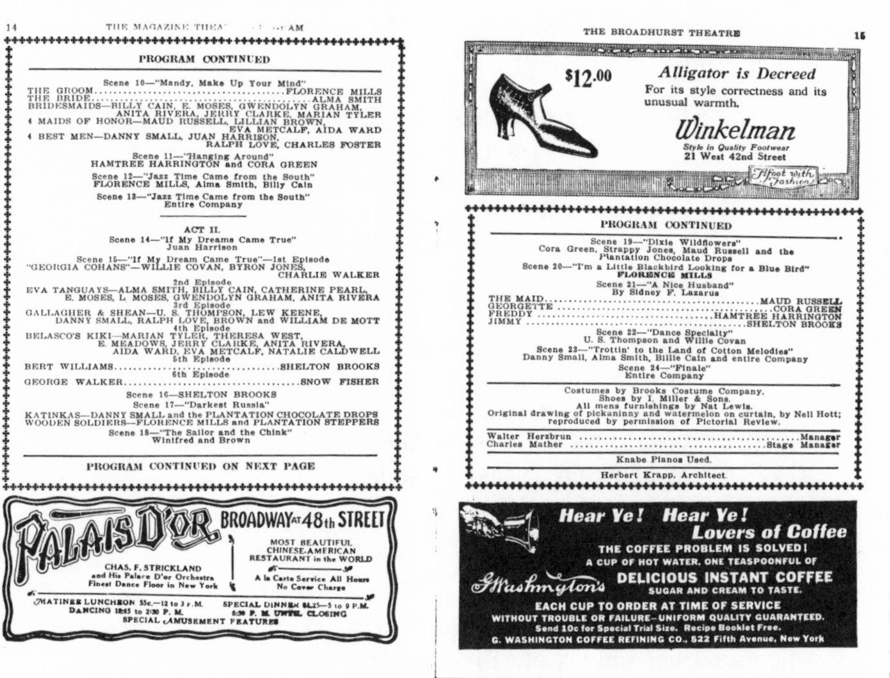

14 THE MAGAZINE THEA[illegible]AM

PROGRAM CONTINUED

Scene 10—"Mandy, Make Up Your Mind"
THE GROOM..........FLORENCE MILLS
THE BRIDE..........ALMA SMITH
BRIDESMAIDS—BILLY CAIN, E. MOSES, GWENDOLYN GRAHAM, ANITA RIVERA, JERRY CLARKE, MARIAN TYLER
4 MAIDS OF HONOR—MAUD RUSSELL, LILLIAN BROWN, EVA METCALF, AIDA WARD
4 BEST MEN—DANNY SMALL, JUAN HARRISON, RALPH LOVE, CHARLES FOSTER

Scene 11—"Hanging Around"
HAMTREE HARRINGTON and CORA GREEN

Scene 12—"Jazz Time Came from the South"
FLORENCE MILLS, Alma Smith, Billy Cain

Scene 13—"Jazz Time Came from the South"
Entire Company

ACT II.

Scene 14—"If My Dreams Came True"
Juan Harrison

Scene 15—"If My Dream Came True"—1st Episode
"GEORGIA COHANS"—WILLIE COVAN, BYRON JONES, CHARLIE WALKER
2nd Episode
EVA TANGUAYS—ALMA SMITH, BILLY CAIN, CATHERINE PEARL, E. MOSES, L. MOSES, GWENDOLYN GRAHAM, ANITA RIVERA
3rd Episode
GALLAGHER & SHEAN—U. S. THOMPSON, LEW KEENE, DANNY SMALL, RALPH LOVE, BROWN and WILLIAM DE MOTT
4th Episode
BELASCO'S KIKI—MARIAN TYLER, THERESA WEST, E. MEADOWS, JERRY CLARKE, ANITA RIVERA, AIDA WARD, EVA METCALF, NATALIE CALDWELL
5th Episode
BERT WILLIAMS..........SHELTON BROOKS
6th Episode
GEORGE WALKER..........SNOW FISHER

Scene 16—SHELTON BROOKS

Scene 17—"Darkest Russia"
KATINKAS—DANNY SMALL and the PLANTATION CHOCOLATE DROPS
WOODEN SOLDIERS—FLORENCE MILLS and PLANTATION STEPPERS

Scene 18—"The Sailor and the Chink"
Winifred and Brown

PROGRAM CONTINUED ON NEXT PAGE

PALAIS D'OR BROADWAY AT 48th STREET
CHAS. F. STRICKLAND
and His Palace D'or Orchestra
Finest Dance Floor in New York
MOST BEAUTIFUL CHINESE-AMERICAN RESTAURANT in the WORLD
A la Carte Service All Hours
No Cover Charge
MATINEE LUNCHEON 55c.—12 to 3 P.M.
DANCING 12:15 to 2:30 P. M.
SPECIAL DINNER $1.25—5 to 9 P.M.
6:30 P. M. UNTIL CLOSING
SPECIAL AMUSEMENT FEATURES

THE BROADHURST THEATRE 15

$12.00
Alligator is Decreed
For its style correctness and its unusual warmth.
Winkelman
Style in Quality Footwear
21 West 42nd Street
Afoot with Fashion

PROGRAM CONTINUED

Scene 19—"Dixie Wildflowers"
Cora Green, Strappy Jones, Maud Russell and the Plantation Chocolate Drops

Scene 20—"I'm a Little Blackbird Looking for a Blue Bird"
FLORENCE MILLS

Scene 21—"A Nice Husband"
By Sidney F. Lazarus
THE MAID..........MAUD RUSSELL
GEORGETTE..........CORA GREEN
FREDDY..........HAMTREE HARRINGTON
JIMMY..........SHELTON BROOKS

Scene 22—"Dance Specialty"
U. S. Thompson and Willie Covan

Scene 23—"Trottin' to the Land of Cotton Melodies"
Danny Small, Alma Smith, Billie Cain and entire Company

Scene 24—"Finale"
Entire Company

Costumes by Brooks Costume Company.
Shoes by I. Miller & Sons.
All mens furnishings by Nat Lewis.
Original drawing of pickaninny and watermelon on curtain, by Neil Hott; reproduced by permission of Pictorial Review.

Walter Herzbrun..........Manager
Charles Mather..........Stage Manager

Knabe Pianos Used.

Herbert Krapp, Architect.

Hear Ye! Hear Ye!
Lovers of Coffee
THE COFFEE PROBLEM IS SOLVED!
A CUP OF HOT WATER, ONE TEASPOONFUL OF
G. Washington's DELICIOUS INSTANT COFFEE
SUGAR AND CREAM TO TASTE.
EACH CUP TO ORDER AT TIME OF SERVICE
WITHOUT TROUBLE OR FAILURE—UNIFORM QUALITY GUARANTEED.
Send 10c for Special Trial Size. Recipe Booklet Free.
G. WASHINGTON COFFEE REFINING CO., 522 Fifth Avenue, New York

greater role in shaping black musical theatre in the 1920s than did the better-known *Shuffle Along*.

A prologue, "Evolution of the Colored Race," began *Dixie to Broadway*. Designed to provide a framework for the entire show, the scene traced Negro history from "Salome to Madame Butterfly to Abraham Lincoln." Despite the lofty educational intentions of this opening scene, most critics agreed that this theme was quickly abandoned in the show. Danny Small, Maud Russell, the Plantation Chocolate Drops (a chorus), and the Plantation Steppers then performed "Put Your Old Bandanna On," one of the evening's many references to the joyous life on the old plantation: "Eight dancing boys, all specialty steppers, but acting as an ensemble, steamed up the house. They completed an encore, and the applause from the encore fused with applause for the entry of Florence Mills."

Mills received a standing ovation. Although she had had few Broadway roles, her reputation (from both Harlem and London) evidently preceded her. She followed the southern theme of the previous number with "Dixie Dreams":

> Dear old Dixieland, how I long for your sunshine,
> Gee, I'm sorry I ever started to roam.
> But when the night comes creeping
> And it's time for sleeping
> I seem to live once more in my Dixie home.
>
> Dixie dreams, forever haunt me,
> Dixie dreams, are fondest of all.
> On my pillow at night,
> I see fields of white
> And mammy's songs and stories, I recall.
> Dixie scenes all pass before me
> And I live my childhood it seems.
> At the close of each day
> Mister dream-man I pray
> Bring back my Dixie dreams.

The audience was not disappointed with Mills's opening number. One critic found her singing of "Dixie Dreams" charming: "The colored songbird's fluty voice rose to high registers, a surprise to some who are not familiar with her varied talent."

After Mills's encore, the Plantation Steppers reappeared. "A Few Steps in Front of the Curtain" was designed to disguise a scenery change. With the few steps completed, the curtain opened on the obligatory graveyard or haunted house sequence, "Treasure Castle," written by Tom Howard. It might be tempting to assume that this standard feature of black revues of the 1920s was a recent white creation for white audiences. Newspaper reviews indicate, however, that such interludes were part of Harlem musicals between 1910 and 1920, and all-black audiences greeted them favorably. These sequences showed primarily blacks' fear of the possibility of spectral appearances in a graveyard at night. White critics heartily approved this latest effort, with the New York *Evening Post* noting that "Hamtree Harrington pulls off one of the most original pantomimes of ghost-fright seen in a long day. He simply becomes too scared to move, and it is effective beyond words." Even Florence Mills agreed with this assessment: "I have watched [the faces of the audience] on many occasions while Hamtree Harrington and Billy Mills were on the stage in the 'Treasure Castle' sketch, in which they enter a haunted house in search of a long lost treasure. Talk of the fountain of youth, why when Hamtree Harrington turns stiff from fright at the sight of a ghost—old men become boys and old women become girls as they rock with laughter."[13]

Cora Green then appeared with her rendition of "He Only Comes to See Me Once in a While," which specialized in double-entendres. Gabriel W. Gabriel found the song "not what you might think nice."[14] As she sang, another scene change took place, allowing Florence Mills to sing "Jungle Nights in Dixieland" with the Plantation Chocolate Drops. The Chocolate Drops wore short blue grass skirts and white wigs, and Mills was adorned in a bright red skirt. Her performance dazzled the critics: "The dusky star of the proceedings—if you can imagine a star glowing darkly—is as much of a startled faun. She can shift from the frenzied war whoop that takes one back to the days of her ancestors on the Congo to the soft easy dribbles of hummed speech that were intoned on the plantations back in those dear old southern times before the war."

A brief dance number, "Prisoners Up-To-Date," introduced the show's most talented terpsichorean, Johnny Nit. Although his name is not well known today, critics often linked Nit and Florence Mills to explain the success of *Dixie to Broadway.* The New York *Sun* described this "rhapsody in brown" in its headline as "Florence Mills, Johnny Nit and Others in a Mulatto Revue." Alexander Woollcott endeavored to explain Nit's genius: "As for Mr. Nit, he is, to our notion, an answer to all the spangles and routine humor that gets into these revues. . . . The dark Mr. Nit, with the toothful smile slides quietly into the rhythm and gives himself over to an artful, beautifully competent soft shoe dance that is the high point of the evening. The lisp of his feet on the floor is rhythm's self, and it was out of the efforts of the honky-tonk pianists to bend their measures to the likes of him that the thing called ragtime was born."[15] In this number, Nit joined Byron Jones and Lou Kean as fellow convicts who execute a clever tap dance while chained together. A comedy skit ("The Right of Way") followed, which featured nefarious doings after a traffic accident. Embellishing the scene was a wrecked automobile, provided by the New York Oldsmobile Company.

13. "Looking Across the Footlights," unidentified article, in "Florence Mills" File, TC/PFL.

14. New York *Evening Mail,* n.d., clipping in "*Dixie to Broadway*" File, TC/NYPL.

15. New York *Sun,* October 30, 1924.

Florence Mills then reappeared in a bridal number, "Mandy, Make Up Your Mind." Contrary to expectations, she was the groom in evening dress, and Alma Smith portrayed the bride:

> June time is drawing near
> The time I long to hear
> Sweet sounds of wedding chimes
> Lonesome times disappear
> Their joyful melody
> Means joy for you and me
> So if you'll just agree
> Happy we will be
>
> Weddin' bells are dandy
> Mandy, make up your mind.
> Preacher man is handy, Mandy
> Easy to find.
> Marchin' down the aisle,
> Your style will make 'em all stare.
> With a little black-eyed Susan
> Stuck in your hair.
>
> Gee, but you're the candy, Mandy
> Won't you decide?
> Ev'rything is dandy, once you're a bride.
>
> In a year or two, there may be three of a kind.
> Mandy, make up your mind.[16]

Hamtree Harrington and Cora Green then sang "Hanging Around" while the scenery was changed once again. The new set featured a gigantic white piano (several years before Busby Berkeley's Warner Brothers fantasies), which provided a backdrop (as well as a dance floor) for Mills, Alma Smith, and Billy Cain. Critics were also stunned by Mills's energetic dancing talents, and asked her to explain:

> It all depends on the audience. I never know what I'm doing. . . . I just go crazy when the music starts, and I like to give the audience all it craves. I make up the dances to the songs beforehand, but then something hap-

16. Acute observers should have noticed that this song was at best an homage to, but more likely a retread of, a classic Irving Berlin number called "Mandy." The song first appeared in a World War I all-soldier show *Yip, Yip, Yaphank* in 1918 and later in the 1919 edition of the *Ziegfeld Follies*. In a similar sex-switch strategy, Marilyn Miller played minstrel George Primrose.

Florence Mills (*center, in tuxedo*) sings "Mandy, Make Up Your Mind" in *Dixie to Broadway*
Courtesy Billy Rose Theatre Collection, New York Public Library

> pens, like one of the orchestra talking to me, and I answer back and watch the audience without appearing to do so. It's great fun. Something different at each performance. It keeps me fresh. Once in New York I fell down literally. Did the split. The audience thought I was hurt. I heard some sympathetic expressions. So I got up and started to limp comically. It got a burst of applause. Then I winked and that got another hand. So the producer ran backstage and asked me to keep it in. I did for several nights, but other things happened and I forgot. I never remember just what to do. I'm the despair of stage managers who want a player to act in a groove. No grooves for me. The stage isn't large enough for me at times. But it is during the midnight performances that I let out most. We all do. Not that we overstep the conventions, you understand. But it's just the feeling that it's after hours, I suppose. And we whoop it up.[17]

Audiences greeted the singing and energetic dancing of "Jazz Time Came From the South" with enthusiasm as the curtain closed on Act I.

"If My Dream Came True" opened the second act. Here the actors began to speak of all the chances they had missed in the theatre. Most expressed their desire to play Shakespeare, but several began to fantasize how they could have become famous stars. A series of impressions began, with cast members endeavoring to copy the leading lights of the Broadway stage. First, several George M. Cohans (Georgia Cohans) entered to the strains of "I'm a Yankee Doodle Dandy." The Eva Tanguays followed, singing "I Don't Care." A black Gallagher and Shean then presented their classic number:

> Your hair has a kink,
> And your face is like ink.
> I'm a brownskin Mr. Gallagher
> I'm a sealskin, Mr. Shean.[18]

Marion Tyler appeared as "Belasco's Kiki" (a 1921 David Belasco Parisian farce starring Lenore Ulric), and then several cast members paid tribute to Walker and Williams, the only black stars in this Broadway pantheon.

Shelton Brooks arrived as the number ended, performing several songs he had written. Theophilus Lewis, drama critic for the *Messenger*, found this "the bright spot of the show," noting that Brooks "is in a fair

17. Philadelphia *Public Ledger*, n.d., in "Florence Mills" File, TC/PFL.
18. *Variety*, November 5, 1924, p. 18.

way to surpass the late Bert Williams, if he can find a producer who can keep him at work and give him his head."[19]

"Darkest Russia" provided "a Negro interpretation of the 'Parade of the Wooden Soldiers' with the exquisite dancing to the march tempo of Florence Mills, accompanied by the perfect ensemble work of a chorus that deserves honorable mention for every talented number." Audiences recognized this routine as a nod to Broadway's popular 1922 revue, *Chauve Souris.* Of Russian (and Parisian) origin, this show featured Nikita Balieff explaining the proceedings in badly fractured English. Its hit number, "Parade of the Wooden Soldiers," was the obvious source of the sequence in the Leslie revue. For those missing the logical connection, the set had a caricature of Balieff painted on the backdrop. Heywood Broun found Mills's rendition even better than the original.

"Sailor and the Chink" represented yet another common theme in black musicals in the early 1920s. From *Shuffle Along*'s "Oriental Blues" to *Dixie to Broadway,* songs or dance numbers referring to Orientals (often unfavorably) were unusually frequent. Cora Green next returned with "Dixie Wildflowers," performed with the Plantation Chocolate Drops.

Late in the second act, Florence Mills sang the number that was to become her trademark, "I'm a Little Blackbird Looking for a Blue Bird," which received a standing ovation every night:

> Never had no happiness
> Never felt no one's caress
> Just a lonesome bit of humanity
> Born on a Friday, I guess
> Blue as anyone can be
> Clouds are all I ever see
> If the sun forgets no one,
> Why don't it shine for me?
>
> I'm a little blackbird looking for a little blue bird, too.
> You know little blackbirds get a little lonesome, too, and blue.
>
> I've been all over from east to west.
> In search of someone to feather my nest.

19. *Messenger,* VII (January, 1925), 18 (billed as a "tardy review"). For information on Lewis, see Theodore Kornweibel, Jr., "Theophilus Lewis and the Theater of the Harlem Renaissance," in Arna Bontemps (ed.), *The Harlem Renaissance Remembered: Essays, Edited with a Memoir* (New York, 1972), 171–89.

Why don't I find one the same as you do?
The answer must be that I am a hoo-doo
I'm a little jazz-bo
Looking for a rainbow too.

The lyrics alone cannot explain the excitement caused by the singing of this song. Theophilus Lewis attempted to convey his feelings to his readers:

> Florence Mills is incomparable. She is the most consummate artist I have ever seen on the musical stage. She has perfect control of both the technique of restraint and the technique of abandon. . . . When she sings her song "I'm Just a Little Blackbird," she lets herself out, and—My God! Man, I've never seen anything like it! Not only that, I never imagined such a tempestuous blend of passion and humor could be poured into the singing of a song. I never expect to see anything like it again, unless I become gifted with second sight and behold a Valkyr riding ahead of a thunderstorm. Or see Florence Mills singing another song.[20]

It was virtually impossible to top Mills, and *Dixie to Broadway* moved quickly to a close. A brief comedy skit ("A Nice Husband") by Sidney Lazarus followed, and then the consummate dancers U.S. Thompson and Willie Covan. The finale, "Trottin' to the Land of Cotton Melodies," returned the show to its Dixie theme as the curtain fell.

It was evident that first-nighters (critics and audience members) enjoyed the show. Although these audiences, often composed of backers, relatives, and friends, were usually quite enthusiastic, even the New York *Times* was particularly stunned by the response: "On several occasions last night the new revue worked its audience up to a high pitch of excitement. The Negro revue has at least one characteristic that other revues have not. When a certain degree of excitement has been developed in the audience it communicates itself to the performers, and endeavor gives way to fervor as the players continue their work. There were times last night when emotional waves crossed and recrossed the footlights."[21]

Alexander Woollcott noticed a similar phenomenon: "Even in the happy and thunderous audience assembled last evening at the Broadhurst there seemed to be a swaying of shoulders and a sympathetic

20. *Messenger,* VII (January, 1925), 18. The praise is all the more striking in the midst of an extremely hostile review.

21. New York *Times,* October 30, 1924.

tapping of feet, so infectious and sociable and generally gay was the spirited revue called *Dixie to Broadway* then and there presented to New York." During the show's tour, Philadelphia critics concurred: "Hardly a performance passes that several in the audience do not rise in their seats as though impelled by some unknown power to take part in the mad revelry, and numerous are the times when applause unrestrained breaks in upon dance and song numbers before their completion."[22]

Perhaps the only reservation among the major reviewers concerned the blurring of the fine line between "black" and "white" revues. Percy Hammond complained in the New York *Herald Tribune* that "in *Dixie to Broadway* the colored folks have gotten away from the fundamental jokes of blackface comedy, and there are fleeting references to razors, craps, and chicken stealing. Which is, perhaps, unfortunate. It leaves them black performers in a white show." Heywood Broun of the New York *World* disagreed:

> There may be some objection that not very much which is pure African is to be seen in *Dixie to Broadway,* but for my part I have always felt that the nearness of Harlem to the jungle mood or thought was slightly exaggerated.
>
> Nor would I say that there is nothing in *Dixie to Broadway* wholly characteristic of the race from which it draws its performers. There is a passionate fidelity to the eternal verities of tempo not in the inheritance of Nordics. When I see a Negro child two or three years old come out and dance better than anybody at the New Amsterdam or the Winter Garden I grow fearful that there must be certain reservations in the theory of white supremacy.[23]

Perhaps the only naysayer was Theophilus Lewis, who, despite his admiration for Florence Mills, found the show an insult:

> This show contains bits of almost everything, a few mites of which are precious, but most of it is extremely shoddy, garish, and vulgar. It is really amazing how a man can take such material as Cora Green, Shelton Brooks, Florence Mills, Will Vodery's jazz orchestra, 247 yards of red silk, two dozen yaller gals, and a couple of junk automobiles, and make a bad show of the ensemble. However, Mr. Leslie contrives to accomplish the feat.

22. "Stirs Emotional Reaction in People," unidentified article, in "*Dixie to Broadway*" File, TC/PFL.

23. New York *World,* October 30, 1924.

> From the unintelligible tomfoolery involving a status of Lincoln and a lot of hands waving to the skit "The Chink and the Sailor," the show is in the main, second-hand and cheap. Its ghost scene, the obligatory scene of colored musical shows, is the worst one I've ever clapped my eyes on. As a spectacle, the show is infinitely inferior to *The Follies* and *Chocolate Dandies* and Mr. Leslie impudently thrusts his show forward as an apologist for the Negro race.

Not all black critics agreed with Lewis. *Variety* invited George Bell, "a Negro first nighter," to review *Dixie to Broadway.* Bell found the show a "credit to the colored race, rather than a ridicule."[24]

Leslie himself disagreed with criticisms such as those from Theophilus Lewis. He explained to one reviewer that "through working with Negro playing so long, [he] has a great respect for the race. The Negro was born without any desire to make money. He devotes his entire efforts towards happiness. Talk about the black man's burden—the white man has all the trouble and bears the burden while the black man knows how to live and laugh." Although doubts can certainly be raised about Leslie's understanding of the "Negro race" (and Lewis often led the critical chorus against his shows), there is no question that Leslie discovered the formula that governed black revues in the 1920s in America, England, and even Paris.[25]

Despite the title *Dixie to Broadway,* the show spent a great deal of time north of the Mason-Dixon Line. The few obligatory southern songs seemed to fade in the context of the whole show, which had a northern and urban focus. As one publicity release explained: "It isn't Africa any more than it is the South. It is America—jazzing, dancing America. Instead of the simplicity of a backward people there is the same hard sophistication that is the bone and sinew of every revue."[26] Leslie's shows tended to stray from the standard southern stereotypes inherent in several of the earlier black musical shows and presented a modern New Negro, the new vision of the Harlem Renaissance. The change was not yet complete, to be sure, and Leslie would long be the target of severe criticism from several black critics. Concentrating on the ghost or razor sequences in his

24. *Messenger,* VII (January, 1925), 18; *Variety,* September 17, 1924, p. 13. Bell viewed the show during a Chicago tryout.

25. "Tastes Differ in Negro Revues; England Prefers Them Artistic, America Wants Them to Be Fast and Funny," unidentified article, in "Lew Leslie" File, TC/PFL.

26. Publicity release, in "*Dixie to Broadway*" File, TC/PFL.

shows, they would ignore what was new in Leslie's modernization and urbanization of the black musical.[27]

"Broadway" often dominated "Dixie" in the Leslie revues. The producer-director capitalized on the growing interest of New York's elite in the culture and history of black Manhattan. The art, music, literature, and poetry of the Harlem Renaissance presented a new image of black life. While the contemporary tone of the music of *Shuffle Along* may have helped to usher in the Harlem Renaissance, as Langston Hughes once suggested, the world of the New Negro and the world of the Broadway musical tended to remain separate.[28]

Indeed, many leaders of the new cultural movement frowned on the impressions of black life that the new musical comedies gave to white audiences. On one occasion, Alain Locke and Charles S. Johnson, two of the "three midwives of the Harlem Renaissance," according to Langston Hughes, interviewed the famed Austrian theatrical director Max Reinhardt for *Opportunity*, the official monthly publication of the National Urban League. When they asked Reinhardt for his opinions of the new musical comedies *Shuffle Along*, *Liza*, and *Runnin' Wild*, he waxed rhapsodic: "It is intriguing, very intriguing . . . these Negro shows I have seen. . . . They are most modern, most American, most expressionistic. . . . To me they reveal new possibilities of technique in drama, and if ever I should try to do anything American I would build on these things." Locke and Johnson were appalled by the director's notions: "We didn't enthuse. . . . What Negro who stands for culture with the hectic stress of a social problem weighing on the minds of an over-serious minority could enthuse. *Eliza* [*sic*], *Shuffle Along*, and *Runnin' Wild!*" While black literary lights tended to dismiss the new black musicals, whites took the image of the Harlem Renaissance and displayed their fascination with it on the New York stage.[29]

27. Rogier Didier gave *Dixie to Broadway* high praise: "It ranks with the best of the current revues with all white performers." His only qualifications had to do with a "comic strip" Negro playing at dice and "the over used razor that crops up as the show goes on" (*Opportunity* [November, 1924], 345–46).

28. Nathan Irvin Huggins, *Voices From the Harlem Renaissance* (New York, 1976), 339–40. When asked about his connection with the Harlem Renaissance, Eubie Blake spoke of his relationship with Langston Hughes, explaining that they had written an (unpublished) song together. Nevertheless, when queried about his "impressions of what was going on in the Harlem Renaissance," Blake mentioned only the white interest in black music, not other aspects of cultural life.

29. Locke, "The Negro and the American Stage," 114–15. See also "Charles S. Johnson," in Bruce Kellner (ed.), *The Harlem Renaissance: A Historical Dictionary for the Era* (Westport, Conn., 1984), 193.

The utilization and exploitation of the New Negro as musical comedy icon often brought fast profits to white producers. Nevertheless, success at the box office obscured what was occurring behind the scenes. Despite the radiant presence of a Florence Mills (or, later, Ethel Waters or Lena Horne), virtually all the backstage talent was white. As early as 1924, a wholly black entertainment was slowly becoming a white commodity. By this date, *black musical* referred more and more to the individuals onstage, and not the talents who created the show. Whether Leslie or George White was in charge, the opportunities for black directors, composers, lyricists, stage managers, and conductors, which had been increasing during the previous two decades, were beginning to fade. The results of this transition were twofold. First, white creative talent assumed an ever-increasing role in determining the images of black Americans that would be shown on the Broadway stage. Second, the change would also have a devastating effect on the evolution of a black theatre for black audiences. Theophilus Lewis voiced his fear in 1926:

> The white producer prefers to select his headliners from the ranks of colored performers who have made good on the white vaudeville stage. He pays higher salaries than the colored actor can earn playing before Negro audiences, and if the show enjoys a modestly successful run, the members of the cast subsequently find it easier to get bookings on the white vaudeville stage as well as from the managers catering to colored audiences. This condition makes a prominent part in a show assembled for white audiences the goal of a colored actor's ambition. . . . They submit to the distorted standards of white vaudeville because becoming popular with its audience is the surest way to catch eyes of white producers.[30]

As a result, the black actor (whether Bert Williams or Florence Mills) was often co-opted by the white world of Broadway, and true black theatre remained in its infancy.

A more subtle change was also beginning to be evident onstage as well. One reviewer titled his opening night criticism "Florence Mills, Johnny Nit and Others in a Mulatto Revue." Color was apparently becoming extremely important in casting the female roles in these white-produced revues. One critic said of *Runnin' Wild*: "It looks good enough to be Ziegfeld's Follies back from Palm Beach with a coat of

30. *Messenger*, VII (September, 1926), 278–79.

tan." The *Messenger* responded, "[He fails to discern] any fundamental difference between Mr. White's chorus of kanaka cuties and Mr. Ziegfeld's chorus of O'fay frails." In 1928, Robert Littell, critic for the New York *Post,* criticized a Miller and Lyles show (*Keep Shufflin'*) for being a copy of "a white folks' musical comedy" because there was an "abundance in its ranks of quadroons, octoroons, and even smaller fractions of colored blood. The girls could, most of them, pass as white anywhere. We noted Jewish types, Italian types, and one head of genuine red hair. When they all danced together, the twinkle of their legs was barely a shade darker than the legs of any Broadway chorus." By 1930, Burns Mantle noted (in his review of Leslie's *Blackbirds of 1930*) that he favored "the dark colored girl in the chorus," which hinted that she was the oddity rather than the standard.[31] Leslie's ultimate contribution to the black musical revue, though widely hailed in the 1920s, was converting it almost entirely from a black to white-controlled enterprise as color became an important factor both on the stage as well as off.

31. New York *Post,* February 28, 1928; New York *Daily News,* October 23, 1930.

VIII

A PASSING FAD?

Rudolph Fisher, a graduate of Howard University Medical School and an incipient novelist, pronounced the spate of black musicals "just a fad" in the August, 1927, issue of the *American Mercury.*[1] In many ways, that was an accurate assessment. Despite a flurry of black musicals in the early part of the 1920s, the genre seemed to vanish by mid-decade.

A 1925 effort, *Lucky Sambo,* premiered during an early June heat wave. Opening night was only sparsely attended, and within ten minutes, some men in the audience removed first their collars and later their shirts. The show, which had traveled on the road as *Aces and Queens,* seemed interminable to the critics. Several noted the ending time (11:22), as though it were highly unusual. *Variety* described the book of *Lucky Sambo* as "like that of other attractions of the kind. There are the inevitable old men with whiskers, and though the grave yard scene was missed, the jail house is still there." Although Tim Moore performed valiantly as a con man who discovers an oil well, first-week receipts were low. As a result, the orchestra refused to play without pay, thus closing the show after one week.[2]

My Magnolia suffered a similar fate the following summer. Despite attractive performances by Eddie Hunter and newcomer Adelaide Hall, critics dismissed the show. A postmidnight curtain did little to improve the critics' humor. The *Herald Tribune*'s judgment was

1. Rudolph Fisher, "The Caucasian Storms Harlem" *American Mercury,* XI (August, 1927), 393–98. Fisher (1897–1934) later wrote *The Walls of Jericho* (1928) and *The Conjure Man Dies* (1932). The latter work was dramatized as *Conjur Man Dies* by Arna Bontemps and Countee Cullen for the Federal Theatre Project in 1936.

2. *Variety,* June 10, 1925, p. 25.

harshest: "*My Magnolia* is an ambitious attempt on the part of a company of colored performers to emulate the musical comedy of Broadway made popular by white actors. . . . Any efforts to create humor here are much like those of children acting out a play in a nursery." Ironically, several scribes noted (though in a left-handed fashion) that black audience members enjoyed the performance. *Variety* attempted to explain this seeming incongruity: "The length of the first night performance is partly blamed on the number of encores, given for any excuse. Colored people were spotted throughout the lower floor and occupied several boxes. From such sources there was ready and always present applause. The encore habit is peculiar with colored shows and becomes flagrant when colored authors and directors have their way."[3] *My Magnolia* received a few favorable comments (for Hunter, Hall, and Catherine Parker), but it wilted after just four performances.

Although few new black musicals appeared on Broadway, Fisher's obituary was a bit premature. As he prepared his article for print, three new black musicals opened on Broadway during the summer, and two opened later during the regular season. One, *Blackbirds of 1928,* became the longest-running black musical of the decade, exceeding *Shuffle Along*'s triumph. What Fisher viewed as the end of a trend was merely a respite.

Two factors clouded Fisher's vision. Black musicals may have been temporarily absent from Broadway, but they were enjoying unparalleled popularity elsewhere. Lew Leslie, for example, returned to London with Florence Mills and presented a *Blackbirds* revue (after a Harlem tryout) in 1926. (He also produced a *Whitebirds* in 1927!) Sissle and Blake invaded Britain to similar acclaim, and Turner Layton (of Creamer and Layton) also joined the transatlantic express.

Second, the mid-1920s witnessed the growing popularity of "Negro cabarets" patronized by whites. Located in Harlem, these clubs presented small-scale revues similar to Lew Leslie's. In the early 1920s the white presence at Harlem clubs was minuscule, but by mid-decade it seemed an invasion. In 1927, Fisher often found himself an oddity at his former haunts:

> Now, however, the situation is reversed. It is I who go occasionally and white people who go out night after night. Time and again, since I've returned to live in Harlem, I've been one of a party of four Negroes who went to this or that Harlem cabaret, and on each occasion we've been the

3. New York *Herald Tribune,* July 13, 1926; *Variety,* July 14, 1926.

only Negro guests in the place. The managers don't hesitate to say that it is upon these predominant white patrons that they depend for success. These places therefore are no longer mine but theirs. Not that I'm barred, any more than they were seven or eight years ago. Once known, I'm even welcome, just as some of them used to be. But the complexion of the place is theirs, not mine.[4]

The top clubs—Smalls' Paradise, Barron Wilkins' Exclusive Club, Connie's Inn, and the Cotton Club—became potent rivals to Broadway in the search for white audiences for black talent. The clubs removed the theatre's proscenium and plunged the audience into close contact with the performers. In some cases the clubs also encouraged their black and white patrons to interact, leading Chandler Owen, a contributor to the *Messenger,* to call the "black and tan cabaret" America's most democratic institution:

> [They] establish the desire of the races to mix and to mingle. They show that there is lurking ever a prurient longing for the prohibited association between the races which should be a matter of personal choice. These cabarets portray even the vanished prejudice of white men lest a Negro man should brush against a white woman. They show as Emerson would say that "every human heart is human; every human heart is big with truth." They prove that the white race is taking the initiative in seeking out the Negro; that in the social equality equation the Negro is the sought, rather than the seeking factor. They prove that there is no sex line in the seeking since both white men and white women attend—not only with their own racial mates but with opposite race mates.

Despite Owen's optimism, his observations were not universally true. Some clubs (Connie's Inn and Barron's, for example) discouraged black customers unless their skin was unusually light. The Cotton Club also presented barriers to its black patrons. Eubie Blake recalled that on one occasion he and Ethel Waters wanted to hear Duke Ellington perform there. The King of Jazz, Paul Whiteman, had to be their host before they could be admitted. If notables such as Blake and Waters experienced difficulties, an average tab of $15 per person also kept less affluent black customers from attending the Harlem nightclub.[5]

4. Fisher, "The Caucasian Storms Harlem," 395. For information on these clubs, see Jim Haskins, *The Cotton Club* (New York, 1977); and Lewis, *When Harlem Was in Vogue,* Chap. 7. For an account of a white drama critic's visit to the Harlem clubs, see George Tichenor, "Colored Lines," *Theatre Arts Monthly* (June, 1930), 485–90.

5. *Messenger,* VII (January, 1925), 97; Huggins, *Voices From the Harlem Renaissance,* 340.

As white audiences moved uptown a Broadway theatre was no longer the only option for black talent. Indeed, the availability of alternate showcases for black performers may have also caused an upgrading in the production quality of black musicals in the latter part of the decade. After all, a Broadway musical would have to supply something that could not be obtained at any Harlem night spot.

The turnaround came in the summer of 1927, when three black musicals opened on Broadway during the traditional slack season. Two achieved modest success and encouraged the return of the black musical to Broadway.

Bottomland began the black musical summer season with a vehicle for the Clarence Williams Trio—Williams, Eva Taylor, and Sara Martin—who were recording artists and radio performers. "Complying to the thousands of requests," wrote Williams, "to see and hear the Clarence Williams Trio in person, I have written a musical comedy in three acts, with special music, entitled *Bottomland.* Eva Taylor and Sara Martin, the world's foremost . . . record artists, have been engaged as co-stars, as well as a pickaninny chorus of fifty" (actual count: eight).[6]

Williams used the skimpiest of story lines. May Mandy Lee (Taylor), "a happy, but ambitious southern woman," migrates from a black slum (Bottomland) to the bright lights of New York City. She heads north in response to the glowing letters from her friend Sally (Olive Otiz), who claims to be a successful singer. When May arrives in the Big Apple, she discovers that Sally has fallen on hard times and is now an alcoholic chanteuse in a second-rate nightclub. While all the difficulties are being resolved, the Williams Trio has ample opportunity to perform old favorites and new songs in a nightclub setting. The New York *Times* wrote: "The music of Clarence Williams is . . . plentiful; so plentiful in fact, that about every tenth line in the book is a song cue."[7] Critics thought "Shootin' the Pistol" and "Bottomland" were the best numbers.

Nevertheless, the critics pounded *Bottomland* for a variety of reasons. First, it failed to fit any preconceptions of a black musical comedy or revue. The *Times* headline revealed this confusion: "*Bottomland* Baffles as a Negro Revue." The review continued: "Contenting itself neither with being essentially racial nor with slavish imitation of the Caucasion [*sic*] song and dance fiestas, it steers a middle course and develops

6. New York *Post,* June 28, 1927. The missing word was "Okeh," the Williams record label. The advertising department of the *Post* argued that this was unpaid advertising. The New York *Herald Tribune* followed suit on this matter, substituting "so-and-so."

7. New York *Times,* June 28, 1927.

into an amorphous presentation whose moments, such as they are, are routine and stereotyped." The *Times* was not alone in its "bafflement." Several other critics found the show's form a mystery. Again the critics' message that seemed strongest concerned the unnecessary baggage of the libretto—*Billboard* argued that "the book would hardly do credit to a child."[8] Apparently, a revue (or a concert) would have been the best forum for the Clarence Williams Trio on Broadway. Nevertheless, the fact that Williams would make such a choice for his initial mass audience showcase revealed that musical comedy had become an available option for the presentation of new black talent.

A second, and somewhat minor, theme of the downbeat reviews revealed that critics were beginning to make comparisons with similar shows and performances in Harlem clubs. The *Herald Tribune* argued that "there is nothing in the show, except, perhaps, some meritorious tap dancing . . . , that you cannot see in more engaging performance at several of the Harlem night clubs; and from much of the material recherche establishments like the 'Nest' [Club] would turn with well-bred scorn."[9] *Bottomland*'s anemic 21-performance run at the Princess may have revealed that ticket purchasers were making similar comparisons. Broadway would have to provide more than a nightclub performance to attract large audiences.

Africana (1927) opened two weeks after *Bottomland* and also featured a major new talent, Ethel Waters. Waters, like the Williams Trio, had made several popular recordings, but she established her career in vaudeville and nightclubs. This native of Chester, Pennsylvania, arrived in New York during World War I and began performing in black clubs. Earl Dancer, later the producer of *Africana,* "discovered" her and urged her to perform in white vaudeville. He got her a booking and helped her construct a new act, and her career blossomed. Her first major break occurred when Florence Mills left the Plantation Club in the summer of 1924 to go on tour, and a replacement was needed. Waters hesitated to audition, since she believed that Mills was an impossible act to follow. Apparently, the managers of the Plantation had the same difficulty, and their search for new talent proved fruitless. Waters finally auditioned, performing "Georgia Blues," and impressed all observers. Songwriters Harry Akst and Joe Howard asked her to sing a new number, "Dinah," which she performed at a rapid tempo.

8. *Ibid.; Billboard,* July 9, 1927.
9. New York *Herald Tribune,* June 28, 1927.

They then asked her to sing it "her" way, and, returning the next day, she made the song her own. As a result, she became Mills's replacement. "Dinah" was also the smash of the Plantation engagement, and audience attention was riveted on the new star.

Unfortunately for Waters, Mills returned in September, and she was forced to leave. She appeared for a short time in a touring version of the Plantation revue, but she quit and returned to Earl Dancer. Their tab show, *Miss Calico,* toured for several months. Waters not only starred, but she also staged several numbers. One of the best sequences was a takeoff on the hit Broadway show *Lulu Belle* (1926), which starred Lenore Ulric in blackface as a Parisian tart whose amorous intrigues help her climb the social ladder. Waters sang "You Can't Do What the Last Man Did" during this parody and later repeated the sequence in *Africana.* Also with Waters on the road was a new young composer, Donald Heywood, who later wrote many of *Africana*'s songs. *Miss Calico* continued its tour around the United States under various names, but Dancer always hoped that he could get a Broadway showcase for Waters. After a disappointing Chicago booking into a Shubert theatre, which left the company without the funds for railroad tickets, Dancer persuaded banker and philanthropist Otto H. Kahn to put up $10,000 to feature Waters in a Broadway revue.[10]

Patched together from Waters' tab shows, *Africana* offered audiences a mainstream revue, using the so-called black qualities that critics tended to favor. One critic decried "the tendency to whitewash the Negro shows these days, that is, instead of giving the production all the racial character that is its most enjoyable quality, to copy the Broadway revue of white folks, and this is not so good." He found this "evident" in *Africana,* in which all the "best scenes are those of darktown extraction." These qualities included "the usual romantic songs about the hypothetical delights of a Dixie paradise . . . and a cake-walk finale—led, according to announcement, by 'Pickaninny Hill, champion cake-walker of the world.' "[11] Amid the rampant Dixiana, Waters and company also provided satiric glances at recent Broadway shows.

Waters, however, dominated the evening, and a few critics began to compare her to Florence Mills. In the middle of the second act, Waters

10. For an account of the genesis of *Africana,* see Waters, *His Eye Is on the Sparrow,* 185–195. David Levering Lewis dubs Otto Kahn a "dollar and cents salon Negrotarian [who] combined noble sentiments with keen market analysis" (*When Harlem Was in Vogue,* 102). A tab show is a "tabloid" or abbreviated vaudeville show.

11. Unidentified review, in "*Africana*" File, TC/PFL.

performed a medley of her hits, including "Dinah," "Shake That Thing," "Take Your Black Bottom Outside," and "I'm Coming Virginia." *Variety*'s critic particularly enjoyed "My Special Friend Is in Town": "It's one of those ditties often found in colored shows, the lines saying just what they mean, raw, of course. The first-nighters ate that one up." *Time* proclaimed Waters "queen," and *Variety* said she was the "kick of *Africana*."[12]

Variety's sharp-eyed critic also noticed the origin and format of many of the songs and skits of *Africana*, calling them "cafe floor show stuff." Certain sequences were traced to Connie's Inn, and others derived from such tab shows as *Black Cargo* and *Miss Calico*.[13] Producer Earl Dancer seemed to be copying the work of Lew Leslie, constructing a show from proven material that could compete with the allure of Harlem clubs. For the critics, at least, the strategy appeared successful. Dancer also deviated from the recent practice, in black musicals and revues, of the "encore habit." He deliberately prohibited encores, and *Africana* moved along at a sprightly pace, ending at an appropriate hour.

Despite the critical raves, *Africana* ran into trouble at the box office. The initial $10,000 dwindled away, and the entire cast was placed on deferred payments. By August 17, Dancer was unable to meet the $1,700 weekly payroll, and he asked John and Harry Cort, the owners of Daly's Theatre, to advance him the money. They refused, and the show closed that weekend. The Shuberts, however, had a vacant theatre (the National) and agreed to advance funds to Dancer if he would move the show. It was a sagacious offer by the Shuberts, since no alternate show was available and an Elks convention, with several black units, had just arrived in town. The Shuberts foresaw a potential audience that could rescue *Africana*. The Corts bristled when their former tenant moved to the National. Arguing that the Shuberts, Dancer, and Waters violated the clause in their contract that stipulated that *Africana* could not move to another theatre within eight weeks of closing at Daly's, they requested an injunction against the move and asked for $24,000 in damages. *Africana* continued for a time at the

12. *Variety*, July 13, 1927.

13. *Ibid*. Black shows, of course, were not the only ones to take this route. *Padlocks of 1927*, which opened the week before *Africana*, featured a replica of Texas Guinan's nightclub in the finale. Guinan appeared in the show and, in this sequence, threw mock snowballs at the audience. Joining in the fun, the audience returned the compliment. One critic was hit in the eye, and turned in an unfavorable notice the following morning. But so did all the other critics who attended the show.

National, but the court case was a major financial burden for Waters and Dancer. Perhaps the only one enriched by the process was Waters' lawyer. The show lasted slightly over a month, but most of the cast remained unpaid.[14]

A few weeks later, *Africana* moved to the road to more acclaim and improving box office receipts. Although its run was short, Waters had clearly become a top star who could carry a major Broadway show on her own.

Contributing to the demise of *Africana* was the arrival of *Rang Tang* on Broadway the evening following *Africana*'s premiere. Featuring the comic heroes of *Shuffle Along,* Miller and Lyles, this show returned to the musical comedy model that had proved so successful in the early 1920s. One critic called it "the best show since *Shuffle Along* and in many ways it is superior to that." The main improvement was the production quality: "Certainly no other darky play ever was given such a handsome production as that provided for *Rang Tang* by Walker and Kavanaugh." The sets and costumes by Swedish artist Olle Nordmark complemented the proceedings and gave the evening a "right fantastic touch."[15]

Miller and Lyles reached into their bag of tricks and continued their tale of Sam and Steve fleeing from their creditors. This time they leave New York in search of treasure in Africa. As they fly to their destination the airplane (shown onstage) slowly begins to disintegrate. Seeing that their end is near, Sam and Steve confess all the dirty tricks (and there are many) that they have played on each other. The airplane's wings are falling off, but Sam and Steve land safely in Africa. They meet the Queen of Sheba and even a hostile Zulu tribe. In the midst of these meanderings, the team discovers a large cache of diamonds. They return to Harlem, pay off their debts, and at last begin to live like kings. Despite the convoluted plot, *Variety*'s critic argued that *Rang Tang* was "a musical played in a revue style." Kaj Gynt's libretto was a "mere thread" that vaguely connected Miller and Lyles's comedy routines and the "tuneful" musical numbers.[16]

Although opening night was sweltering, critics enjoyed the show. The score by Ford Dabney and Jo Trent was praised as "bright and rhythmical," making "the feet crazy to dance." The reviewers estab-

14. *Variety,* August 17, 31, 1927.

15. New York *Evening World,* July 13, 1927; unidentified review, in "*Rang Tang*" File, TC/PFL.

16. *Variety,* January 18, 1928, p. 50.

lished *Rang Tang* as the summer's black hit and predicted a long run.

Unlike *Bottomland* and *Africana, Rang Tang* lasted through the summer heat and continued into the winter months. When it closed in January, with back salary owed to most cast members, Miller and Lyles redoubled their efforts and returned in late February in *Keep Shufflin',* yet another reprise of their standard formula from the days of *Shuffle Along.* This time, Steve and Sam take the initiative and form a utopian society, the Equal Got Club, which entitles every member to an equal portion of the town's wealth. Since the main source of money in Jimtown is the bank, Sam and Steve devise a foolproof plan for dynamiting the institution and stealing all the money. Unlike most of their previous schemes, this one is wildly successful. They then distribute their ill-gotten gains to the many members of their club. With all the newfound wealth, no one in Jimtown has to work ever again. Sam and Steve begin plans to refurnish their tumbledown apartment, and, in one of the most humorous scenes, they destroy virtually every piece of furniture and dishware they have. They march down to the swankiest department store, but it is closed because no one has to work. So, for a change, Sam and Steve have some money, but they are unable to do anything with it. They must try to swindle the funds away from all the members of their utopian organization. The *Wall Street News* found the new show a joy, informing readers that "if [they] want to slum among the negro set for an evening, and wish to save [themselves] a trip to Harlem, I can think of nothing better than a trip to *Keep Shuffling.*" Most other critics thought that the show "reverted more to the inchoate and jazzy hodgepodge of the older type of colored revues" but still had "the required number of laughs that this team deserves."[17]

After the opening of *Rang Tang,* the *Evening World*'s critic proposed that Broadway change its name to the "Great Black Way," since the two-year drought for black musicals on Shubert Alley seemed to be ending. As autumn approached, there was another omen: Florence Mills at last returned to New York after a lengthy European tour with the *Blackbirds* company. While talk of new shows was in the air, Mills became ill and underwent an emergency appendectomy in October, 1927. Something went awry, and she had a second operation at the Hospital for Joint Diseases. She died on November 1, 1927.

Mills's sudden death shocked her countless admirers. Nearly three

17. Unidentified review, in "*Keep Shuffling*" File, TC/PFL; *Wall Street News,* March 1, 1928; New York *Herald Tribune,* February 28, 1928.

thousand people attended her funeral service, and the black theatrical world was represented by Ethel Waters, Miller and Lyles, Edith Wilson, Evelyn Preer, Will Vodery, Gertrude Saunders, Abbie Mitchell, and many others. The body lay in state at Howell's Mortuary on 137th Street and Seventh Avenue, and almost ten thousand people paid their respects. The funeral was on Sunday afternoon at Mother A.M.E. Zion Church. Harry Burleigh, Abbie Mitchell, and Hall Johnson led the spirituals. Louis Howard sang "Face to Face"; A. A. Haston, "Free as a Bird"; Jessie Zackery, "Come Unto Thee"; Julius (Jules) Bledsoe, "Lead Kindly Light"; Clarence Tisdale, "Keep Her in Perfect Peace"; Louette Chapman, "I Know That My Redeemer Liveth"; and the Carolina Choir, "I'm a Pilgrim of Sorrow."

Most moving was "Florence," a song specially composed by Juanita Stinette, who had appeared in *Plantation Revue* with Mills. "Facing toward the coffin Mrs. Stinette began in a voice that was hardly audible. 'Florence' each short stanza began. Each time she raised her voice a little higher and threw more feeling into the appeal. As the crowd stirred and a few persons rose to their feet, it became a frantic cry, 'Florence!' " The singer swayed, but struggled on to the climax. 'The hours you spent for us—Florence!' She threw back her arms, screamed, and collapsed into a heap upon the floor. Outside the door a great wail arose, penetrated by a shrill cry."

Several newspapers estimated that nearly 150,000 accompanied the funeral procession. As the cortège moved through the streets of Harlem an airplane released a flock of blackbirds in tribute to Mills's shows and her classic song, "I'm a Little Blackbird Looking for a Blue Bird." She was buried in Woodlawn Cemetery. There was a tower of red roses four feet wide and eight feet high; the card was signed "From a Friend." Pundits suggested that the flowers were from the Prince of Wales, who saw Mills perform thirteen times while she was in London.

James Weldon Johnson attempted to describe the qualities that had so endeared Mills to the theatrical world, but he found her "indefinable":

> One might best string out a list of words such as: pixy, elf, radiant, exotic, Peter Pan, wood-nymph, wistful, piquant, magnetism, witchery, madness, flame; and then despairingly exclaim: "Oh, you know what I mean." She could be whimsical, she could be almost grotesque; but she had good taste that never allowed her to be coarse. She could be risquee, she could be seductive; but it was impossible for her to be vulgar, for she

> possessed a naivete that was alchemic. As a pantomimist and a singing and dancing comedienne she has no superior in any place or any race.[18]

With Mills's death at thirty-two years of age, the black musical theatre suffered yet another of its grievous losses. George Walker, Bob Cole, Ernest Hogan, and Bert Williams all died way before their time. Mills left yet another gap that would be almost impossible to fill.

Broadway later paid tribute nightly to Florence Mills in a show intended for her, *Blackbirds of 1928,* produced by Lew Leslie. Prior to the finale, Aida Ward in male evening dress performed "A Memory of 1927," an obvious paean to Mills, though her name was never mentioned. She then sang one of Mills's classics, "Mandy, Make Up Your Mind" from *Dixie to Broadway. Variety*'s critic found it "a sentimental gesture, one appreciated by the first nighters and finely accomplished by the Ward girl." Robert Garland, however, critic for the *Mirror,* thought that the evening had "a sad wistful side. For as one was introduced to Mr. Leslie's new Blackbirds, memories of the first and greatest of them all—the late Florence Mills—hovered over them all."[19]

Despite the difficulty caused by the loss of its star, *Blackbirds of 1928* eventually became the longest-running black musical show of the 1920s. Although Florence Mills was absent from the cast, Lew Leslie's new revue had several factors working in its favor. First of all, its format was tried and true. The show, in one version or another, had been continually tested throughout the mid-1920s. The current edition of *Blackbirds* had links, of course, to *Dixie to Broadway,* but it was the immediate spiritual heir of a traveling version of the show that began in Harlem in 1926. Florence Mills starred in *Blackbirds of 1926,* which opened at the Alhambra Theatre on West 126th Street for a six-week run prior to a European tour. Formerly a film house, the building was converted to a theatre in a mere forty hours.

After a sell-out run in Harlem, Leslie moved the company to London, where it received considerable acclaim. Several changes were introduced for British audiences. "The average Englishman," noted Leslie, "looks on the Negro singer as the real exponent of native American music. [He] thinks of a Negro show in terms of art and wants to hear spirituals sung in the rich warm manner of Paul Robeson. When I

18. Johnson, *Black Manhattan,* 197–201. Johnson retained a scrapbook of all the newspaper articles on Mills's death. These are available in Theatre Scrapbooks, JWJP. See also "Florence Mills" files, TC/PFL and TC/NYPL.

19. *Variety,* May 16, 1928; New York *Mirror,* May 10, 1928.

put on a revue in England I have plenty of the 'Old Black Joe' and 'Go Down Moses' type of spirituals. Even the dancing is of the less low-down type." After the tour of the Continent was completed (and after the death of Mills), Leslie put on *Blackbirds* in his nightclub, Les Ambassadeurs, on West Fifty-seventh Street. Revisions were again necessary: "Americans think of Negro revues in terms of fast dancing and swing songs. They seem to prefer the traditional Negro comedian with the burnt cork make-up, big shoes and a razor, who plays craps and steals chickens."[20] Leslie emphasized these characteristics in his advertisements for *Blackbirds*. One noted the inclusion of the "Famous Poker Scene," in which one "darkey (producing a razor as another darkey makes an attempt to touch chips)" comments, "Brother, if you lay your hand on those chips, the next time you buy gloves just ask for one!" Another flyer stressed the "Famous Graveyard Scene." The "1st Darkey" warns the other, "Don't get scared. That's the voice of a dead man and you know a dead man can't hurt you." The "2nd Darkey" replies, "Maybe not, but they kin make you hurt yourself!"

On May 9, 1928, *Blackbirds of 1928* settled at the Liberty Theatre, where it remained for 518 performances. One reason for its success was that its tryout run in major metropolitan centers was one of the longest of any black musical show in the 1920s. This fact, coupled with the show's evolution in a New York City nightclub (a growing source for black entertainment), helped to mold *Blackbirds* into a hit.

After Mills's death, Leslie conducted an extensive search for new talent that could carry the revue. Some, such as Aida Ward, were recruited from rival nightclubs (Connie's Inn); others flocked to Leslie for a chance to perform. Joseph Attles, who appeared in the chorus of *Blackbirds of 1928*, recalled: "They didn't have regular auditions for [the show]. You just heard about it by word of mouth, and you went over and tried out. Black performers didn't have much to work with then except spirituals." Adelaide Hall was lured from the Broadway stage (*My Magnolia*), but the most fortuitous pick was Bill ("Bojangles") Robinson, a fifty-year-old tap dancer from vaudeville. This casting coup virtually made the new *Blackbirds*: critics praised Robinson as the "King of Tap Dancers." A late addition to the cast, Robinson forgot the words of his big song on opening night, but everyone forgave him the minute he started to dance.[21]

20. "Tastes Differ in Negro Revues; England Prefers Them Artistic, America wants Them to Be Fast and Funny," unidentified article in "Lew Leslie" File, TC/PFL.

21. New York *Times*, April 22, 1977, C-2; *New Yorker*, October 6, 1934, p. 27.

The opening moments of *Blackbirds of 1928* seemed a tribute to *Dixie to Broadway.* An early song asked: "Why did I go away from Dixie? / Heart of the South / My mammy used to call me Dixie / Part of the South." Yet, like the earlier show, *Blackbirds* soon replaced its supposed Dixie origins with the urbanized sophistication of the new northern nightclub revue.[22]

Many critics complained of the weakness of the skits, but they all praised the exceptional music and dancing. As was true of other Leslie shows in the 1920s, the score was by whites—Jimmy McHugh and Dorothy Fields. But the cast made each number a showstopper. The top hit, "I Can't Give You Anything But Love," performed by Ward, Hall, and Willard McLean, was actually rescued from a previous flop, *Delmar's Revels* (1927). It had been a tribute to Charles Lindbergh ("I Can't Give You Anything But Love, Lindy"), but it languished in obscurity. *Blackbirds,* however, made it a hit. Ironically, the song also may have rescued *Blackbirds* itself. After five weeks of steady, but unspectacular grosses, the show moved toward capacity. When asked to explain this unusual trend, Leslie credited the McHugh and Fields hit, noting that the song was "beginning to be sung everywhere."[23] Yet, on opening night, this classic was only one of the many songs cited by the critics. "I Must Have That Man," "Diga Diga Do," and "Doin' the New Low Down" were picked as possible hits.

Bill Robinson overwhelmingly carried the dancing honors for the show. Alexander Woollcott warned those who might be tempted to leave *Blackbirds of 1928* before the final curtain to remain until 10:45 so they could see Robinson's big number. Robinson's work differed from the fast-paced action of other tap artists. His slow, smooth movements seemed to express a variety of emotions. Most critics seemed to think that Robinson talked with his feet. Also receiving special praise was Earl Tucker: "Has he got snake hips—and how! Tucker is a marvel in his way, for no such weaving of the hips has been shown. That boy certainly smacked them hard." Milton Crawley was cited as well for combining his acrobatic dancing with a clarinet solo.[24]

While *Blackbirds of 1928* continued its marathon run an unusual musical comedy with a score by Joe Jordan, Homer Tutt, and Henry

22. New York *World,* May 10, 1928.

23. Miles Kreuger, "*Blackbirds of 1928*" liner notes, Columbia Records, OL-6770; Nat N. Dorfman, "The Failure That Became a Hit," unidentified newspaper, in "*Blackbirds of 1928*" File, TC/PFL.

24. *Variety,* May 16, 1928, p. 48.

Poker scene in *Blackbirds of 1928*
Courtesy Billy Rose Theatre Collection, New York Public Library

Typical Lew Leslie decor from *Blackbirds of 1928*
Courtesy Billy Rose Theatre Collection, New York Public Library

Creamer and a libretto by Salem Whitney and Tutt opened the following January. Unlike recent efforts, *Deep Harlem* (1929) attempted to include serious ideas about black history and black life. The *Herald Tribune* critic, Arthur Ruhl, noted that "Whitney (with the cavernous voice of an old-fashioned southern Negro preacher) had the air throughout his work of being somewhat a philosopher and of letting his more or less solemn thoughts about the history and present thoughts about his race come to the front as much as he thought practicable in a musical show on Broadway." Whitney and Tutt's libretto traced black history from "ancient Abyssinia, the African desert, the jungle, the slave ship, the slave market" to present-day Savannah, Georgia, and the "cabarets and streets of Harlem." A majority of critics dismissed the enterprise: "What audiences may think of *Deep Harlem* remains to be seen. But most of the critics brushed aside the experiments in ancient Africa as grotesque mumbo-jumbo, while the comparative quiet tone and tempo of the piece was lamented as a waste of good material, which, being black, must necessarily be without sense or real human feeling, and at the rise of the first curtain explode like a piece of fireworks and go on meaninglessly whirling and fizzing with 'pep' and 'speed' until the end." Perhaps the only portions of the show the critics favored were the modern sequences, many of which borrowed the chorus line from Connie's Inn to enliven the proceedings. *Variety*'s critic noted: "There the show is always at home—as Harlem is always at home in Times Square and Times Square is always at home in Harlem."[25]

Straying from standard conceptions of the black musical or revue, *Deep Harlem* lasted barely a week. Only critic Arthur Ruhl discovered the true novelty of the show: "It was interesting nevertheless because of its attempt to make something out of what wideawake Negro minds have been thinking of as possibilities for genuine black drama, and in its very ingenuousness there was a kind of charm which is generally quite drowned out by the hullabaloo and brassy cocksureness that Broadway has come to expect and demand from black shows." Ruhl defended the show in a special article in the Sunday *Herald Tribune*, but he failed to excite any interest in *Deep Harlem*. By differing so radically from the concept of a 1920s black musical, the show was doomed from the start. Nevertheless, *Deep Harlem* was an early attempt

25. New York *Herald Tribune*, January 8, 1929, p. 34, January 13, 1929, Sec. VII, p. 1; *Variety*, January 9, 1929, p. 62.

to use musical comedy to present a black perspective on history and culture.[26]

Messin' Around followed *Deep Harlem* by just a few months, but it returned to the format typical of black revues in the 1920s. Typical, however, was not enough when *Blackbirds of 1928* was still on view a few blocks away. The *Sun* noted that the comparison was "hardly fair to *Messin' Around* because *Blackbirds* was such an exceptional negro revue." Most critics, however, ignored this advice. Obviously needing a gimmick to rescue the show from the fate of other recent second-rate black revues, *Messin' Around*'s producers decided to add an unusual twist to this conventional revue. John C. Fitzgerald described the bizarre goings-on:

> A surprise came in the second act when the curtains dropped back to disclose a regulation ring into which two young ladies, answering to the names of Aurelia Wheeldin, "world's female bantamweight champion," and Emma Maitland, "world's female junior lightweight champion," soon clambered. They were introduced, shook hands, and with the well-known trainer Grupp as the referee, they started slugging. Well, we've seen *Ringside* and *Hold Everything* and Jack Dempsy's *The Big Fight.* But if there was a prize fight in any one of those stage plays that was put on with anywhere near the ferocity that marked the combat of Emma and Aurelia, we'll buy the drinks. Both good-looking colored girls, each did her utmost to obliterate the other's features. It was a fight that had the audience on its toes.[27]

The exciting prizefight grabbed most of the headlines, but the critics praised several sequences in *Messin' Around.* The score by James P. Johnson and Perry Bradford received high marks, with universal agreement that "Your Love Is All I Crave" should be the season's biggest hit. "Shout On," "I Don't Love Nobody," and "Get Away from My Window" were also selected as the best songs of the evening, and Cora La Redd and Hilda Perleno received nods for their exciting vocal styles. Despite these favorable notices, *Messin' Around* failed to compare with the ever-popular *Blackbirds.* Even with the dramatic fight sequence, the show did not last the month.

Pansy, which opened the month after *Messin' Around,* also felt compelled to resort to a gimmick. Instead of a heavyweight bout, *Pansy* offered the Broadway debut of singer Bessie Smith. Unfortunately, her

26. New York *Herald Tribune,* January 13, 1929, Sec. VII, p. 1.
27. New York *Sun,* April 23, 1929; New York *Evening World,* April 23, 1929.

appearance was delayed until the second act of a mediocre college musical, which critic Wilella Waldorf described as "a sort of colored *Good News.*" Most of the audiences seemed to ignore the onstage proceedings for much of the evening, except for an occasional attempt to laugh at the jokes. However, when Bessie Smith finally arrived, the audience "rose up and roared." She began her performance with "If the Blues Don't Get You" and repeated the number to thunderous applause. Since the college capers eventually had to continue, Smith was forced to leave the stage. She returned later in the second act for "A Stranger Interlude," a parody of a recent O'Neill play, but that was the last to be seen of her. *Pansy* itself received little attention in the reviews, though some critics acknowledged that Maceo Pinkard's songs might sound better in a different show. *Pansy* also suffered the *Blackbirds* backlash: "*Blackbirds of 1928,* like most successful ventures, has inspired a horde of imitators. The time is ripe, it is argued, for negro musical productions of all sorts to burst upon Broadway. Several have burst already and half a dozen others are said to be in preparation. Unless the coming events are a great improvement over the recent ones, it is going to be a harder summer than we had anticipated."[28]

Hot Chocolates, originally dubbed *Tan Town Topics,* may have followed *Pansy,* but it was a *Blackbirds* at heart. Primarily of nightclub origin, this revue brewed and simmered at Connie's Inn. Then Connie (George Immerman) took the show downtown to the Hudson Theatre. From the moment the audience entered the theatre, the ties to the nightclub were evident. The Prologue, "At Connie's Inn," featured a porter (Jazzlips Richardson), a head waiter, a doorman, waiters, attendants, and a master of ceremonies (Jimmie Baskette), as well as "guests, an orchestra, and entertainers." Paul and Thelma Meeres performed their classic "Waltz Divine," as they did at the club, and this segued into a lengthy section entitled "The Club Revue." For a time, members of the Broadway cast migrated northward after the show to perform the same numbers in Connie's Inn, but after exhaustion took its toll, the practice was discontinued.

Strong attention focused on the musical numbers and the performers. With Thomas ("Fats") Waller, Andy Razaf, and Harry Brooks providing the score, the success of the show was virtually assured. The Waller score included, of course, his classic "Ain't Misbehavin'," but not all critics immediately appreciated its merits. *Variety* found it the

28. New York *Post,* May 15, 1929.

"hit of the score," but the New York *World* was quite reserved: "There is a song called 'Ain't Misbehavin'' on which much reliance is placed. Almost everybody in the show sings it at one time or another, and as there are a good many in the show, the song gets sung pretty often. It is tuneful and pleasant, and I should feel like giving everyone a great deal of credit for it if it were not so strikingly reminiscent of something I seem to remember from a year or so ago." "Black and Blue," "Sweet Savannah Sue," and "Can't We Get Together?" also received high marks from the critics.[29]

Madagascar-born Andy Razaf supplied the lyrics for Waller's melodies. His trademark, double-entendre lyrics, gave *Hot Chocolates* a raunchy humor lacking in several recent black revues. Critics commented on the eroticism in the show. Robert Garland's headline read "Fun and Frankness Run Through Dialogue, with Here and There Dubiously Chaste Wisecracks Interjected, in Presentation at the Hudson Theatre." Bide Dudley of the *Evening World* noted: "In the stepping division, one Jazzlips Richardson stopped the proceedings with his unique gyrations, and a very scantily clad young woman named Louise Cook shook and twisted until I was reminded of a certain sideshow on the Midway Plaisance at the Chicago World's Fair. Little Egypt had nothing on Louise Cook, who as indicated, had very little on herself." *Variety*'s critic agreed: "Connie's floor show is certainly hot in spots and hasn't been toned down much, if any, for Broadway. There is an example in 'Pool Room Papa,' as done by Edith Wilson and Billy Maxey. It is a double-meaning lyric, made distinctively suggestive. That goes for a number in the 'Traffic in Harlem' skit, Miss Wilson . . . again having blue, blue lines."[30]

Despite all the comments on the blue material in *Hot Chocolates*, there were few complaints. The clubs in Harlem had accustomed reviewers and audiences to material of this sort, as well as a more exotic style of dancing than was practiced in the *Ziegfeld Follies*. Also, *Hot Chocolates* was not the first show to emphasize these qualities. The critic for the Brooklyn *Daily Eagle* gave *Harlem* (1929) credit for loosening the moral strictures in the Broadway theatre. *Harlem*, one of the three dramas by black dramatists on Broadway during the 1920s, attempted to provide a realistic picture of black life in New York City. Eschewing the myths propounded by white writers such as Paul Green in *In Abraham's Bosom* (1926), black playwright Wallace

29. *Hot Chocolates* program, in TC/NYPL; New York *World*, June 21, 1929; *Variety*, June 26, 1929.

30. New York *Evening World*, June 21, 1929; *Variety*, June 26, 1929.

Thurman came closest to portraying the actual behavior of Harlem's blacks during the decade. The frank language and unusual idioms (explained in a glossary handed out with the playbills) prepared Broadway audiences for *Hot Chocolates,* which opened a few months later.[31]

Although Broadway's next black musical, *Bamboola* (1929), billed itself as "a unique Afro-American musical comedy," most critics found it rather conventional. Authors D. Frank Marcus and Bernard Maltin used a fairly weak tale of Savannah-born actress Anna Frost (Isabell Washington), who responds to her friend's urging to come to New York to appear in a new musical revue, *Bamboola.* In the big city, she is romanced by the show's juvenile lead. She nevertheless decides to marry her sweetheart from back home, an aspiring composer. The plot was cast aside at various points to allow for the musical numbers. At the beginning of Act II, it was announced that numbers from the revue *Bamboola* would be presented, and at last the chorus did its singing and dancing. Whenever another excuse was needed for a song, the budding composer would say, "I just wrote a new song. Would you like to hear it?" Despite these plot contortions, *Bamboola* had a few interesting musical numbers. One, a Harlem rent party scene, excited the audience, and a tribute to Bojangles (already a legend) featured a chorus dancing up and down stairs in the Robinson manner.[32]

Bamboola burned out at the box office, and the management could not pay the orchestra by the second week of the show. The management then diverted funds from the cast's salaries in order to keep the musicians working. The actors, obeying the dictum "The show must go on," agreed to partial payments. So $490 remained from the two-week gross to pay a cast of sixty-five. The lead actors received $5 to $10, and the chorus accepted $1. By the third week, the musicians refused to perform unless they received $142 by 4:00 each afternoon, but the cast remained loyal with its token payments. Nevertheless, producer Irving Cooper, a former vaudeville agent and co-producer of the 1929 hit play *Harlem,* pulled the plug on *Bamboola* after he and his two brothers were over $30,000 in debt because of the show.[33]

31. Brooklyn *Daily Eagle,* June 21, 1929. *Harlem* was written in collaboration with W. J. Rapp, a white. It played ninety-three performances in its initial run, and was revived in October for sixteen additional performances. The other two dramas written by black authors that appeared on Broadway during the 1920s were Garland Anderson's *Appearances* (1925) and Frank Wilson's *Meek Mose* (1928).

32. New York *Post,* June 27, 1929.

33. *Variety,* July 3, 17, 1929.

Ginger Snaps, the final black revue of the decade, opened on New Year's Eve of 1929, but it was hardly cause for celebration. The New York *Times* dismissed it as an "amateur night"—curtains failed to rise and spotlights failed to shine. Thus the golden decade of the black musical ended with a whimper.[34] *Ginger Snaps* having a Broadway berth meant that it had all the prime qualities for a black show in the late 1920s. As a result of Lew Leslie's efforts, the majority of black musical comedies finally rid themselves of the encumbrance of a book and moved toward a revue form. Even those shows that retained the classic structure of a book musical could discard the book at any time during the evening. *Bamboola* dismissed its libretto by the second act in order to present a mini-revue, and Miller and Lyles used the merest trace of a plot to include their old vaudeville routines. Consequently, the libretto of the black musical became nearly invisible by the end of the decade. What succeeded on Broadway was clearly the revue, which maintained a close structural relationship to the increasingly popular Harlem nightclubs of the 1920s. First-rate talent, top-drawer songs, and excellent choreography became the keys to popularity, rather than reliance on a libretto as in the popular white musicals of the age. While the revue format was popular and sometimes financially successful for black musical shows, it remained to be seen whether a formula based on the prosperity of the 1920s could succeed during the Great Depression, which was clearly not a time of "ginger snaps."

34. New York *Times,* January 1, 1930.

IX

"WALL ST. LAYS AN EGG"

When *Variety's* headline proclaimed "Wall St. Lays an Egg" after the stock market crash in October, 1929, many wondered whether this catastrophe could fail to hit Broadway and the rest of the entertainment business as well. If the sumptuous musicals and revues of the 1920s could no longer be financed as easily in an uncertain economic climate, what would happen to black musical productions? Even in the best of times, these were precarious investments. A few, such as *Shuffle Along* and *Blackbirds of 1928,* had earned a healthy profit, but most black shows had a perilous existence. One might therefore expect the black musical or revue to be one of Broadway's first casualties in the Great Depression. Indeed, matters seemed bleak as early as mid-summer of 1929, months before the crash. Oppressive heat waves devastated the summer business on Broadway (as *Bamboola* discovered), and the growing popularity of talking pictures was beginning to dent the theatre business. Not only were audiences attending motion pictures in record numbers, but more and more legitimate theatres were converting from stage productions to showing films. And some even added air-cooling techniques to keep a summer audience captive. Passers-by gasped in wonder at the cool air wafting from the Paramount Theatre as they walked down the street. When the economic collapse of the end of the decade combined with these trends, the black musical seemed to face an uncertain future.[1]

Despite these auguries of disaster, black musical theatre maintained an unusual strength during these difficult times. More black musicals and revues appeared in the early 1930s than at any time since the

1. *Variety,* July 10, 1929.

golden age of the early 1920s. Six black musicals shows appeared in the 1930–1931 season, and five during the following season.

Several factors sheltered the black musical from the economic storms early in the decade. First, these shows were comparatively inexpensive to produce. As black musicals became more and more similar to nightclub presentations in the late 1920s, several expenses were pruned. Out-of-town tryouts were rarely needed, as local clubs from Manhattan to Brooklyn served the purpose. Additionally, the shows did not use much scenery or many costume changes because they concentrated on musical elements. At times, such as in *Rhapsody in Black* (1931), the set was reduced to a mere black backdrop.

Black shows also offered producers low labor costs in the early days of the Great Depression. In the past, black actors had often resisted a producer's request that they accept a wage reduction to keep a show running. However, as early as May, 1929, in an article entitled "Colored Musicals on Boom Since Casting for White Shows Harder," *Variety*'s theatre reporter commented: "The dark epidemic is a logical outcome of uncertainty among producers in producing white shows, knowing the hazards entailed by the talking picture draw on stars, directors, and songwriters. There is no fear from those quarters in producing a colored attraction. Producers find plenty of co-operation from the negroes who are more than willing to gamble with them on the outcome of a presentation. It is rumored that one producer paid off the ensemble of his show in $5 bills, one to each, last week."[2] With the worsening economic situation in the early 1930s, these practices became more frequent. There were few examples of actors refusing to play without pay.

Changes in Actors Equity rules as the depression continued also led to lower wages for black performers. Earl Carroll wanted to hire fifty black actors for his new *Vanities* revue. He received a special waiver to hire them as "atmosphere" rather than as performers. By changing their status from "chorus" to "atmosphere," he could pay them $19 each week. In normal times, *Variety* would have expected a storm of protest from Equity in response to this semantic (and salary) change, but on this occasion the union offered no resistance. No doubt the worsening market for actors, both black and white, contributed to the docile acceptance of whatever wages were offered.[3]

These economic factors did strongly enhance the appeal of black

2. *Ibid.*, May 15, 1929.
3. *Ibid.*, August 4, 1931.

musicals and revues. In addition, Broadway critics and audiences welcomed one of the biggest hits of the decade, an all-black show entitled *The Green Pastures,* on February 26, 1930. The show was not a musical, though it did have music. The success of this unlikely show opened doors for other black shows. *Variety* noted: "Quick Vogue of *Green Pastures* Brings Cycle of Colored Plays."[4]

Virtually no one had faith in the enterprise, an adaptation of Roark Bradford's *Ol' Man Adam an' His Chillun.* Marc Connelly, who dramatized the stories and directed the stage production, recalled: "Innumerable Broadway managers declined to produce *The Green Pastures* on what to them was a reasonable assumption: that anyone would be insane to finance a religious fantasy in which the principal character, God, would be played by a Negro. They were convinced of the insanity of Rowland Stebbins, the theatrically inexperienced Wall Street broker who finally produced it [along with Laurence Rivers], when they learned that the play would open in New York without an out-of-town tryout."[5] Adding to the incredulity of the Broadway savants was the fact that God would be played by Richard B. Harrison, a former Pullman porter who had little acting experience.

From the modern viewpoint, *The Green Pastures* is chockablock with stereotypes in this white vision of a black heaven. Connelly's program notes in the playbill gave the inevitable hints of the direction the drama would take:

> *The Green Pastures* is an attempt to present certain aspects of a living religion in the terms of its believers. The religion is that of thousands of negroes in the deep south. . . . They accept the Old Testament as a chronicle of wonders which happened to people like themselves in vague but actual places, and of rules of conduct, true acceptance of which will lead them to a tangible, three-dimensional Heaven. In this Heaven, if one has been born in a district where fish frys are popular, the angels do have magnificent fish frys through an eternity somewhat resembling a series of earthly holidays.

Despite this tomfoolery, contemporary critics raved. Brooks Atkinson declared the play a "masterpiece" in the New York *Times,* and the New York *World* noted: "It will move you to tears, and make you gasp with the simple beauty of Old Testament pageantry, and give you a sort of laughter that you never had before." Richard Watts, Jr., then with the

4. *Ibid.,* March 19, 1930.
5. *Show Business Illustrated,* September 5, 1961, p. 99.

New York *Herald Tribune*, attempted to explain what gave *The Green Pastures* its greatness: "Perhaps the quality . . . that stands out in the memory most strikingly is what Mr. Brooks Atkinson calls its 'compassionate comedy.' Seldom in the theatre, or anywhere else, have those two virtues of sympathy and laughter been allied so closely that you can never tell where one leaves off and the other begins. There is no condescension in the sympathy and no mockery or cruelty in the laughter; there is a lovely good nature in the compassion and there is a gallant tenderness in the comedy."[6]

In addition to the high quality of the writing (Connelly won the Pulitzer Prize), critics were also stunned by the magnificent performances. Richard B. Harrison, as De Lawd, provided the essential dignity that held the work together. Harrison, the son of former slaves who had fled to Canada, had only the slightest education in the public schools of London, Ontario, but he did attend a drama school for a brief period. He used his talents to earn the odd dollar by giving Shakespearean readings for black audiences in Canada. These dramatic readings supplemented the income he received from being a dining car waiter, a porter, and a police station handyman. After traveling through the Deep South for a time, he began teaching drama in several black colleges and high schools. When Connelly discovered him, he was working for the New York Federation of Churches as a director of church festivals in Harlem. He played the leading role in *The Green Pastures* for almost five years in New York and on the road. He became ill before his 1,658th performance, and his understudy went on for the first time. Harrison died shortly thereafter at age seventy.[7]

While Harrison dominated the proceedings, the entire cast deserved praise. James Weldon Johnson, who did not comment on the stereotypes in the play, argued in *Black Manhattan*:

> [*The Green Pastures*] established conclusively [the Negro's] capacity to get the utmost subtleties across the footlights, to convey the most delicate nuances of emotion, to create the atmosphere in which the seemingly unreal becomes for the audience the most real thing in life. *The Green Pastures* is a play so simple and yet so profound, so close to the earth and yet so spiritual, that it is as high a test for those powers in the actor as any play the American stage has seen—a higher test than any of the immor-

6. Playbill, in "*The Green Pastures*" File, TC/NYPL; New York *Herald Tribune*, March 12, 1930.

7. *Time*, March 4, 1935; unidentified articles, in "Richard B. Harrison" File, TC/PFL.

> talized classics. It is a play in which the line between the sublime and the ridiculous is so tenuous that the slightest strain upon it would bring the whole play tumbling down.

Johnson was able to think of at least twenty performers who deserved mention, but he included the show's program in his book so all would receive praise.[8]

The final factor creating the mood of Connelly's play was the work of the Hall Johnson Choir, which sang the numerous spirituals. For James Weldon Johnson, it "served to blend all the efforts into a magical whole." DuBose Heyward, the white author of *Porgy* (1927), agreed: "It seems to me that in this play the spiritual has come into its own in the theatre. Sung by a splendidly trained choir of thirty voices it is used after the manner of a Greek chorus, and the songs rise so naturally and appropriately out of the action in the various scenes that they convey the impression of spontaneous creation, and carry the mood from scene to scene with an effect of unity unobtainable by any other possible means."[9]

White critics uniformly praised *The Green Pastures*, but there were murmurs of discontent among black writers and audiences. Critic John Mason Brown of the New York *Evening Post* received a letter from a black writer who stated that "the general mood [of the play] is one of unconscious patronizing, as if the author were constantly asking the audience the question, 'Isn't this childlike simplicity utterly charming and captivating?' " Yet initial doubts were erased for many black critics after seeing the play. Randolph Edmonds explained this phenomenon in *Opportunity*:

> Negroes who have never seen this play criticize it sharply. They could not see how a fish fry could represent the Negro's side of heaven when they have been told all their lives about pearly gates and golden stairs. God being black is something they have never heard except as a humorous part of the Garvey movement. The Lord accepting a ten cent cigar seems to them the height of absurdity, and the spirituals are just those old slave songs sung for the benefit of white people. In short, they conclude that it is just another show making fun of the race. Very rarely are these comments heard after they have seen the spectacle, however. Somehow the spiritual message forces its way through the comedy, music, setting and the violent contrasts of its episodes. There comes a feeling, even among

8. Johnson, *Black Manhattan*, 221–24.
9. Brooklyn *Daily Eagle*, March 9, 1930.

> the harshest critics, that here is something beautiful and powerful acted by Negroes and told in a Negro dialect, and of which they need not be ashamed.

Sterling Brown, who wrote for the same magazine, also approved of the show, but he had one major complaint. In the 1920s and early 1930s most of the Broadway plays about black life were by white authors, so distorted images of black life for theatre audiences were inevitable.[10]

Although the controversy in New York was rather muted, passions flared as *The Green Pastures* took to the road. Major cities faced the difficulty of welcoming the black cast of a top Broadway play into segregated theatres and public accommodations. Usually the show was housed in the newest theatre in town, but many performers were unable to find hotel rooms. Often the cast performed to all-white audiences as it moved from city to city. In Washington, D.C., it appeared that no blacks would be allowed to attend the performances. After all, as Langston Hughes wrote, "they couldn't even allot a corner in the upper gallery—there was such a heavy demand from white folks." There were threats of a strike, but a contingent of police and private detectives quelled the rebellion before the premiere. Johnny Logan, who portrayed an angel in the show and had organized the opposition, was arrested for disturbing the peace, and the performance went on as planned.[11]

Whatever the controversies concerning *The Green Pastures,* it did shelter black actors, actresses, songwriters, and other creative talents somewhat from the ravages of the depression. The show itself was a

10. New York *Evening Post,* March 21, 1930; Randolph Edmonds, "Some References on the Negro in American Drama," *Opportunity* (October, 1930), 304; Sterling Brown, "Concerning Negro Drama," *Opportunity* (September, 1931), 284. Howard Bradstreet wrote the monthly theatre review for *Opportunity.* He, too, joined the raves: "To see *The Green Pastures* once is to desire to see it again. To stand through the performance in the absence of seats, is not a test of endurance inasmuch as one forgets he is standing. Both statements label it a remarkable play" (*Opportunity* [May, 1930], 150–51).

11. Langston Hughes, "Trouble With the Angels," *New Theatre* (July, 1935), 6–7. Hughes's criticism of the play was scabrous. He called it the famous "Negro" play about the charming darkies who drink eggnog and fry fish in heaven and sing all the time. He also heaped criticism on God (Harrison), who refused to urge Washington theatres to allow blacks to attend the performance: "But Negroes have always been stupid about God, even when he is white, let alone colored. They still keep on expecting help."

Washington temporarily relaxed the segregation of theatres during the 1936 visit of *Porgy and Bess.* Black patrons could purchase orchestra seats. See *Theatre Arts Monthly* (May, 1936), n.p., in SCCF/NYPL.

vast employment agency for actors and singers, both in New York City and later on the road. But the ultimate success of *The Green Pastures* was its ability to convince investors that they should continue to support black shows—both musicals and dramas—during Broadway's hardest decade. As a result, Broadway audiences saw more black musicals in the three years following *The Green Pastures* than they had since the early 1920s. Blacks remained big business in the white world of Broadway—at least for the time being.

Black musicals of the early 1930s were certainly notable for their quantity, but they were not remarkable for their quality. Producers flocked to the tested formats, and this led to a flood of carbon copies of earlier hits. *Change Your Luck* (1930) was the first black musical to open in the wake of the *Green Pastures* euphoria. Opening-night critics agreed that the new production still needed considerable rehearsal, as patrons began leaving the theatre long before the final curtain. This show had the thinnest thread of a plot: the undertaker in the town of Sundown decides to move into a new (and obvious) business after the start of Prohibition. Nevertheless, the libretto seemed to vanish in a matter of moments: "We assume that there was some idea of a book when the authors started, but this was fortunately kicked over the footlights with the first entrance of what *Shuffle Along* used to call 'syncopating sunflowers' and 'magnificent magnolias.' It would never be missed." Dancing came to dominate the evening with the appearance of the Four Flash Devils, who performed so "tirelessly and nimbly that you feel human energy cannot accomplish more. Indeed, you wonder if they are not just puppets with strings attached and one man on the platform above to dangle each joint, such amazing agility do they achieve."[12] The brisk choreography stopped suddenly in the second act, when a familiar sight appeared. A referee announced the rematch between those battling beauties of *Messin' Around* fame, Emma Maitland and Aurelia Wheeldin. This gimmick did not save the earlier show, and it did not change the luck of this latest effort. Despite valiant performances by Hamtree Harrington and Alberta Hunter, *Change Your Luck* had only a seventeen-performance run.

Hot Rhythm (1930) finished the summer black musical season with disastrous results as well. White producer Will Morrissey, in an attempt to save money, opened his new show without a tryout or even a dress rehearsal. Opening night was a shambles. Morrissey, who "su-

12. New York *Evening World*, June 7, 1930; Philadelphia *Record*, January 15, 1930.

pervised" the production, actually appeared onstage several times to bark instructions at the cast and make sly remarks to the audience. Morrissey billed the show as a "Sepia Tinted *Little Show,*" a reference to the 1929 musical hit by Howard Dietz, Arthur Schwartz, and George S. Kaufman. He often reminded the audience of *Hot Rhythm*'s supposed kinship to that earlier show. During a tender love duet, Morrissey told the assembled crowd: "Look at them—just like Jack Buchanan and Gertie Lawrence. Only a lot cheaper!" Amid the wreckage, a Eubie Blake interpolation in the score, "Loving You the Way I Do," was sung beautifully by Revella Hughes. Also, one critic said that Edith Wilson provided the evening's only "genuine encores." But *Variety*'s critic noted more than one hundred walkouts during the ramshackle premiere.[13]

While audience members judged the show on its merits (or lack of them) on opening night, they did not know that two cast members had recently died. Both actors had been in an "electric chair" comedy skit. The first actor to accept the role, thirty-two-year-old James Jackson, was found asphyxiated in his room two days before opening night. There was some reluctance among other performers to step into what was already being seen as a "jinx part," so dance director Nat Cash volunteered. The forty-two-year-old actor was found dead the next day of heart failure in his Newark apartment.[14]

Brown Buddies (1930), the first black musical to open during the regular season in some time, almost rescued the genre from its string of failures. Reuniting the stars of Lew Leslie's *Blackbirds of 1928,* Bill Robinson and Adelaide Hall, the show garnered high praise. A few days before the premiere, however, it was doubtful that the show would open. When Robinson was about to board a train in Pittsburgh, he noticed a woman in distress. He quickly ascertained that a man had snatched her purse, so he ran after the thief and pulled his gold-plated gun from his pocket. A Harlem detachment of police had given Robinson the gun for his support of their crime-fighting efforts. The Pittsburgh constabulary, unaware of the supposed hero's activities, shot the man waving a pistol. When the situation was disentangled, Robinson received ample apologies, but his wounded arm was in a sling that was strapped to his body. Despite the injury, Robinson agreed to perform. Critics noted that he seemed to have some slight trouble with his balance due to the inability to use his arm. The audience, however,

13. New York *Times,* August 22, 1930; *Variety,* August 27, 1930.
14. Unidentified article, in "*Hot Rhythm*" File, TC/PFL.

forgave all—Robinson brought his much-heralded step-dancing number to his new show. After a stirring performance on a broad stairway, Robinson was joined by ten dancers who echoed his now-classic routine.

Brown Buddies followed the adventures of a group of black soldiers during World War I who at first remained stationed in St. Louis, but later joined the war effort overseas. The high point of the show was a YMCA entertainment unit, consisting of the girlfriends of the St. Louis soldiers, visiting the troops in France. Here, as in other black musicals, the libretto was temporarily forgotten, and a string of song-and-dance numbers ensued. Despite some vivid depictions of the horrors of war in Act II (especially in the scenery which displayed a devastated land marked by shell holes and withered trees), all ended happily as the soldiers return to St. Louis on the day before Prohibition went into effect. This naturally provided the opportunity for a rousing finale that featured Robinson's tap-dancing.

The performances of Robinson and Hall dominated the evening. Critic Richard Lockridge gave Robinson credit for one-third of the success of *Brown Buddies*: "And now we move to the feet of Mr. Robinson—the subtle feet, the amazingly rolling eyes, the strange chuckling sounds with which he applauds the feet when they perform, always to his apparent surprise, some peculiarly difficult evolution. He croons with his feet and laughs with them and watches them in wide-eyed amazement as they do things which apparently surprise him as much as they do the rest of us, and please him, if possible, even more." Hall then received credit for the success of "a large share of the remaining two-thirds" of the show for her renditions of "Give Me a Man Like That" and "My Blue Melody." After finishing the love letters to Hall and Robinson, some critics also praised the libretto, which remained intact, and often funny, for much of the evening. The sprightly reviews (and the well-acknowledged talents of Hall and Robinson) helped *Brown Buddies* run for 111 performances during the height of the difficult 1930–1931 season.[15]

Since Robinson and Hall were performing at the Liberty Theatre, Lew Leslie was without his potent box office draws from *Blackbirds of 1928*. He, too, was interested in joining the rush of black revues with a new edition of his classic show, *Blackbirds of 1930*. After hiring Flournoy Miller, the Berry Brothers, and Buck and Bubbles, Leslie began to

15. *Variety*, October 15, 1930; "*Brown Buddies*" File, TC/PFL; New York *Evening World*, October 8, 1930; New York *Post*, October 8, 1930.

put out feelers to Ethel Waters concerning a job in his new show. Leslie, who had never wanted Waters previously, no doubt felt that the lack of a strong female presence in the show (like Mills or Hall) could hurt box office prospects. Waters joined the show and, as usual, experienced a traumatic rehearsal period. This time, funds were so tight, producer Leslie found himself distributing bus fare to the cast members so they could travel home to Harlem after rehearsal.

Opening night was a shambles, with the oft-noted "encore problem" driving critics to distraction. Percy Hammond caustically commented: "If I were inclined to censor the play I should suggest to Mr. Leslie . . . that he give it more speed and variety. He should limit the songs to eight or ten verses, and try to have them sing something in less than half an hour. He should restrict the encores, and prevent his artists from exhausting themselves and their audience by laboring overtime. As it was last evening a dropped playbill or a sneeze was enough to bring the entire troupe back again in turning repetitions." Leslie followed the reviewer's suggestions, and in just a few nights, he trimmed almost one hour from the show. *Variety*'s critic, who viewed the third performance, noted the changes favorably, but it was perhaps too late to contain the damage from the reviews.[16]

The show resembled its predecessors of the 1920s perfectly. It began on a levee on the Mississippi to the accompaniment of "Roll, Jordan," sung by Cecil Mack's Blackbird Choir, and then moved slowly northward (with a slight African detour) as the evening progressed. By scene six, the *Blackbirds* cast arrived in New York with "Take a Trip to Harlem" and parodies of *The Green Pastures* and *All Quiet on the Western Front* (called "All's Quiet on the Darkest Front"). The comic scenes took the harshest beating from the critics, several of whom said they were tired of the prevailing style of blackface comedy in these revues. Richard Lockridge, critic for the *Sun,* seemed particularly exasperated:

> It would be interesting to discover, and quietly murder, the man who first convinced Negro comedians that the way to be a comic lies in blacking brown faces. You take a Negro, who is apt to have naturally certain qualities which the white race cannot acquire, and black him up. You lay on his dialect with a trowel—and with no closer relationship with the actual dialect of the Negro than may be found in the phonetic idiosyncracies of the average white writer about him. You tell him it is funny to twist words, using, for example, "evict" in place of "convict," which

16. New York *Herald Tribune,* October 23, 1930; *Variety,* October 29, 1930.

> ninety-nine times out of a hundred, it isn't. You make him, in short, a bad imitation of what was not a very good imitation in the first place, and you tell him to make the people laugh. He—and I shall never know why—believes you.[17]

Critics did have kind words for Ethel Waters and songwriters Eubie Blake, who also conducted the orchestra, and Andy Razaf. "Lucky to Me," "Baby Mine," and "Dianna Lee" received high praise, and "My Handy Man Ain't Handy No More" caused the most controversy. An audible buzz passed through the first-night audience as Waters sang this sly and wicked torch song. The combination of the king of the double-entendre lyric (Andy Razaf) and the queen proved electrifying, causing one critic to entitle his review "Hot Stuff Is 1930 'Blackbirds' at the Royale." Some found the combination too torrid, but the *New Yorker* praised Waters for her "innocence and cleansing quality to her personality which make even a song like ["Handy Man"] almost permissible."[18] The lyric is perhaps the prototype of the Razaf style:

> Once I used to brag about my handy man,
> But you'd better believe I ain't braggin' no more.
> Something strange has happened to my handy man,
> He's not the man he was before.
>
> I wish somebody would explain to me,
> About this dual personality.
>
> He don't perform his duties like he used to do,
> Never hauls my ashes les' I tell him to,
> And before he hardly gets to work, baby,
> He says he's through,
> Well, my handy man ain't handy no more.
>
> He's forgotten his domestic science,
> And he's lost all of his self reliance.
>
> Now, you used to turn in early, you used to get up at dawn,
> All full of new ambitions
> How you would trim my lawn!
> But now when you ain't sleepin', all you do is yawn.
> My handy man ain't handy no more.

Leslie's using Blake and Razaf as a song-writing team for *Blackbirds of 1930* was an oddity, since he stated in several interviews that white

17. New York *Sun*, October 23, 1930.
18. *New Yorker*, November 1, 1930, p. 26.

artists could write better songs than could blacks. Shortly after the premiere, Leslie claimed to have changed his mind, voicing hopes that an "annual edition of 'Blackbirds' will spur ambitious authors to greater efforts with the result that the Negro race will in a short time develop a group of authors comparable to Rodgers and Hart, Irving Berlin, George Gershwin, B. G. DeSylva, Ray Henderson, Lew Brown, and others." Nevertheless, Leslie promptly dropped his visions of a vast black training program just a few months later, as he returned to using white composers for the rest of the decade.[19]

Despite praise for some portions of the latest Leslie effort, the show faltered at the box office. Ethel Waters recalled: "*Blackbirds* opened . . . at a theatre right next to a flea circus. Our show was a flop and the fleas outdrew us at every performance. The Depression came in and made our business worse. But it didn't dent the take of the flea circus at all. It reminded me of the old vaudeville joke about the flea circus that became so prosperous each flea was given his own private dog."[20] After a two-month run in New York, the troupe traveled to Philadelphia and Newark, where all funds disappeared. Waters was forced to take several cast members back to Harlem in her automobile.

Leslie again attempted to capture an audience for a black revue at the end of the 1930–1931 season with *Rhapsody in Black* (1931), a "symphony of blue notes and black rhythm." For the first time, Leslie broke from his standard *Blackbirds* pattern, which had failed earlier in the season. Leslie explained the new format in a newspaper interview, which portrayed him as a member of the theatre's avant-garde:

> *Rhapsody in Black,* however, is a new step forward in Negro entertainment. It is not a revue in the accepted term of the word. It dispenses with the routine chorus of dusky maidens, the comedians, and the sketch. In its stead there are artists, each a specialist, a plenitude of original ideas, humor in song and dance peculiarly native, voices that blend in spiritual harmony and an orchestra that expresses the soul of the Negro.
>
> "Knowing the Negro as I do," states Mr. Leslie, "I know his very soul has been crying for emancipation. The routine Negro show is passe. The caricature has become obnoxious. The Negro is fitted for better things in the theatre. Even before I produced my last 'Blackbirds' I saw the light ahead of me. It took courage to drop the formula, hackneyed as it was,

19. "Sees Colored Revues Written By Members of Own Race," unidentified article, in "*Rhapsody in Black*" File, TC/PFL.

20. Waters, *His Eye Is on the Sparrow,* 214.

> because it had spelt success to me in the past. I do not mean by this that 'Blackbirds' is to be no more. But when there is a new 'Blackbirds' next season it will be fashioned along the lines of my *Rhapsody in Black.*"

This self-congratulatory excerpt appeared in an article entitled "Negro Taken Out of Jungle in *Rhapsody in Black.*"[21]

Leslie's hyperbole might be interpreted in a different fashion. When *Blackbirds of 1930* failed, a formula that had been successful since the days of *Plantation Revue* began to falter. And since his image as a successful producer was fading, Leslie no longer had easy access to funds for his latest theatrical ideas. As a result, Leslie concentrated on what had proven most popular in his shows, the music and the artists. All else was eliminated. The Washington *Post* noted at the tryout that *Rhapsody in Black* was "presented in a single simple setting of black velvet drapes and a silver curtain, unembellished by elaborate costuming." But this spartan setting did not prevent the audience from blowing "the theatre roof off with applause."[22]

Although Waters had been popular in the *Blackbirds* revues, Leslie moved to eliminate her from *Rhapsody in Black* because of her high salary. While Waters was on a vaudeville tour, Leslie built the show around a talented newcomer, Valaida (Snow), who not only played the trumpet but also conducted the orchestra in one number. Waters, who was under contract for Leslie's new production, suddenly found herself without anything to do, and she complained bitterly. When Leslie suggested that she just sing some of her "off-color" songs, she turned the matter over to her lawyer. He reminded Leslie of a clause that stated that Waters had to be satisfied with her material for the show, so they searched for the appropriate songwriter. They discovered a new husband-and-wife team, Mann Holiner and Alberta Nichols, who gave Waters the biggest song hits of the show, "Washtub Rhapsody (Rub-sody)," "Dancehall Hostess," "What's Keeping My Prince Charming?," and "You Can't Stop Me from Loving You." Not only were these songs successful (especially the last), they also revealed a new side to the Waters persona. Everyone was expecting the traditional off-color numbers, but these songs emphasized her acting ability. She created new and believable characters for each sequence. Leslie, of course, later took credit for this change, recounting events in this fashion. Leslie told Waters that "I'm going to have you sing char-

21. Unidentified article, in "*Rhapsody in Black*" File, TC/PFL.
22. Washington *Post*, April 13, 1931.

acter songs, and give character portraits of your people. No more "hot" numbers for you.' Ethel Waters was stunned. 'But you can't do that, Mr. Leslie,' she protested. 'I've always got by with scorching lyrics.' Leslie, however, was adamant and as much as Miss Waters dreaded losing her identity by venturing into a new field, she accepted the assignment and in *Rhapsody in Black* emerged a new and far superior actress."[23]

Once the material was agreed upon, Waters went through tough negotiations with Leslie on salary. She wanted $1,250 per week, but Leslie refused. Waters was willing to accept half her weekly vaudeville salary, because the prestige of a leading role on Broadway often led to better and higher-paying bookings. Instead, they agreed on $700 per week and 10 percent of the gross. The surprise success of *Rhapsody in Black* on Broadway, on the road, and in a briefer vaudeville presentation brought Waters twice her original salary demands.

Rhapsody in Black was certainly different. As the New York *Times* critic said, there "were no sketches in which a big Negro draws a formidable razor from his pocket and starts off after his smaller companion. There was likewise no chorus of tawny Harlem belles, specializing in stomping and other abandoned exercises calling for a display of hot feet and there were no elaborate production effects." There was, however, a mélange of musical styles, from black spirituals to Victor Herbert ("Dance of the Wooden Soldiers") and George Gershwin ("Rhapsody in Blue"). The true oddities of the evening were Spanish and Russian numbers sung by Valaida, and the Yiddish "Eli Eli," sung by Avis Andrews, Eloise Uggams, and the Cecil Mack Choir. The latter number brought cries of sacrilege from the audience on opening night, though on succeeding evenings no unusual catcalls were heard.[24]

Some critics found the proceedings a bit calm compared to the traditional black revues, but Leslie had no hesitation about the show. Delighted with increasing box office revenues during the first three weeks, he had tickets printed for the entire summer. He claimed to be gratified by the success of *Rhapsody in Black* "because [playgoers] are accepting a new and novel idea in Negro musical plays. Veteran pro-

23. Compare Waters, *His Eye Is on the Sparrow,* 215–16, and "Negro Star Changed Her Familiar Style—(As Result Ethel Waters Has Scored New Hit in *Rhapsody in Black*)" unidentified article, in "*Rhapsody in Black*" File, TC/PFL.

24. New York *Times,* May 6, 1931; Robert Garland, "Second Thoughts on *Rhapsody in Black,* Not to Mention Ethel Waters and Valaida," New York *World,* n.d., in "*Rhapsody in Black*" File, TC/PFL.

ducers told me Broadway only wants to see the Negro stage artist in caricature. I disagree with them and am now presenting the Negro in a show which raises him to the highest level yet attained by his race on the musical comedy stage."[25] Although Leslie avoided the stereotypes of his and others' black revues, he still did not allow black talent to write songs or scripts. The content of *Rhapsody in Black* therefore was white, though the performers were black.

Waters' triumph in *Rhapsody in Black* catapulted her into Broadway's top-drawing and highest-paid elite. After the Leslie show folded, Waters received an offer from the Cotton Club at the highest salary the club had ever paid. Here Harold Arlen offered her his new song, "Stormy Weather," which continued to spread her fame. After Irving Berlin saw her perform the classic number, he gave her a role in his new revue, *As Thousands Cheer* (1933), which featured Clifton Webb, Helen Broderick, and Marilyn Miller, Broadway's favorite musical comedy stars. Waters sang "Heat Wave," "I've Got Harlem on My Mind," and "To Be or Not to Be" in her traditional style. She stopped the show with "Supper Time," the story of a black woman who is preparing supper for her absent husband, who has just been lynched. Her moving rendition of this song furthered her growing reputation as both a singer and an actress. During this year, Waters became the highest-paid woman on Broadway.

As the first full season of the depression era ended on Broadway, the black musical was still a potent draw, though critics were beginning to complain of the sterility of the formulas developed during the 1920s. The success of *Rhapsody in Black* partially reflected its willingness to break from those patterns. Resembling a concert more than a revue, it offered hope that the black musical or revue might seek out new directions. But, then again, the depression was not the most auspicious time to experiment.

For the first time in several years, no new black musicals opened during the traditional summer season of 1931. Yet two new musicals premiered in September, which seemed to indicate that the interest in black musicals was continuing. *Fast and Furious* started the season on the fifteenth with a new revue produced by Forbes Randolph, a self-proclaimed savant of Harlem who had previously sponsored black acts in vaudeville. The show resembled many of the classic black revues in

25. "*Rhapsody in Black* Now All Set For a Summer Run," unidentified article, in "*Rhapsody in Black*" File, TC/PFL.

Ethel Waters sings "Heat Wave" in *As Thousands Cheer*
Courtesy Billy Rose Theatre Collection, New York Public Library

the 1920s, reproducing the tried-and-true skits—among them, a courtroom sequence and yet another Maitland-Wheeldin bout. Perhaps the only major difference was a tendency to give greater weight in the musical numbers to black spirituals and to offer more sequences about life in black heaven and hell. This one variation on the 1920s formula reflected the influence of *The Green Pastures*. White songwriters Mack Gordon and Harry Revel provided most of the evening's melodies, but a few black composers participated in this effort. Most notable was the reappearance of J. Rosamond Johnson, hero of the black musicals of the first decade of the century, providing "Jacob's Ladder," "So Lonesome," and "Boomerang." The *Herald Tribune* critic took special notice of his songs, proclaiming him "one of the sweeter psalmists of his people."[26]

Most critics, however, dismissed the show. Robert Garland said in his headline that "*Fast and Furious* Arrives Only to Prove It Is Nothing of the Kind." Gabriel W. Gabriel, writing in the *American,* went one step farther: "It is possible that the so-called colored show is going definitely out of fashion. It is also possible that I've had bad times at most of them, and have failed to appreciate the geniality and animal humor and vivid athletics of their jumbles, that I can't forgive some of them for being so successful in the past"[27]

Singin' the Blues, which opened the night after *Fast and Furious,* seemed to break with the patterns of black musical theatre developed in the 1920s. Billed as a "melodrama with music," this new show by John McGowan had the strongest libretto of any black musical show in recent memory. During a dice game in Chicago, Jim Williams (Frank Wilson) has the misfortune to shoot an off-duty policeman and is forced to flee the Windy City. He arrives in Harlem, where he hides with Susan Blake (Isabell Washington), an entertainer at Dave Crocker's Club. Blake outwits the police and club owner Crocker (Jack Carter) in her attempt to save Williams. Both eventually return to his hometown in Georgia. Several nightclub sequences provided a musical backdrop for this Harlem melodrama. Eubie Blake conducted the orchestra, and Isabell and Fredi Washington offered first-rate songs by Jimmy McHugh and Dorothy Fields (of *Blackbirds of 1928* fame).

In its attempt to fuse drama and music, *Singin' the Blues* utilized some of the top black actors of the 1920s. Frank Wilson, who was Broadway's first Porgy in 1927, received raves for his performance, which created sympathy for a murderer on the run from the law. The strength of the performances, from the leads to the supporting players, gave *Singin' the Blues* its appeal. With the addition of top-notch musical talent, the show pleased virtually all the critics, and several recommended that it not be missed.[28] Nevertheless, this novel experiment, like others before it, lasted only forty-five performances during this

26. *Variety,* September 22, 1931; New York *Herald Tribune,* September 16, 1931.
27. New York *American,* September 16, 1931.
28. *Variety,* September 22, 1931; New York *Times,* September 17, 1931.

difficult depression period, as favorable notices could not save the show.

Meanwhile, at the Royale Theatre, whites were still appearing in blackface in Mae West's latest show, *The Constant Sinner,* which featured a romance between the voluptuous actress and a Harlem numbers king (played by white actor George Givot). *Variety* noted that Givot "walks on for a bow in whiteface at the finish to square the mixing as much as it possibly could be squared for theatrical usage." Despite the long and continuous presence of real black performers on Broadway, several barriers still remained.[29]

Sugar Hill (1931), Broadway's Christmas present from Miller and Lyles, reunited the comic stars of the 1920s. Absent as a team from Broadway since *Great Day* in 1929, they hoped that reviving the *Shuffle Along* tomfoolery would make them famous once again. Yet, *Sugar Hill* strayed from the expectations of audiences and critics, and disappointment was inevitable. *Sugar Hill* actually revealed a closer kinship to *Singin' the Blues* than to any of the earlier Miller and Lyles shows. Although they included some of their classic routines, the new show had a serious theme. It borrowed from real life the tale of a baby's accidental murder in Harlem during a gangland shoot-out and the attempt to bring the murderer to justice. The mixture of melodrama and music confounded audiences and critics, and led to an eleven-performance run for *Sugar Hill.* An added difficulty for the comic duo was an "Amos 'n' Andy" backlash. As the new radio show grew in popularity, Miller and Lyles found themselves compared unfavorably to the white comedy team of Freeman Gosden and Charles Correll, who were no doubt inspired by the early Sam Peck and Steve Jenkins routines.[30]

Blackberries of 1932, which opened in April, attempted to revive the black revues of the 1920s. Despite the similarity in title to the *Blackbirds* shows, Lew Leslie was not involved with this latest effort, though he did attend on opening night. Conceived by Lee Posner, a press agent for several Harlem nightclubs, *Blackberries of 1932* copied the format of the 1920s revues. Even the program billed the show as "a dancical revue presented to you as you expect to see it." From the opening (a levee number with fleeting clouds against the backdrop) to the Act II finale

29. *Variety,* September 22, 1931.

30. See *Time,* August 10, 1931, or New York *Times,* July 29, 1931, for an account of the child's death. Four other children were injured in the crossfire (*Variety,* December 29, 1931).

("Those Good Old Minstrel Days"), *Blackberries* failed to supply even the slightest hint of originality. Tim Moore, Mantan Moreland, and Eddie Green offered some humor, but the critics panned the show. The *Sun* described it as a "nightmare."[31]

Yeah Man (1932) attempted to redeem the black revue after *Blackberries of 1932*'s twenty-four-performance flop. Mantan Moreland, a veteran of the black musical revues in the 1920s who resurfaced in the lead role, garnered most of the favorable comments for the show: "The head man is Mantan Moreland, without whom none of these blackamoor capers is ever quite official. Mr. Moreland is still tireless. His smile is one of the friendliest omens the theatre has to offer, and he can smoke a cigar, take the falls, or feign wide-eyed terror with stout results. But the authors, for all the four deferred openings, have not found time to think up much for him to do." Despite his valiant efforts, critics dismissed the show. The New York *Times* said that *Yeah Man* "struck out for Harlem by way of Dixie. It is a well-worn trail, that Dixie-Harlem highway, and has been ever since *Shuffle Along* of cherished memory set the pace some years ago when this identical hideaway [the Park Lane Theatre] bore the less flossy name of Daly's Sixty-Third Street Theatre."[32]

Yeah Man thus ended the season with fond memories of that 1921 hit, *Shuffle Along*, but there was no new show to take its place as a model. The 1931–1932 season confirmed the fears of the worst pessimists after the stock market crash. Although several factors had sheltered the black musical from the early days of the depression, the toll was being paid. Producers and writers attempted to revive tested formulas in an effort to make a safe and hefty profit. But critics and audiences tired of repeated copies of past hits. Indeed, several critics seemed to idealize the hits of the earlier decade, making them seem even better in the nostalgic glow of memory. *Yeah Man* closed within a week, and no new black musical productions were announced for the summer. It seemed that the depression, combined with a lack of innovation, had finally killed one of the more popular theatrical forms of the 1920s, the black musical.

31. New York *Times*, April 5, 1932; New York *Sun*, April 5, 1932.
32. New York *Times*, May 27, 1932.

X

THE IRONY OF *PORGY AND BESS*

Although George and Ira Gershwin's *Porgy and Bess,* which opened on October 10, 1935, is often remembered as the best black musical of the 1930s, several qualifications are in order. Heralded in retrospect for its daring and innovation, it actually symbolizes the end of the black musical tradition that flourished in the early part of this century. While the faces onstage were clearly black, this musical version of the 1927 DuBose and Dorothy Heyward Broadway play revealed the height of white usurpation of what had initially been a black cultural form. Despite the impressive cast onstage, virtually all the creative talent backstage was white. This transition had been occurring slowly, to be sure, throughout the 1920s, but black artists had often worked in a variety of creative capacities. Although white money had supported black musicals, black talent often provided the songs, dances, skits, sets, or costumes for many of these entertainments. Thus *Porgy and Bess* became a "black musical" in its most minimalist sense, merely as a definition of the color of the cast members. Neither the plot nor the music was of black origin, though its creators insisted on the "Negro inspiration" for its themes.

Nevertheless, *Porgy and Bess* should not in any way be blamed for the death of black musical comedy. It seemed certain, by the early years of the Great Depression, that the genre had its own problems. As critics nostalgically yearned for the heyday of the black musical in their reviews of *Yeah Man* or *Blackberries of 1932,* they recalled either the book musical *Shuffle Along* or the great revues, such as *Blackbirds of 1928,* and, naturally, the newer shows paled in comparison.

The critics' fears were validated by two new black musical stepchildren. *Shuffle Along of 1933,* which opened the day after Christmas in

1932, offered the first glimmer of hope, as much of the talent of the original *Shuffle Along* remained. Eubie Blake and Noble Sissle wrote the songs, and Flournoy Miller concocted the book, which once again presented the misadventures of Steve Jenkins, who is trying to make a fortune with the U-Eat-Em Molasses Company of Jimtown. Aubrey Lyles had also helped plan the show, but he died of tuberculosis in July, 1932, before rehearsals began. Mantan Moreland attempted to replace Lyles in the comedy team. Although the critics found some bright moments in the show, they ripped the book to shreds. Robert Garland of the *World-Telegram* proclaimed that the "new arrival needs . . . an operation on its libretto."[1]

Lew Leslie's efforts to revive his successful black revues met a similar dismal fate. *Blackbirds of 1933,* which opened on December 2, 1933, returned several of Leslie's discoveries, such as Bill Robinson, Edith Wilson, and Eddie Hunter, to the stage of the Apollo Theatre, but to no avail. Reviewer Richard Lockridge noted the fatal flaw: "The harshest critic . . . will hardly deny that the show is lively. Funny it is not, by one of the widest margins ever recorded; particularly musical it is not and its lack of any spark of originality is almost embarrassing. But lively, yes, it is full of clatter and bright colors. And the chorus girls are tireless, having there an edge, one fears, on the members of the audience." Most critics observed the "lack of any spark of originality"—Leslie's enslavement to earlier versions of his show seemed to preclude any experimentation. Therefore, if one had seen an earlier, and no doubt better, *Blackbirds,* there seemed to be almost no reason to visit the Apollo.[2]

The only exception to the negative reviews was the unanimous praise for Bill Robinson, who was billed a "guest star" in the new *Blackbirds.* Brooks Atkinson virtually ignored the show and offered a paean to Robinson: "After all these years he has perfected his act to a point where it is no longer an accomplishment but the expression of his personality. It seems to require no effort. . . . No matter how complicated the dancing rhythm, the crease in his trousers never loses its knife-edge and his jacket never flares out vulgarly from the waist. There is no feeling of exertion; he has plenty of vitality and talent in reserve. . . . [His] feet are inspired. Whatever he is doing they preserve that light rapid mocking patter that dominates the audible world." But

1. New York *Daily News,* December 27, 1932; New York *World-Telegram,* December 27, 1932.

2. New York *Sun,* December 3, 1933.

Robinson's two brief appearances could not save the show, which Atkinson called "a feeble imitation of itself."[3]

The negative reviews for these 1920s clones suggested a double irony for black artists interested in the Broadway musical. The theatrical genres represented by *Shuffle Along* and *Blackbirds* had been heralded by major newspaper critics as the models for black artists. Harsh reviews discouraged any deviation from these norms. With the ultimate dismissal of these two black musical staples, it seemed that no options remained. Experimentation was frowned on, and so was dependence on these classic shows of the 1920s. As a result, any new directions for black artists in musical theatre seemed risky at best.

While this critical response doomed the black musical comedy as it had existed in the 1920s, it did offer one avenue of hope. As musical comedies seemed to be passing out of vogue, black dramas with music, and particularly spirituals, remained in fashion. *The Green Pastures* is perhaps the best-known example of this trend, but it is just one of many. As dramas about black life (whether by black or white artists) assumed greater importance in the 1930s, they often borrowed from the musical comedy traditions of the 1920s. Serious drama, about black life in the rural South or in northern cities, managed to integrate music into its structure. This was not an entirely new phenomenon. Paul Robeson always included singing interludes in his dramatic appearances. Even *Black Boy,* a 1926 drama about a world championship fighter, offered Robeson a chance to display his vocal prowess. In similar fashion, *Singin' the Blues* was primarily a drama of Harlem night life, but it allowed for the inclusion of several songs in its nightclub sequences. Thus in many of the dramas in the 1920s that had to do with black life, music became a staple. In the 1930s this trend prevailed: musical elements of Afro-American culture were showcased primarily in dramas rather than in musicals. *The Green Pastures* no doubt encouraged the popularity of music within dramatic forms, but it was not the first show to do so.

Black artists who might have contributed to musical comedies in the 1920s often shifted their attention to musical dramas or dramas with music in the 1930s. Donald Heywood, who provided some of the more interesting musical experiments of the decade, was the first black to attempt to dramatize black folklore in *Ol' Man Satan* (1932). Heywood's work explored Satan's wanderings on Earth, to the accom-

3. New York *Times,* December 3, 1933.

paniment of a variety of black spirituals. Despite an excellent performance by A. B. Comathiere, critics dismissed the enterprise as a Marc Connelly copy.[4]

Hall Johnson had greater success the following year with *Run, Little Chillun!*, which opened on March 1, 1933. Johnson, a skilled musician who had studied at the New York Institute of Music, the Juilliard School, and the Philadelphia Music Academy, received acclaim in the 1920s for his musical compositions and for the Hall Johnson Choir, which appeared in *The Green Pastures*, on radio, and in films. When Johnson began the preparation of *Run, Little Chillun!*, a folk drama indebted to the works of Zora Neale Hurston, he brought his musical talents to bear. The show enjoyed a well-attended and profitable 126-performance run during the harshest days of the depression.[5]

Johnson's drama concerned the conflict between the Christian and African religious heritage in black life. It featured the beautiful Sulamai (Fredi Washington), who tempts Pastor Jones's son Jim (Aston Burleigh) to leave his wife and religion. She introduces Jim to the rituals of the African-oriented New Day Pilgrims, but he eventually returns to the fold. In the climactic scene, the pregnant Sulamai confronts Jim in the Baptist church and is struck by lightning as her lover rejects her. Critics tended to ignore the plot, for the true genius of the evening was the marvelous choral music. *Variety* noted: "When Mr. Johnson . . . reaches the spirituals, he is on familiar ground. Some of them deserve—without the usual equivocation—the adjective superb, and all of them are more than good. Partly they are haunting and wistful, and partly ringing; partly they take their tempo from the old church litanies. And in their singing the voices of men, women, and children are blended perfectly." While Johnson called his work a drama, *Time* suggested that he had written an opera, a goal rarely achieved or even considered by black artists working in Broadway's environs.[6]

Although the thought of an opera with a black cast and created by black talent was relatively rare, it was not unprecedented. Bob Cole had spoken about an opera based on *Uncle Tom's Cabin*, but the work remained uncompleted at his death. Scott Joplin, the noted composer of ragtime music, had written an opera, *A Guest of Honor*, while living in St. Louis in 1903. The opera enjoyed a few performances in Mis-

4. *Ibid.*, October 4, 1932.
5. Ronald P. Ross, "Hall Johnson," in Woll, *Dictionary of the Black Theatre*, 221.
6. *Variety*, n.d.; *Saturday Review of Literature*, July 29, 1933; *Time*, March 13, 1933.

souri, but it did not travel beyond the state's borders. Joplin's second opera, *Treemonisha,* composed between 1905 and 1907, seemed somewhat more promising, and Joplin moved to New York in order to obtain backing for his work. Although New York publishers welcomed Joplin's ragtime works, they ignored *Treemonisha.* Joplin labored until 1915 in order to have his opera performed, but with the exception of auditions in Harlem, he never saw his work given a professional production. Joplin died in 1917, his dream unfulfilled.[7]

Despite these initiatives by black creative artists, the honor of presenting the first black-performed opera on Broadway must be given to Virgil Thomson and Gertrude Stein for *Four Saints in Three Acts* on February 20, 1934. Although receiving a mixed critical reception, the production ran for forty-eight performances, the longest continuous run of a modern American opera to that date. In 1927, Thomson suggested to Stein that they write an opera based on the lives of Saint Teresa and Saint Ignatius. The most provocative feature of this production was that the cast would be black. Carl Van Vechten credited the inspiration for this idea to the aftermath of a performance of Hall Johnson's *Run, Little Chillun!*: "Virgil turned and said to me, 'I am going to have *Four Saints* played by Negroes. They alone possess the dignity and poise, the lack of self-consciousness that proper interpretation of opera demands. And they are not ashamed of words.'" John Houseman, the director of *Four Saints,* acknowledged another version in his autobiography, *Run-Through.* He claimed that the decision was reached in Jimmy Daniels' Harlem nightclub. No matter which story is true, these anecdotes reveal the continuing white interest in black theatre and music during the Harlem Renaissance and the consequent influence on white theatrical productions.[8]

The bizarre proceedings on the stage of the 44th Street Theatre soon

7. Vera Brodsky Lawrence, "Scott Joplin and *Treemonisha,*" *Treemonisha* liner notes, Deutsche Grammophon, 2707–083. Lawrence is responsible for the rediscovery and publication of many of the unpublished works of Louis Moreau Gottschalk and Scott Joplin. *Treemonisha* finally reached Broadway on October 21, 1975, at the Uris Theatre. The Houston Grand Opera Association production directed by Frank Corsaro had sixty-four performances. The following year, when the Metropolitan Opera abandoned plans for a Bicentennial presentation of *Porgy and Bess,* the Houston Grand Opera again came to the rescue with a Broadway production of the Gershwin work.

James Weldon Johnson also experimented with opera after leaving the Cole and Johnson team. He provided an English translation for the opera *Goyescas,* which was performed at the Metropolitan Opera House. See R. G. Doggett, "*Goyescas* Brings Colored Man to Front in New Role," unidentified newspaper, March, 1916, in "James Weldon Johnson" File, SCCF/NYPL.

8. John Houseman, *Run-Through* (New York, 1972), 105.

became the vogue in New York. John Anderson, critic for the *Evening Journal,* provided an appropriate headline for his review: "Brain Scrambling Words Draw Sophisticates to Opera of Naive Appeal."[9] "Brain scrambling" was perhaps the most polite description of Gertrude Stein's poetry, since the maddening libretto was virtually incomprehensible to all and had little relationship to the lives of the saints in the title. As a result, the saints in this show often avoided religious symbolism in favor of more worldly locutions. Particularly irksome to the critics was the depiction of Saint Ignatius' vision of the Holy Ghost as: "Pigeons on the grass alas. / Short longer grass short longer longer shorter yellow grass. / Pigeons large pigeons on the shorter longer yellow grass alas pigeons on the grass."

With the entire production of *Four Saints in Three Acts* wrapped in a decor of colored cellophane by Florine Stettheimer, few critics noted that Houseman, Thomson, and Stein had provided a operatic vehicle for black talent. While the singers received praise for their meritorious efforts to make sense of Stein's verbiage, few commented on the supposed novelty of the black cast. What perhaps seems novel to modern eyes had become commonplace to theatregoers of the 1920s and 1930s.

The success of the works by Hall Johnson and Virgil Thomson no doubt encouraged Donald Heywood's 1934 production of *Africana.* He had used the same title in 1927 for a musical revue with Ethel Waters, but the new presentation was billed as a "Congo operetta." *Africana* presented a tale of cultural conflict: an African prince is forced to understand his Oxford-educated son, who has adopted all the habits of Europeans. Heywood directed the show and wrote the music, lyrics, and libretto. His was an ambitious work that, unlike many of the earlier black musical efforts, tackled a serious and uncompromising subject. Unfortunately, this proved a dangerous course. One critic after another attacked the libretto for making the cast "behave like white folks." As George Ross noted in his review, *Africana* had "not even the virtue of decent Harlem rhythms or an excitable tap dancer."[10]

Adding to the negative response from the critics was an unusual opening-night episode. Shortly after the overture began, a man in evening dress rushed down the aisle, shouting at the conductor. Most of the audience assumed that this interruption was part of the show, but when the intruder pulled an iron bar from his coat and swung it at the conductor, chaos ensued. The police arrived and arrested the six-

9. New York *Evening Journal,* February 21, 1934.
10. Unidentified newspaper, November 27, 1934, in *Africana* File, TC/PFL.

foot-tall Almany Dauoda Carmaro, who explained that he had served in the French Foreign Legion with Heywood, and they had jointly conceived the idea for this production of *Africana.* Carmaro wanted to protest what he termed Heywood's "plagiarism" and receive credit for his ideas. An injunction barred Carmaro from future performances, and he agreed to settle the argument in court. The theater audience eventually calmed down and the performance continued, but the damage had been done. Critics paid more attention to the offstage adventures than to the onstage drama. This was merely the beginning of a run of bad luck for Heywood, the opening of whose 1936 show, *Black Rhythm,* was interrupted by a stink bomb. As a result of the chaos, *Africana*'s second-act curtain did not rise before 10:30, helping to condemn the show to a three-performance run.[11]

The disastrous opening and prompt closing of *Africana* further dimmed the interest in black musical shows. Not until one year later did Broadway see another example of the genre, *Porgy and Bess.* This 1935 production differed from earlier black musicals in a variety of ways. *Porgy and Bess* had virtually no blacks involved in either its production or the creation of the musical. The show was also a prestige item, produced by the Theatre Guild; earlier musicals were often mounted on a shoestring. Additionally, this musical version was billed as an "opera" or a "folk opera." Indeed at one point it seemed that the Metropolitan Opera would present the show.[12]

At first glance, therefore, it seems that *Porgy and Bess* had no direct creative links with its black musical predecessors. Nevertheless, without their presence it is quite possible that the show might never have existed. Although the immediate origin of the show was the Heywards' hit play, *Porgy* (1927), it was clear that the genesis of the project harked back to an earlier date. George Gershwin had been interested in the rhythms of black music throughout the prewar years, and he had attended many gatherings of black musicians, poets, and authors during the Harlem Renaissance. He first attempted to create a jazz

11. New York *Herald Tribune,* New York *Daily News,* New York *World-Telegram,* November 27, 1934.

12. For information on George Gershwin in general and the writing of *Porgy and Bess* in particular, see Robert Kimball and Alfred Simon, *The Gershwins* (New York, 1973); Edward Jablonski and Lawrence D. Stewart, *The Gershwin Years* (New York, 1973); and Merle Armitage (ed.), *George Gershwin* (New York, 1938). For information on Heyward's contributions to *Porgy and Bess,* see Frank Durham, *DuBose Heyward, the Man Who Wrote "Porgy"* (Columbia, S.C., 1954). The text of *Porgy and Bess* can be found in Stanley Richards (ed.), *Ten Great Musicals of the American Theatre* (Radnor, Pa., 1973), 75–113.

opera about black life in the early 1920s. Entitled *Blue Monday Blues,* this "Opera ala Afro-American" was prepared by Gershwin and lyricist Buddy DeSylva for the second-act opening of *George White's Scandals of 1922,* Gershwin's third stint as a *Scandals* composer. This normally carefree and escapist revue may seem an odd place for a twenty-five-minute opera, but it must be remembered that a new and surprising interest in black musical productions was occurring in the aftermath of such shows as *Shuffle Along, Put and Take,* and *Strut Miss Lizzie.* White was one of the first to see the profit potential of these new black shows, and he hired Miller and Lyles for his own production, *Runnin' Wild,* in 1923. Whether Gershwin saw these earlier shows is unknown, though Eubie Blake claimed to have known Gershwin during this period. Interestingly, Gershwin's choice as the arranger for *Blue Monday Blues* was Will Vodery, who performed the same task for *Shuffle Along.*

Unlike *Shuffle Along,* however, *Blue Monday Blues* had white performers in blackface, which was the norm on Broadway at the time. Jack McGowan, Coletta Ryan, and Richard Bold appeared in this variation on the "Frankie and Johnny" legend set in a Harlem bar. *Blue Monday Blues* concerns Vi's jealous love for Joe, a gambler. Joe decides to visit his family, particularly his ill mother, down south after a lengthy absence. He sends a telegram about his intentions and awaits a response. The villainous Tom arrives and suggests to Vi that Joe is expecting a telegram from another woman. She believes Tom, and when the telegram arrives she shoots Joe. She then pries the telegram from her former lover's fingers and discovers that it was from Joe's family. Joe's mother has been dead for three years, and there is no need for him to make the trip.

Although the real black musicals were attracting audiences at this time, the pseudo-black *Blue Monday Blues* was yanked from *Scandals* after the opening-night performance. Some have suggested that the show was overlong; others have contended that the opera was too serious for a musical revue. While there might be some truth to these explanations, in fact the sequence received the worst notices of the entire production. Several critics, finding the evening too long, suggested cutting *Blue Monday Blues,* which "delays the second act from getting started." Words such as "painful" and "long-drawn" were frequent, but Charles Darnton of the *Evening World* spared no blows, finding the Gershwin piece "the most dismal, stupid, and incredible blackface sketch that has ever been perpetrated." There was a hopeful note in the *Sun*, however. Its critic considered the sketch a "very clever burlesque of grand opera. . . . Very seriously the singers intone their little arias, while the orchestra comments on their doings after the manner of the modern veristic school. . . . It is all done in the excessive manner of grand opera singers and is a delicious bit of musical fun." This must have been peculiar solace for Gershwin—one of the few favorable reviews totally misunderstood his intentions.[13] Critics otherwise ignored Gershwin's operatic endeavor and selected his "I'll Build a Stairway to Paradise" as the hit of the show.

Nevertheless, *Blue Monday Blues* refused to die. Paul Whiteman, who conducted the orchestra for the 1922 *Scandals*, presented a Carnegie Hall revival of the opera, with new orchestrations by Ferde Grofe in 1925. Again, white singers, McGowan, Blossom Seely, Charles Hart, and Benny Fields, were used. The new version of *Blue Monday Blues*, entitled *135th Street*, seemed to make little impression, but it clearly reveals that Gershwin had been interested in the creation of a black-themed opera at an early date, some thirteen years before *Porgy and Bess*.

Gershwin's operatic endeavors were frustrated, but the composer continued his work on Broadway. During the next ten years he wrote several hits, including *Lady, Be Good!* (1924), *Oh, Kay!* (1926), *Funny Face* (1927), *Girl Crazy* (1930), and *Of Thee I Sing* (1931), the first musical to win the Pulitzer Prize in drama. Accompanying George in these successful efforts was his brother Ira, his latest collaborator. Using the pseudonym Arthur Francis during his cautious early days in the song-writing profession, Ira soon began to equal his brother's considerable talents. Despite the deluge of hit songs and shows during the 1920s, George Gershwin was unable to forget his commitment to the world of classical music. He composed and performed such heralded works as *Rhapsody in Blue* (1924), *Concerto in F* (1925), and *An American in Paris* (1928) at the same time that he was writing "Fascinating Rhythm," "Someone to Watch Over Me," "Strike Up the Band," and "Liza." In his classical and popular works, jazz themes and rhythms were pervasive.

In the mid-1920s, Gershwin once again expressed interest in a new theatrical property about black life, a novel called *Porgy*, written by

13. New York *Evening World*, New York *Sun*, August 29, 1922. See also New York *Mail*, New York *Globe*, New York *Evening Journal*, New York *Telegram*, August 29, 1922. The Vodery orchestrations (often presumed lost) are located in Box 8, George Gershwin Collection, MC/LC.

DuBose and Dorothy Heyward in 1924. When Gershwin suggested to Heyward that they write a musical version, Heyward demurred, since he and his wife were embarking on their own dramatization of the work for the Theatre Guild. *Porgy* premiered on Broadway in October, 1927, and experienced one of the healthiest runs of any play with a black cast during the 1920s. This story of a legless cripple, Porgy, and his love for the faithless Bess on Catfish Row in Charleston, South Carolina, received generally favorable reviews. Not all black critics were enthralled, however. The prevalence of superstition, gambling, and spirituals seemed to spring from stereotypes that were common in white plays about black life that had appeared on Broadway since the early 1920s.[14]

Porgy did excel, however, in its acting talent. Director Rouben Mamoulian, a young Russian-Armenian immigrant who had trained at the Moscow Art Theatre, sagaciously reviewed the black plays and musicals of the 1920s in his search for performers. He managed to find the most promising actors for even the smallest roles from this vast talent pool. Frank Wilson (Porgy) had appeared in *All God's Chillun Got Wings* (1924) and *In Abraham's Bosom* (1926); Evelyn Ellis (Bess), in *Roseanne* (1924) and *Goat Alley* (1927 revival); Georgette Harvey (Maria), in *Runnin' Wild* (1923); and Rose McClendon (Serena), in *Roseanne, Deep River* (1926), and *In Abraham's Bosom. Time* magazine referred to this troupe as "seized from the dusky depths of the vagrant Negro theatre." When Mamoulian was asked how he, a Russian, had managed to direct a black cast with such astounding skill, he noted that he, too, was a southerner—from the Caucasus.[15]

Both Mamoulian and Heyward also displayed an unusual willingness to receive suggestions from the cast, so characters and sequences not in the original novel appeared in the stage version. For example, Leigh Whipper (who played the undertaker) provided the idea for the crab vendor, a character based on his and fellow Charlestonian Heyward's recollections of black waterfront life. C. Wesley Hill, a veteran of the *Shuffle Along* cast, improvised a key scene that had both Heyward and Mamoulian at a loss.[16]

James Weldon Johnson found this production of *Porgy* of major significance in the history of black theatre: "In *Porgy* the Negro per-

14. Edwin D. Johnson, "The Jewel in Ethiope's Ear," *Opportunity* (June, 1928), 167.
15. *Time*, October 24, 1927.
16. DuBose Heyward, "The Casting and Rehearsing of *Porgy*," New York *Times*, October 16, 1935.

former removed all doubts as to his ability to do acting that requires thoughtful interpretation and intelligent skill. Here was more than the achievement of one or two individuals who might be set down as exceptions. Here was a large company giving a first-rate even performance, with eight or ten reaching a high mark. The evidence was massive and indisputable."[17]

Although frustrated at first by the Heywards' inability to participate in a musical version of *Porgy,* Gershwin kept on thinking of the play's possibilities. He wrote to DuBose Heyward again in 1932, expressing his continued interest: "I am about to go abroad in a little over a week, and in thinking of ideas for new compositions, I came back to one I had several years ago—namely, *Porgy,* and the thought of setting it to music. It is still the most outstanding play that I know about the colored people." He learned by return mail that he was not the only musical comedy composer interested in *Porgy.* Jerome Kern and Oscar Hammerstein II considered setting the play to music for the consummate pseudo-black talent, Al Jolson. The news both distressed and confused Gershwin. On one hand, Jolson was a long-standing champion of Gershwin's music; he had even attended the premiere of *Blue Monday Blues* in the 1922 *Scandals.* Gershwin wrote: "I think it is very interesting that Al Jolson would like to play the part of Porgy, but I really don't know how he would be in it. Of course, he is a very big star, who certainly knows how to put over a song, and it might mean more to you financially if he should do it—provided that the rest of the production were well done. The sort of thing that I have in mind is a much more serious thing than Jolson could ever do." Even at this early date, Gershwin voiced his preference for an "all-colored cast" for *Porgy.*[18]

Gershwin was less surprised by Kern and Hammerstein's interest in the property, since it was certainly inspired by their success with *Show Boat* (1927). This multiracial musical based on the Edna Ferber novel explored life along the Mississippi and provided Jules Bledsoe the opportunity to immortalize "Ol' Man River" in his performance as Joe. (Paul Robeson had been the first choice for the role, but previous commitments prohibited his joining the New York production of *Show Boat.* His opportunity to perform "Ol' Man River" was finally realized in the London presentation of the show.) Kern and Hammerstein ulti-

17. Johnson, *Black Manhattan,* 212.

18. George Gershwin to DuBose Heyward, March 29, September 9, 1932, both in Box 17, George Gershwin Collection, MC/LC.

mately dropped their option, allowing Gershwin to begin developing the Heywards' work.[19]

Both Gershwin and DuBose Heyward rearranged their schedules in the early 1930s, trying to alleviate any money problems that might hinder their work. Heyward turned to Hollywood, working on screenplays for *The Emperor Jones* and *The Good Earth,* and Gershwin signed a lucrative radio contract with Feen-A-Mint, which reportedly paid $2,000 per week for two fifteen-minute shows. The only problem was that the Heywards were hesitant to leave their Charleston home for an extended period, and Gershwin had to be in New York for his radio show. Ira Gershwin, who had recently joined the project, offered a solution. He became a go-between, shuttling from Manhattan to Charleston in order to resolve problems in the early months of the collaboration. George finally moved to Folly Island, a small barrier island almost ten miles from Charleston, in order to observe the people of Heyward's *Porgy* and continue working with the southern author. The composer spent the summer of 1934 listening to the Gullahs' speech, a regional dialect with strong African survivals, and their music.

On his return Gershwin spent almost eleven months in the composition of his new work, and another eight months in the orchestration. For the first time in his career he also tackled the vocal arrangements. Heyward also extended his original talents, providing the lyrics for songs in the first act of the new show and collaborated with Ira on the remaining two acts. As their work continued *Porgy* became *Porgy and Bess.* The change reflected the increased emphasis on Bess, but it also calmed Theatre Guild producers who worried that the audience might confuse it with the earlier version. Gershwin was also pleased with the "operatic sound" of the new title—he compared his hero and heroine to "Pelleas and Melisande, Tristan and Isolde, and Samson and Delilah."[20]

As *Porgy and Bess* began to take shape, Gershwin explored the possibility of a Metropolitan Opera production. After initial negotiations, the Gershwins decided to offer the show to the prestigious Theatre Guild. They felt that their new show would reach a wider audience on

19. Miles Kreuger, *Show Boat: The Story of a Classic American Musical* (New York, 1977).

20. New York *Times,* October 6, 1935, Sec. XI, p. 3; DuBose Heyward, "*Porgy and Bess* Return on the Wings of Song," *Stage* (October, 1935), 25–29. See also Kimball and Simon, *The Gershwins,* 170–91.

the Broadway stage, as tickets were more affordable than they were at the Met. The Guild also offered Gershwin a lengthier rehearsal period. Finally, the Met claimed that it was too difficult to find a large cast of black operatic talent. This seemed an insurmountable problem for Met officials, for they had made a similar search in the production of Louis Gruenberg's opera, *The Emperor Jones* (1933). Based on the 1920 Eugene O'Neill play, which featured Charles Gilpin as Brutus Jones, the opera ultimately had white performers in most of the leading roles. Lawrence Tibbett was hailed by the New York *Times* for his "superb" blackface performance. Actual blacks were confined to the background and dancing roles. Gershwin, who had abandoned the disastrous approach of blackface entertainment after the *Blue Monday Blues* fiasco, found this a major reason for preferring Broadway to the Met.[21]

Rouben Mamoulian was once again recruited as director for the new version of *Porgy.* In the interim Mamoulian had proven himself as a Hollywood director who had great sensitivity to the uses and possibilities of the new sound medium. His skills were displayed in a variety of works, but Rodgers and Hart's *Love Me Tonight* (1932), with Maurice Chevalier and Jeanette MacDonald, showcased his talent for the musical comedy form. While most film musicals of the early sound period (and there were many) tended to copy Broadway models, Mamoulian is often credited with creating the first musical for film. The barriers of theatrical conventions disappeared as Mamoulian used song as an editing device that definitively moved the Hollywood musical from its stage origins. Mamoulian, therefore, seemed doubly qualified for this latest task. He knew the *Porgy* story intimately from his 1927 experience, and, by 1935, he had become extremely knowledgeable about the newest directions in musical film.[22]

In general, Mamoulian began the casting of *Porgy and Bess* much as he had *Porgy.* Yet, there was a vital difference in this current work. Singing talent was virtually unnecessary in the earlier play. Here, Porgy, Bess, and Crown would have some of the toughest vocal assignments on Broadway in many years. As a result, Gershwin handled the casting of the major singing roles, and Mamoulian sought out the rest of the cast.

21. New York *Times,* January 8, 1933, p. 1. See also Frederick S. Roffman, "At Last the Complete *Porgy and Bess,*" New York *Times,* September 19, 1976, Sec. II, p. 1. Only in Philadelphia in 1935 did the Hedgerow Playhouse experiment with alternating white and black performers in the Brutus Jones role. For information on Gruenberg's work, see "Opera—*The Emperor Jones*" File, SCCF/NYPL; and *Afro-American,* January 14, 1933.

22. Allen Woll, *The Hollywood Musical Goes to War* (Chicago, 1983), 27–29.

Director Rouben Mamoulian (*center*) and the cast of *Porgy and Bess*
Courtesy Billy Rose Theatre Collection, New York Public Library

Although Paul Robeson was the inevitable first choice for the role of Porgy, Gershwin eventually chose Todd Duncan for the lead. Abbie Mitchell, who was cast as Clara, suggested that Gershwin audition a talented young music teacher from Howard University in Washington, D.C. Duncan, who had received a bachelor's degree from Butler College in Indianapolis and a master's from Columbia, had appeared with Mitchell in a one-night performance of *Cavalleria Rusticana.* Gershwin summoned him from Washington with the offer of a minor role in *Porgy and Bess.* After the audition, he became the top candidate for Porgy. Gershwin found him "the closest thing to a colored Lawrence Tibbett [he] had ever heard."[23] A second audition for the Theatre Guild executives brought him the title role. Anne Wiggins Brown (Bess) and Ruby Elzy (Serena) were recruited from Juilliard, and Edward Matthews, who had distinguished himself in *Four Saints in Three Acts,* was cast as Jake.[24]

For the rest of the cast, Mamoulian scouted the talent of black musicals and dramas. Two of his choices reflected the long history of the black musical. Abbie Mitchell and J. Rosamond Johnson were costars of the 1909 hit *The Red Moon.* John W. Bubbles, of the vaudeville team of Buck and Bubbles, had no training in the legitimate theatre, but he sparkled as the rakish Sportin' Life. Only Georgette Harvey, as Maria, repeated her original role. Harvey, who had sung for many years in both the Soviet Union and the United States, was one of the few original cast members with the vocal ability to appear in the new version of the show.

Of all the backstage talents, only Eva Jessye, who trained the chorus for *Porgy and Bess,* was black. She had traveled from coast to coast for years with her famous choir before coming to Broadway. She performed similar duties for *Four Saints in Three Acts* and *Hallelujah!,* Hollywood's first all-black musical, directed by King Vidor for MGM in 1929.

Despite Gershwin's strong links to the worlds of Broadway and Tin

23. New York *Herald Tribune,* December 8, 1935. A later interview attributes the recommendation to Olin Downes, the critic for the New York *Times.* See Kimball and Simon, *The Gershwins,* 179. The Theatre Guild officials were strong proponents of Robeson. See George Gershwin to DuBose Heyward, March 8, December 17, 1934, both in Box 17, George Gershwin Collection, MC/LC.

24. DuBose Heyward suggested that Gershwin talk to J. Rosamond Johnson about his plans for *Porgy and Bess,* and urged that he listen to Abbie Mitchell as well (Heyward to Gershwin, March 2, 1934, in Box 17, George Gershwin Collection, MC/LC). Gershwin was familiar with *Four Saints in Three Acts* and noted that "there might be one or two in the cast that would be useful to us" (Gershwin to Heyward, February 26, 1934, *ibid.*).

Todd Duncan (Porgy) and Anne Wiggins Brown (Bess)
Courtesy Billy Rose Theatre Collection, New York Public Library

John W. Bubbles (Sportin' Life) and Anne Wiggins Brown (Bess)
Courtesy Billy Rose Theatre Collection, New York Public Library

Pan Alley, he insisted that *Porgy and Bess* was a folk opera. After many requests from interviewers, he explained his argument in a by-lined article in the New York *Times*:

> *Porgy and Bess* is a folk tale. Its people naturally would sing folk music. When I first began work on the music I decided against the use of original folk material because I wanted the music to be all of one piece. Therefore I wrote my own spirituals and folksongs. But they are still folk music—and therefore, being in operatic form, *Porgy and Bess* becomes a folk opera.
>
> However, because *Porgy and Bess* deals with Negro life in America it brings to the operatic form elements that never before appeared in opera and I have adapted my method to utilize the drama, the humor, the superstition, the religious fervor, the dancing, and the irrepressible high spirits of the race. If, in doing this, I have created a new form, which combines opera with theatre, this new form has come quite naturally out of the material.

Gershwin's insistence brought an unusual response from the New York press. While drama critics had naturally covered Gershwin's earlier musicals, music critics would also be asked to judge this new work. Several newspapers copied the format of the New York *Times*, in which drama critic Brooks Atkinson and music critic Olin Downes offered their views in adjoining columns. As a result, *Porgy and Bess* had twice the coverage of any musical offering in recent memory. To a certain extent, this double survey of opinion hurt *Porgy and Bess*'s possibilities. Since this show was clearly not a traditional opera, it appeared caught between two genres. Downes thought that the style of *Porgy and Bess* was "at one moment of opera and another of operetta or sheer Broadway entertainment." Most music critics disliked the show's musical comedy elements, and the drama critics abhorred its operatic tendencies. Atkinson, in particular, dismissed the operatic form as "cumbersome": "Why commonplace remarks that carry no emotion have to be made in a chanting monotone is a problem in art [I] cannot fathom. . . . Turning *Porgy* into an opera has resulted in a deluge of casual remarks that have to be thoughtfully intoned and that amazingly impede the action. Why do composers vex it so? 'Sister, you going to the picnic?' 'No, I guess not.' Now, why in heaven's name must two characters in an opera clear their throats before they can exchange that sort of information?"[25]

25. George Gershwin, "Rhapsody in Catfish Row," New York *Times*, October 20, 1935; Atkinson, New York *Times*, October 11, 1935.

The music critics attacked Gershwin's acknowledged strengths in the realm of musical comedy. Lawrence Gilman of the New York *Herald Tribune* led the attack on the score: "Perhaps it is needlessly Draconian to begrudge Mr. Gershwin the song hits he has scattered throughout his score and which will doubtless enhance his fame and popularity. Yet they mar it. They are a cardinal weakness. They are a blemish on its musical integrity. Listening to such sure-fire rubbish as the duet between Porgy and Bess, 'Bess, You Is My Woman Now,' and 'I Loves You Porgy,' you wonder how the composer of the magnificent choral scenes of this opera could stoop to such easy and such needless conquests."[26]

While most of the white reviewers devoted most of their criticism to Gershwin's score, black critics continued to decry the presence of stereotypes. Hall Johnson offered his analysis in *Theatre Arts Monthly* shortly before *Porgy and Bess* closed. He found Gershwin the perennial outsider in his view of black southern life: "The informing spirit of Negro music is not to be caught and understood merely by listening to the tunes and Mr. Gershwin's much-publicized visits to Charleston for local color do not amount even to a matriculation in the preparatory-school that he needed for his work." Once one accepted that the music had almost no "Negroid" quality, only then could *Porgy and Bess* be evaluated on its own terms. Indeed, Johnson argued that the music had more similarities to Russian opera than to black folk music. Second, the same lack of understanding that Gershwin brought to his music existed also in the characters Heyward created. The actions, the dialogue, and the lyrics failed to reflect black life accurately. The characters, imprisoned in white Broadway's conceptions of black culture, perverted a "true Negro operatic idiom." The only saving grace seemed the performances, as the veteran talent managed to surmount the difficulties inherent in their roles by improvisation and ad-libbing, which managed to inject humanity and character in their characterizations. Nevertheless, Johnson imagined that the predominantly white Broadway audience would admire *Porgy and Bess*:

26. New York *Herald Tribune*, October 11, 1935. Gershwin's "Rhapsody in Catfish Row" article is in part a response to Gilman and Downes: "It is true that I have written songs for *Porgy and Bess*. I am not ashamed of writing songs at any time as long as they are good songs. . . . Songs are entirely in the operatic tradition. Many of the most successful operas of the past have had songs. Nearly all of Verdi's operas contain what are known as "song hits." *Carmen* is almost a collection of song hits. And what about 'The Last Rose of Summer,' perhaps one of the most widely known songs of the generation? How many of those who sing it know that it is from an opera?"

> Manufactured and presented by such a brilliant array of names and performed with such faithful earnestness by such a clever cast, it affords quite adequate fare for the average uncritical audience without too much interest in either opera or Negroes. This audience admires Gershwin, as I do, for his nice tunes, whether they appear singly, in rows, or in clusters, like a bunch of grapes. At the moment, it also admired the Broadway Negro style because it does not know the real and its intelligence is not yet insulted when Negro folk-material is mis-stated in foreign terms.[27]

Despite the harsh words of Gilman and Downes, the general tone of the initial reviews was positive. Most critics admired what Gershwin had done, whatever its classification. Although John Mason Brown of the New York *Evening Post* made several negative comments, he ended his review with considerable praise: "But it is a good thing, a memorable production, if you ask me, and one of the far-famed wonders of the 'Melting Pot' that can be found. It is a Russian who has directed it [*Porgy and Bess*], a Russian who has set it, two southerners who have written its book, two Jewish boys who have composed its lyrics and music, and a stageful of Negroes who sing and act it to perfection. The result is the most American opera that has yet been seen or heard."[28] Even so, *Porgy and Bess* had only a 124-performance run. After ten weeks of respectable grosses in the $25,000 range, the show began to falter at the box office. Lowering ticket prices failed to stem the decline in attendance. *Porgy and Bess* remained on Broadway for the crucial Christmas to New Year's Day period, but afterwards the receipts dropped below the break-even point. *Porgy and Bess* failed to recoup its investment for the Theatre Guild, and Gershwin found that his share would not even cover the costs of printing the musical score.

The cause for the failure of the Gershwin folk opera is often said to be the reviewers' inability to see the classic stature of the work. Admittedly, both music critics and drama critics found *Porgy and Bess* trapped between genres, faulting the show's musical comedy or operatic structure. Yet the tone of the reviews was generally enthusiastic. Perhaps there is another reason for the show's modest run. In the context of the history of black-performed musical comedy, *Porgy and Bess* premiered as the genre seemed to be dying. While black-performed revues or book musicals had achieved considerable success during the 1920s,

27. Hall Johnson, "*Porgy and Bess*—A Folk Opera," *Theatre Arts Monthly* (January, 1936), 24–28.

28. New York *Evening Post*, October 11, 1935.

few succeeded in the early years of the depression. *Porgy and Bess*, therefore, opened as the second great period of the black musical was sputtering to a close, offering few novelties to audiences that had been seeing black-performed musicals for over a decade.

Similarly, as an opera, *Porgy and Bess* was hardly new. Operatic elements had already been introduced in black-performed shows. *Four Saints in Three Acts* was perhaps the best-known example, and Gruenberg's *The Emperor Jones* (though performed mostly by whites in blackface) was an operatic version of a Broadway play with black performers almost two years before *Porgy and Bess*. While the Gershwin show received mixed, but basically favorable, reviews, *The Emperor Jones* was proclaimed a "triumph." The New York *Times* reviewed the show on the front page, a rarity for any musical or dramatic production, and called it an "instant and sweeping success." While Gershwin's music was later dismissed as a mixture of Tin Pan Alley and Broadway, critics heralded Gruenberg's score as "prodigiously sure, headlong, fantastical, brutal in its approach; yet masterly in contrast of mood and in its major proportions; sheer emanation, as it seems, of the play and of the glimmerings, the shadows, the hallucinations and the strength of the jungle."[29] Whether opera, musical comedy, or experimental black musical, *Porgy and Bess* remained a work in a genre that had had its major innovations earlier.

While *Porgy and Bess* languished in the 1930s, it began to be acclaimed as a classic during a period in which black musicals and black-performed operas were a rarity on Broadway. Producer Cheryl Crawford brought *Porgy and Bess* back to Broadway in 1942 with a smaller orchestra and all the recitative removed. The new production more than doubled the 1935 run, making it the longest-running revival to that date. An international touring company enjoyed similar success after a 1953 Broadway run, visiting the Soviet Union, Latin American, the Middle East, and several European capitals.[30] These revivals turned a 1935 financial failure into a classic. With little competition from black musical shows and operas, *Porgy and Bess* seemed

29. New York *Times*, January 8, 1933. See David Mason Greene, *Greene's Biographical Encyclopedia of Composers* (New York, 1985), 1027, for a modern evaluation of Gruenberg's works.

30. Green, *Encyclopaedia of the Musical Theatre*, 337–39. For Crawford's theories on the new popularity of *Porgy and Bess*, see New York *Times*, February 15, 1942. Truman Capote chronicled the 1953 *Porgy and Bess* revival in Moscow in *The Muses Are Heard* (New York, 1956).

unique, a quality that had been lacking in the Broadway atmosphere of the mid-1930s.

The final symbol of the original failure of *Porgy and Bess* was that it inspired no copies. Had the art of the black musical been thriving, the Gershwin show would have encouraged other producers, writers, and composers to experiment further. But Gershwin's show was yet another failure in a dying genre. If the Theatre Guild and Pulitzer Prize–winning composers could not reverse the fortunes of black-performed musical shows, what hope could there be for others? In this fashion, *Porgy and Bess* marked the nadir in the history of black musical comedy, symbolizing the end of tradition and experimentation in black musical theatre on Broadway.

XI

SWINGING THE CLASSICS— OR THE FTP MEETS GILBERT AND SULLIVAN

As the depression decimated the Broadway theatre, plays and musicals, whether black or white, found survival difficult by the mid-1930s. Hordes of playwrights, actors, singers, dancers, and technicians were jobless, primarily in New York, but throughout the country as well. Among the plethora of New Deal projects designed to buttress America's cultural heritage and help its artists and intellectuals survive was the Federal Theatre Project (FTP) of the Works Progress Administration (WPA). Hallie Flanagan, a graduate of Grinnell College, where she was a classmate of WPA head Harry Hopkins, and director of Vassar's Experimental Theatre, was named director of the FTP in 1935. Her daunting task was to return an estimated ten thousand theatre people to work. The mandate of the FTP was nationwide, and it attempted to reach Americans of all ages, races, and ethnic origins. Flanagan's organization encouraged a wide variety of theatrical programs, including children's entertainment and vaudeville shows as well as legitimate theatre. Fairly early in its existence, the FTP established a Negro Unit, with programs in New York, Seattle, Hartford, Philadelphia, Newark, Los Angeles, Boston, Raleigh, Birmingham, San Francisco, and Chicago. Ultimately, FTP programs existed in twenty-two cities.[1]

The Negro Unit was established with the advice of several prominent black actors and actresses. Rose McClendon, who had dis-

1. For surveys of FTP productions, see Jane DeHart Mathews, *The Federal Theatre, 1935–1939: Plays, Relief, and Politics* (Princeton, 1967); John O'Connor and Lorraine Brown (eds.), *Free, Adult, Uncensored: The Living History of the Federal Theatre Project* (Washington, D.C., 1978). For a survey of the plays by black authors produced by the FTP, see E. Quita Craig, *Black Drama of the Federal Theatre Era* (Amherst, 1980).

tinguished herself in such Broadway plays as *Deep River, In Abraham's Bosom, Porgy,* and *Mulatto* (1935) and had also organized a drama school in Harlem, was summoned to Washington to give her thoughts on the proposed organization. When Flanagan asked whether she thought a black actor should direct the program, McClendon replied that "since Negroes had always been performers and had had no previous means of learning direction and design, they would prefer to start under more experienced direction." This explanation, which erases a great portion of black theatrical history, actually glossed over several major differences within the black theatrical community. A core of veterans of Harlem's Lafayette Theatre and black theatre in general argued that a black should run the program. These seasoned performers understood that blacks had been active in all aspects of theatrical life since the turn of the century, and they saw no reason for a change at this point. Nonetheless, several members of Harlem's intelligentsia argued for a white in the key role, claiming that the Negro Unit would otherwise be overlooked in Washington's bureaucratic machinations and in Broadway theatrical circles. Black advisers, however, would be able to keep the director on a proper course.

Rose McClendon eventually emerged as a compromise candidate, but she wanted a white associate with theatrical experience. Whether this indicates a belief in her earlier statement to Flanagan is somewhat in doubt. McClendon realized by this time that she was dying of cancer. Her participation in this new theatrical venture was therefore limited, and her associate, John Houseman, director of *Four Saints in Three Acts,* became the director of the program when she died some months later. Houseman designed the direction of the Negro Unit with the assistance of whites and blacks. The theatrical talents advising him included Orson Welles, Edward Perry, and Carlton Moss.

Despite the disagreement over the leadership of the Negro Unit of the FTP, there seemed to be one area of consensus. All black participants had tired of the changes in the black musical in recent years, especially its becoming more of a white entertainment. Partisans of both the Left and the Right dismissed the standard musicals and revues as "handkerchief-head," and encouraged the Negro Unit to avoid them completely. As a result, this new production group fostered an interest in developing new black drama, often with a social message. The Negro Unit sponsored plays by veteran playwrights and newcomers such as Theodore Ward (*Big White Fog*), Hughes Allison (*The Trial of Dr. Beck*),

Theodore Browne (*Natural Man*), Abram Hill (*Liberty Deferred*), J. Augustus Smith (*Turpentine*), and Frank Wilson (*Walk Together Chillun*).[2]

Although the Negro Unit avoided musical comedies, the FTP included a few musicals with black casts. The first, *Swing It* (1937), written by Eubie Blake, Cecil Mack, and J. Milton Reddie, was presented by the Variety Theatre Unit of the FTP. Most critics said that the show was yet another pale echo of *Shuffle Along*. It dealt with black chicanery in an attempt to move a showboat up the Mississippi to the Harlem River (the rivers do not connect), where the captain would present a musical show. The cross-country trek seemed a minor problem compared to everyone's desire to star in the show. The captain, his wife, and the show's backers all had different visions of the play-within-the-play. Charles Dexter of the *Daily Worker* lambasted the show, "a hodgepodge of the old and alleged jokes and traditional vaudeville banalities about the Negro. He is represented as lazy, shiftless, stupid, and deceitful, a joyful child happy because, even if he hasn't got any money, 'Ain't I (We) Got Love,' as the song puts it." Shortly after the disastrous Broadway premiere, Variety Unit director Frank Merlin was forced to resign for using the word *nigger* to refer to cast members. *Swing It* closed in the summer of 1937, dampening hopes for an FTP musical triumph.[3]

The only FTP musical comedy success with a black cast ultimately launched a new genre of black musical theatre. This unusual and seemingly improbable effort involved the modernization of Gilbert and Sullivan's classic operetta, *The Mikado,* for black performers. This was not the first attempt by black entertainers to tackle English operetta. Boston theatregoers had seen "The Black Mikado or The Town of Kan-Ka-Kee" performed by Thatcher, Primrose, and West's black minstrels in 1886. Other Gilbert and Sullivan operettas were also fair game, as Washingtonians saw a first-rate black *Pirates of Penzance* in 1900. In Berlin in 1927, there was an attempt to integrate the Charleston into the operetta's score. But this new black *Mikado* was the first American version to adopt the latest musical rhythms. *Swing*

2. For a history of the Negro Unit, see Ronald P. Ross, *Black Drama in the Federal Theatre, 1935–1939* (Ann Arbor, 1972). For the politics of the FTP, see Hallie Flanagan's memoir, *Arena: The Story of the Federal Theatre* (New York, 1985), 63; and Houseman, *Run-Through,* 175–209. For a description of other WPA programs for black performers, see J. F. McDougald, "The Federal Government and the Negro Theatre," unidentified article, in "WPA" File, SCCF/NYPL.

3. New York *Times,* July 23, 1937; *Variety,* July 28, 1937; *Daily Worker,* July 24, 1937; Brooklyn *Eagle,* July 24, 1937.

Mikado (1939) also included some alterations to accommodate the black cast. The action was moved to the South Sea Islands, and the performers wore Fiji Island garb. George Jean Nathan later found this an ironic touch. In his *Newsweek* column entitled "The G. and S. Blackbirds," he wrote: "Is it any greater distortion of [*The Mikado*'s] values to cast its Japanese with Negroes than it is to cast them, as conventionally, with English? Is directing several of its dance numbers in the Negro rhythm any more absurd than directing them in the old-time, established pitter-patter which stage tradition has bogusly associated with all Nipponese terpsichorean movement?"[4]

This new version, sponsored by the Illinois FTP at the Great Northern Theatre in Chicago in 1938, took audiences by storm, breaking all FTP records: it played to 250,000 people and cleared $35,000, and the top ticket price was $1.10. The word from Chicago led to a bidding war. Theatrical producers Mike Todd and Alfred de Liagre, Jr., attempted to mount their own swing versions of the public-domain *Mikado* in New York. Chicagoans Bernard Ulrich and Melvin Ericson attempted to "buy" the show from the government. When that failed, they offered the players contracts with salaries ranging from $160 to $350 a month, considerably more than the $94 WPA average. WPA officials blocked the attempt to sign their actors, and Mike Todd charged that the government was "impeding private enterprise" in difficult times. The FTP's response was to sponsor the show's move east. Salaries were raised to an average of $180 for the New York run. De Liagre gave up when he heard about these developments, but Todd merely accelerated his plans. For an insurance policy, Todd hired one of the top draws in black musical theatre, Bill Robinson, for his *Mikado*. Undaunted, the Chicago production closed early and moved eastward to the New Yorker Theatre, beating Todd to the punch by three weeks.[5]

Eleanor Roosevelt attended the opening night of *Swing Mikado*, a relatively unusual outing for her since her husband had been elected president. However, in the aftermath of her criticizing the DAR's ban on Marian Anderson's performance in Constitution Hall in Washington the previous spring, she made a concerted effort to attend two all-black shows during her New York visit. She also honored Ethel

4. "*Swing Mikado*" File, TC/PFL.

5. "Producer Criticizes WPA 'Mikado' Deal," "WPA *Swing Mikado* To Go Commercial," "WPA Swings 'Mikado' East After 22 Consecutive Weeks in 'Chi'; Opens in New York," unidentified clippings, all in "*Swing Mikado*" File, TC/PFL. Ericson is listed alternately as Melville and Melvin.

Waters in her smashing dramatic debut in *Mamba's Daughters* (1939).

Although *Swing Mikado* was a financial success in New York, several critics complained that the show did not swing enough. In fact, with few exceptions, the show played as the D'Oyly Carte troupe might have done it. The New York *Times* felt that the show came alive only when the Mikado (Edward Fraction) "burst out into a cakewalk" and the three little maids from school "strutted what they had learned there." Indeed, the *Times* critic was correct. As the show was being planned Harry Minturn, director of the Illinois FTP, brought in Gentry Warden to examine the score and see what could be modernized. He argued that only five numbers could accommodate swing reinterpretations. As a result, most of the score remained as Gilbert and Sullivan had written it.[6]

Mike Todd, however, refused to be limited by the original authors' intentions. Opening at the Broadhurst three weeks after the FTP production, Todd's *Hot Mikado* swung more than the earlier show had dared. For a time, New York theatregoers could actually choose the black swing version of *The Mikado* they wished to attend. This situation was hardly new for Gilbert and Sullivan devotees, since the lack of an Anglo-American copyright treaty made these operettas an American staple shortly after they opened in London. In 1886, there were three rival productions of *The Mikado* in New York City, and the show was performed by over 170 companies throughout the nation. Todd claimed that he had masterminded the original updating of *The Mikado* some five years earlier, when he sponsored a "straight" version of the show in the Midwest. Forced to abridge his presentation for a showing in a vaudeville theatre, Todd added a dancing female chorus and dubbed his show *Hot Mikado.* Several critics have doubted this explanation. Ethel Waters noted in her autobiography that Will Vodery had written a jazz version of *The Mikado* for a 1924 revue at the Plantation Club. Waters sneered that Todd "must have been a tiny street gamin who was playing with his toy balloons" at the time.[7]

Critics reviewed both *Mikado*s and gave the nod to the "hot" version. Clearly, the presence of Bill Robinson and a cast of talented Broadway veterans tilted the balance toward the private-sector *Mikado.* Todd and

6. "He Had a Lot of Negroes Handy, So He Heated Up the Sullivan Music," New York *Herald Tribune,* March 26, 1939; *Time,* March 13, 1939.

7. "Berlin Heard First 'Mikado' to Be Jazzed Up," "It's Happened Before—Boston Saw a Black 'Mikado' back in 1886—Of Course It Wasn't So Hot as This One," unidentified clippings, and playbill, all in "*Hot Mikado*" File, TC/PFL; Waters, *His Eye Is on the Sparrow,* 184.

Bill Robinson as the Mikado in *Hot Mikado*
Courtesy Billy Rose Theatre Collection, New York Public Library

company could employ Broadway's best, but FTP rules stipulated that their productions had to use primarily unemployed actors. Since the FTP could not cast the ideal person for each role, characterizations were often shaped by the available players. In Illinois many of the available black artists had appeared in straight versions of *The Mikado,* so the show moved toward a more formal structure. Todd's version, however, faced no such restraints, and it featured top talent in a more swinging version.

Robinson, as always, received raves from the critics, and Brooks Atkinson, a perennial admirer, led the chorus: "He has been a great man all these years in black dancing shoes and a black derby hanging on one ear. But Bojangles is a creature of wonderful effulgence when he is caparisoned in gold. Yes, that costume becomes him. He struts. He taps sharply and lightly according to the way he feels about a scene, and he gleams at the audience with the gusto that has crowded New York with his friends." Robinson also garnered raves for his rendition of the updated and quite topical lyrics by Dave Greggory and William Tracy:

> Whenever I find things are not copecedic,
> In this domain of mine,
> I'll double the taxes, and frame up an axis,
> Between me and Father Divine.
> Those Auctioner Fakirs
> Who clip you I'll torture
> With Hot Foots, until they squirm.
> Joe Louis is gotta
> Be the Vice Mikado
> If I choose to take a third term.
>
> My object all sublime, I shall achieve in time
> To let the punishment fit the crime,
> The punishment fit the crime.[8]

Hot Mikado had a Broadway sheen that the FTP show could not hope to duplicate. Hassard Short, a noted director of Broadway musicals, gave the Robinson *Mikado* a veneer of professionalism. The costumes by Nat Karson were wildly extravagant—Robinson had a solid gold uniform. And the pace of the dance numbers, by Truly McGee, never slackened, speeding the show to a rousing finish.

8. New York *Times,* March 24, 1939; lyrics reprinted in *Hot Mikado* souvenir booklet, in "*Hot Mikado*" File, TC/PFL.

Nonetheless, the seemingly modest qualities of *Swing Mikado* caused Alain Locke to prefer it. He argued that the Broadway "octopus formula" had "crushed such a promising new thing back into the conventional mold" in the Todd show. The government-backed *Mikado* was ultimately shaped for and by its actors. *Hot Mikado,* however, "told the other side of the story." White creative talents once again imposed their own image of black life on the cast. Locke foresaw "the new horizons of Negro musical comedy" in *Swing Mikado,* but, unfortunately, few endeavored to duplicate what was "novel and spontaneous" about that show.[9]

Despite the extensive public relations campaign about the battle of the *Mikado*s, the runs for both shows were fairly modest. The rivalry became complicated when legislators learned that the FTP had rejected private offers to take over *Swing Mikado* and thus remove eighty actors from the welfare roles. Additionally, congressional hostility to those WPA programs it viewed as "boondoggles" had grown considerably by 1939. As a result, Congress mandated that the government *Mikado* be turned over to private investors as soon as a bona fide offer was made. Chicagoans Ulrich and Ericson saw their opportunity and finally gained control of the show at a fairly low cost. Their only new expenditure would be for new scenery, since government property could not be given to the private sector. The new management moved the show from the New Yorker Theatre to the conveniently located 44th Street Theatre, just across the street from *Hot Mikado.* The admission price was lower than that for the Todd show ($2.20 versus $3.30 top ticket prices), and Ulrich and Ericson hoped to beat Todd in the competitive world of free enterprise that he had so often praised. Unfortunately, the move hurt both productions. *Swing Mikado* lasted only twenty-four performances at the new site before box office revenues dictated its closing. The producers then sought to take the show through major East Coast cities, but other black *Mikado*s had started touring earlier. Philadelphia, for example, enjoyed a show entitled *Mikado in Swing.* Nevertheless, a few cities had not been hit by the *Mikado* bug, and the Chicago producers managed to tour their show for a short period. Mike Todd ultimately saved his show from a financial loss by a quick move to a theatre at the site of the famed 1939 New York World's Fair.[10]

The Mikadization of New York prompted *Pins and Needles,* the Inter-

9. Locke, "Broadway and the Negro Drama," 745–50.
10. *Variety,* April 12, 1939.

national Ladies Garment Workers Union topical revue, to supply its own rendition of the classic operetta. In its 1939 version, *Red Mikado* jabbed the nation's conservatives by transforming the three little maids into three little DAR's who prohibited the appearance of Marian Anderson in Constitution Hall. The little maids are eventually decapitated by the lord high executioner, and the ghosts of Gilbert and Sullivan appear and picket in front of posters of proposed future "Mikados," such as a "Hollywood Mikado," a "Strip Mikado," and even a "Flea Mikado."[11]

Both *Mikado*s seemed to engender more publicity than financial success, but they did set a pattern for future black musical shows. Producers sought to swing available classics in their search for theatrical success. This new subgenre in black musical theatre lasted well into the 1970s—London enjoyed *Black Mikado* in 1975. *Swingin' the Dream* was the first carbon copy. Composers Jimmy Van Heusen and Eddie De Lange attempted to swing *A Midsummer Night's Dream* in a November, 1939, production. The kings of swingdom were recruited for the show, which featured Benny Goodman, Louis Armstrong, and Maxine Sullivan. Librettists Gilbert Seldes and Erik Charell (who had earlier tried to option *The Swing Mikado,* but to no avail) moved the action to New Orleans in the 1890s, but failed to enliven the show. Despite an excellent cast, most critics dismissed the new *Dream*. John Chapman of the *News* objected strongly to the show: "For foolish casting, take Louis Armstrong, dressed as a fireman and always carrying his trumpet, as Bottom. Or Maxine Sullivan, with a World's Fair Guide chair as her throne, as Titania. Butterfly McQueen as Puck, carrying a flit gun with which to charm her sleeping victims. . . . Juan Hernandez as Oberon, who slides down a hollow tree on a fireman's pole." This uninspired tomfoolery sank *Swingin' the Dream* after only thirteen performances.[12]

Oscar Hammerstein II also tossed his hat into the revision ring, by attempting to update Bizet's *Carmen* with a black cast. Hammerstein claimed to have considered the possibility of modernizing the opera after listening to a Hollywood Bowl concert performance of the work. Assuring himself that "if Bizet and Verdi were alive today they'd be the first persons to insist upon" revising their classic works, Hammerstein began to look for a modern equivalent for the gypsies of Bizet's opera. The lyricist ultimately chose to present a black version of the original,

11. Green, *Ring Bells! Sing Songs!*, 153.
12. New York *News*, November 30, 1939.

Louis Armstrong in *Swingin' the Dream*
Courtesy Billy Rose Theatre Collection, New York Public Library

since he found the "Southern Negro" and the Spanish gypsies similar—they were "emotional, colorful, and passionate." In this fashion, *Carmen* became *Carmen Jones* (1943), and the locale shifted to South Carolina during World War II. The tobacco factory was abandoned in favor of a parachute factory; toreador Escamillo is now Husky Miller, a prize fighter; and Don Jose becomes Corporal Joe, a soldier. The score, however, remained intact, and the songs were performed in the same order as in the original opera. Hammerstein eliminated the recitative, a part of *Porgy and Bess* that had so irritated the critics. He claimed that such a transformation had a certain historical validity, for Bizet had originally written the opera with extended narrative portions, and the recitative was added after the fact. Nevertheless, Hammerstein's main reason was that "we don't like recitatif. The tradition of singing unpoetic plot exposition is a senseless relic of another day. It should be eliminated from all operas."[13]

Producer Billy Rose used Broadway's top designers for the new *Carmen,* and Hassard Short was recruited as director. Work proceeded quickly in preparing the show, but casting was a formidable obstacle. Despite the modernization of *Carmen*'s lyrics, the music was operatic, and singer-actors trained for a show of this nature were few. Since the major American operatic societies had rarely admitted black performers, there was often little incentive for those blacks interested in opera to undergo the rigorous training that might be required for a show such as *Carmen Jones.* As a consequence, conventional recruiting methods continually drew a blank. Finally Rose and Hammerstein prevailed upon John Hammond for assistance. Hammond, a Vanderbilt heir and a Yale dropout, had become a devotee of black jazz and blues in the early 1920s and eventually brought hitherto unknown black artists into the recording studios. One of Hammond's contemporary legacies is the heritage of black popular music of the 1920s and 1930s, which might have remained unrecorded and might have been lost without his efforts. His discoveries spanned the decades, from Billie Holiday to Bob Dylan and Bruce Springsteen.[14]

When Rose and Hammerstein approached Hammond about casting the show, they learned that he had been reclassified 3-A and was about

13. New York *Times,* November 14, 1943. Most music critics, however, tended to discount Hammerstein's historical accounts of the writing of the Bizet opera. See also Hugh Fordin, *Getting to Know Him: A Biography of Oscar Hammerstein II* (New York, 1977), 204–10.

14. See John Hammond and Irving Townsend, *John Hammond on Record* (New York, 1977), 241–43.

Muriel Smith and Luther Saxon in *Carmen Jones*
Courtesy Billy Rose Theatre Collection, New York Public Library

to leave for the army. Rose asked the head of the Washington Square draft board to defer Hammond until the show could be cast. Hammond, who had no part in the request, hesitated since it might seem inappropriate in time of war. Rose and Hammerstein, however, had a considerable investment in the show. Hammond soon received word that his induction would be delayed for a time.

Hammond began a nationwide recruiting journey of his own, visiting twenty-five black colleges—among them, Fisk, Howard, Spelman, and Tuskegee—that had noted music departments, glee clubs, or choirs. He found the lead, Muriel Smith, in a Philadelphia camera store, and the role of Escamillo went to a former New York City policeman who needed special permission to take a leave from the force. Luther Saxon (Joe) arrived in New York from the Philadelphia Navy Yard, and Buell Thomas had been marking time in a Los Angeles post office. Drummer Cozy Cole, the highest-paid member of the cast, had the longest professional career as a performer. He had provided solos for Billie Holiday, Artie Shaw, and Benny Goodman. Cleveland's Karamu House supplied much of the dancing talent. Hammond had to find two individuals for each principal role, since it was virtually impossible for one person to handle the complex arias for eight performances each week. Most of the talent chosen for the show had never appeared onstage before. This caused *Phylon* drama critic Miles Jefferson to suggest that Hammond deserved a laurel wreath for his efforts. When Hammond finished his task, he left for Fort Dix, New Jersey. Life in the army proved to be quite a change for him. Although he was drafted on the same day as his friend Buck Clayton (of the Count Basie Band), regulations prohibited fraternization with the black draftees. As a result, Hammond had to sneak over to the black barracks at Fort Dix to visit his old friends.[15]

Although several critics expected the new show to swing, they were pleasantly surprised at Hammerstein's careful and literate treatment of Bizet's opera. Most reviewers declared the show the best of the year, and Howard Barnes of the New York *Herald Tribune* led the chorus to raves: "It is magnificently performed and ably sung by an all-colored cast, and it has been staged with cunning and splendor. *Carmen Jones* is something more than a major theatrical event. It opens infinite and challenging horizons for the fusion of the two art

15. Miles Jefferson, "The Negro on Broadway," *Phylon*, VI (1945), 42.

forms [opera and musical comedy]." Even the music critics, who had savaged *Porgy and Bess* with faint praise, could hardly restrain their enthusiasm for the Hammerstein show. Olin Downes, who had disliked the Gershwin work, found *Carmen Jones* "audacious and original," though he objected to "too much white man's training in it all." He preferred shows that featured "a Negro performance in the natural creative way of that race of born actors and singers." Nevertheless he, too, had strong words of praise for both cast and the creative team.[16]

Carmen Jones enjoyed continued success both in New York and on the road. It was one of the shows most often revived during the late 1940s, and it returned to Broadway twice within a year of its closing. Across the United States, the show was equally popular. At the same time, it became a rallying point for the NAACP in its continuing effort to eliminate segregation in theatres. When the touring company traveled from St. Louis to Kansas City, it was greeted by pickets. The issue was that black patrons were segregated while black artists were being permitted onstage. Louisville hoped to avoid any problems by announcing in advance that there would be no segregated seating. It was soon discovered that all blacks were being seated in a separate section. As a result, the show was greeted by protests on opening night there as well. Although newspaper coverage was considerable and often sympathetic, the practice of audience segregation remained in force in several cities during *Carmen Jones*'s post-Broadway tour.[17]

Memphis Bound! (1945) returned the black musical adaptation to familiar ground. Despite the title, the show was primarily a jive version of *H. M. S. Pinafore.* The hero of the evening was, once again, Bill Robinson, who was born in the same year Gilbert and Sullivan composed their operetta. Here Robinson portrays a man living a luxurious life in jail, where he is hiding from a woman who wants to marry him. Eventually he leaves jail and persuades a Tennessee riverboat owner to

16. "A Negro Cast Will Sing 'Carmen,'" New York *Times*, August 23, 1942; "*Carmen Jones* Defies All Opera Traditions," undated article, in "*Carmen Jones*" File, TC/PFL; Howard Barnes, "The Theatre: *Carmen Jones*," New York *Herald Tribune*, December 3, 1943; George Freedly, New York *Morning Telegraph*, December 4, 1943; *Women's Wear Daily*, December 3, 1943. For a photo essay of the show, see *Collier's*, January 15, 1944, pp. 14–17. *Carmen Jones* inspired the Mexican painter Covarrubias to paint several portraits, which were reprinted in *Life*, May 8, 1944.

17. St. Louis *Globe-Democrat*, November 18, 1946; Kansas City *Times*, December 26, 1946; Louisville *Times*, November 15, 1946.

present a swing version of *Pinafore.* Assisting Robinson in his efforts were some of the past heroes of black dramas and musicals—Frank Wilson, Avon Long, Billy Daniels, and Edith Wilson.

Critics approved of the swing *Pinafore,* but objected to the plot convolutions that inspired the showboat performance. Excerpts from *Trial by Jury* brought some respite but they were too brief to save the evening. Only Robinson won raves from the critics. Most reveled in the fact that this gentleman was celebrating his sixty-seventh birthday during the run of *Memphis Bound!.* John Chapman, critic for the *News,* was stunned by that revelation: "It's true, alright, but I don't believe it anyhow. Nobody sixty-seven years old could have such bounce, emanate such stage presence, and have such a happy time and tap dance so wonderfully. Bill is famous for a stunt of running the hundred yard dash backwards and beating opponents running forward, and this may be his secret. Maybe he is running backward inside, too, and he is steadily becoming younger." Some reviewers thought it was better than George S. Kaufman's rival *Hollywood Pinafore, or The Lad Who Loved a Salary* with William Gaxton and Victor Moore. But *Memphis Bound!* ran aground after only forty-five performances.[18]

My Darlin' Aida (1952) terminated the rage for converting classics. This show, one of Broadway's most expensive at $350,000, managed to move *Aida* from ancient Egypt to the Deep South during the Civil War. Verdi still provided the music, but Charles Friedman wrote the libretto. Although critics noted the close resemblance to the spirit of *Carmen Jones,* there was one marked variant. While *Carmen Jones* featured a black cast in the 1940s, this early 1950s musical presented whites in most of the lead singing roles that seemed ideal for black performers. Among the major roles, only Aida's father, Adam Brown (Amonasro in the original), was portrayed by a black, William Dillard. Aida, a mulatto slave in the revised version, was played by Elaine Malbin in the evenings and Eileen Schauler at the matinees. Blackface makeup supplied the appropriate racial heritage.

This casting decision brought continual complaints from black actors during auditions. When producer Robert L. Joseph hinted that a white woman would play the lead, because of "the inability to find a Negro qualified to sing the title role," the Coordinating Council of Negro Performers lodged a protest. This new organization was formed to help black performers find employment in the theatre and in motion

18. New York *News,* June 10, 1945; *Time,* June 4, 1945, p. 85; *Life,* June 20, 1945.

pictures. The members were Frederick O'Neal, a vice-president of Actors Equity; J. Rosamond Johnson; Lester Walton, a producer during the 1920s and former ambassador to Liberia; and Dick Campbell, a concert manager and head of the USO Camp Shows Negro Division. Since the casting of *Carmen Jones* revealed that an ample pool of operatic talent was clearly available for any producer who would take the trouble to discover it, the council urged Joseph to widen his search. Joseph called the demands "racism in reverse," vowed to hire "the most qualified performer" for the role, and dismissed the protest as "un-American." Walton, chairman of the council, countered Joseph's charge by asking whether it was un-American to note that "the employment of Negroes on stage, screen, radio, and television is at a low ebb" and to undertake a "determined effort to secure the selection of a competent Negro singer for the role of Aida." Although Joseph auditioned Muriel Rahn (of *Carmen Jones*) and New York City Opera talents Camilla Williams and Margaret Tynes, he hired a relatively inexperienced, twenty-two-year-old white singer. *Variety* ultimately objected to the casting, since Malbin was "unmistakably a white girl in the consciousness of the audience, so the situation tends to be synthetic." With Broadway so accustomed to actual blacks having roles in musical comedies, operas, and revues, burnt cork makeup appeared incongruous in 1952, and *My Darlin' Aida* was one of the last Broadway musicals to use nonblacks in obviously black roles. The show, which closed swiftly, became one of the most costly flops of the season and helped end the modernization of classics for many years on Broadway.[19]

Although the days of the new black versions of *The Mikado* or *Carmen* were long gone, Broadway experienced a brief revival of these efforts in the late 1960s and 1970s. Here, however, the classics were often white Broadway musicals. *Hello Dolly* (1967) provided the impetus with its rendition by an all-black cast starring Pearl Bailey and Cab Calloway. Despite the changeover in performers, the libretto and music remained essentially the same, though Calloway managed to take several liberties with the score. *Guys and Dolls* (1976) featured Robert Guillaume, Norma Donaldson, Ken Page, and Ernestine Jackson. Unlike *Hello Dolly,* this new version of the 1950 Pulitzer Prize musical was

19. *Variety,* July 23, October 29, 1952; Miles Jefferson, "The Negro on Broadway, 1952–1953: Still Cloudy; Fair Weather Ahead," *Phylon,* XIV (1953), 269; New York *Times,* July 19, 24, 27, 1952. For Charles Friedman's account of the writing of *My Darlin' Aida,* see *Theatre Arts* (June, 1953), 33–34.

modernized with a black cast in mind. New orchestrations, more reminiscent of the 1970s, were created, and new choreography by Billy Wilson updated this version considerably. Despite a healthy run through the summer of the Bicentennial year, few endeavored to follow in the footsteps of *Dolly* or *Dolls,* as new and original black musicals began to appear on the scene. The all-black swing versions or modernizations of the classics were efforts during a time of crisis when no black alternatives were feasible or available. Once a new black theatre began to blossom in the late 1970s, these makeshift modernizations were consigned to the dustbin.

XII

BLACK AND WHITE BROADWAY

After the *Mikado* mania calmed down, black musical theatre entered its second period of exile. A once thriving cultural tradition faded to a mere whimper on Broadway. Black-performed musical shows did not disappear during the next twenty years, but they existed on the fringes of Broadway as oddities, exotica, or nostalgic reveries. Black musicals, which had once enlisted the talents of black artists both onstage and off, became a white-owned and white-created form that bore little resemblance to the Williams and Walker entertainments or the high jinks of the age of *Shuffle Along.* Sissle and Blake epitomized the black musical in the 1920s, but it ultimately became a vehicle for white songwriters—among them, Harold Arlen (*St. Louis Woman, House of Flowers,* and *Jamaica*), Vernon Duke (*Cabin in the Sky*), Kurt Weill (*Lost in the Stars*), Oscar Hammerstein II (*Carmen Jones*), and William Archibald (*Carib Song*)—who wanted to explore black life and culture. During this period, black composers, lyricists, and writers were virtually absent from Broadway's musical stages. As a result, these new white-black musicals lost any connection with the heritage of black entertainment, black history, and black culture. Instead, they evolved from the history of white visions of black Broadway.

Cabin in the Sky (1940) became the modern musical heir to both *The Green Pastures* and *Porgy and Bess.* Like the authors of these earlier shows, Vernon Duke, John LaTouche, and Lynn Root constructed an otherworldly affair. Here the Lawd's general (Todd Duncan) and Lucifer Jr. (Rex Ingram) fight for the soul of the lovable but weak Little Joe Jackson (Dooley Wilson). Little Joe often strays the minute any woman appears, particularly with Katherine Dunham as Georgia

Brown. But his faithful wife Petunia (Ethel Waters) ultimately helps to save his soul from perdition.

While the plot (and even some of the cast) hearkened from the earlier Marc Connelly hit, the creative team bore a closer resemblance to the *Porgy and Bess* backstage contingent. Composer Duke, designer Boris Aronson, and choreographer George Balanchine seemingly knew more of life in the Soviet Union than in the American South. Duke submitted the libretto to Balanchine, who claimed not to understand it and returned it to the composer for deciphering. Duke initially hesitated when asked to write the score, arguing that he was not "sufficiently attuned to Negro folklore." Even Duke's publisher attempted to discourage him: "I don't need you for colored shows. For those I already have the right Duke—Ellington." Nonetheless, all the prospective collaborators were won over by the humanity of the libretto. Like the Gershwins, the *Cabin in the Sky* team undertook a creative sojourn to the South to imbibe black culture. After two weeks at a Virginia Beach retreat, where most of the time was spent imbibing highballs, Duke and lyricist John LaTouche returned to Westport, Connecticut, to complete the score. Resolving to stay away from "pedantic authenticity," they decided to write their "own kind of Negro songs instead."[1]

Brooks Atkinson declared *Cabin in the Sky* "the peer of any musical in recent years." The reason for its success was that it broke away from what Atkinson called "Broadway's Negro formula: hot dancing, hot singing, dark-town comedy about poker playing and fried chicken." The authors' model resembled Broadway's black passion plays of the early 1930s that featured a white reconstruction of black myths and fables. Providing the anchor for the new show was a new and different Ethel Waters. During the 1920s she could always be counted on for a bawdy lyric and a sensuous song. Waters began to alter her image in the early 1930s in such shows as Irving Berlin's 1933 revue, *As Thousands Cheer.* While Waters could belt out a song with the best of them as in "Heat Wave," she also was able to move the audience with a quiet "Supper Time," a housewife's lament for her recently lynched husband. By the late 1930s, Waters attempted a switch to dramatic roles. She appeared in *Mamba's Daughters* by *Porgy* authors Dorothy and

1. George Ross, "Russian Harangue Jars Rehearsal," unidentified newspaper, October 19, 1940, in "*Cabin in the Sky*" File, TC/PFL; Vernon Duke, *Cabin in the Sky* liner notes, Capitol Records, SW-2073.

DuBose Heyward. Initially several producers had resisted casting Waters in a dramatic role, since she was widely known as a singer. Once the show opened on Broadway, praise for Waters' portrayal of Hagar, who attempts to give her daughter Lissa (Fredi Washington) all the opportunities she never had, was virtually unanimous. Only the all-important New York *Times* critic Atkinson found her performance lacking. In protest, Carl Van Vechten, author of *Nigger Heaven* and a patron of many Harlem Renaissance authors, purchased a full-page ad in that newspaper to encourage Atkinson to reconsider. Signing the letter of protest were Judith Anderson, Dorothy Gish, Oscar Hammerstein II, and Tallulah Bankhead. Atkinson returned to *Mamba's Daughters* and gave his stamp of approval.[2]

Had *Cabin in the Sky* been produced in the early 1930s, Waters would certainly have played the sultry temptress Georgia Brown. Yet, by 1940, Waters moved to portray Petunia, the woman whose faith sustained both her and her husband. In the original Lynn Root libretto, Petunia was a modestly humorous figure. Waters changed the character to a woman of inner strength. Waters explained the transformation in a 1940 interview when she noted that the producers realized that she was the only one "who could speak to the God [she] reveres without being ridiculed." Petunia's steadfast faith was a strong and somewhat unexpected center for the show. And the role furthered Waters' growing reputation as a dramatic actress.[3]

Cabin in the Sky was the first black-performed Broadway musical to be filmed by Hollywood. While film musicals had avoided all-black casts for over a decade, partially out of fear of adverse reaction in the South, *Cabin in the Sky* became a beneficiary of the wartime emphasis on racial harmony in motion pictures. With slight government prodding, major studios featured top black talent in two spectacular all-black musicals, *Stormy Weather,* which featured Lena Horne and Bill Robinson, and *Cabin in the Sky.* MGM retained Ethel Waters as Petunia and provided such able assistants as Eddie (Rochester) Anderson, Lena Horne, Louis Armstrong, Rex Ingram, the Hall Johnson Choir, and the Duke Ellington Orchestra for added box office appeal. Although one might regret that earlier black-written and -performed musicals escaped preservation, the 1944 MGM version directed by novice Vincente Minnelli must be applauded as a historical record of one of

2. New York *Times,* November 3, 1940; Waters, *His Eye Is on the Sparrow,* 247–48.
3. "Petunia Has Her Way," unidentified clipping, in "*Cabin in the Sky*" File, TC/PFL.

Todd Duncan (*top*), Ethel Waters, and Dooley Wilson in *Cabin in the Sky*
Courtesy Billy Rose Theatre Collection, New York Public Library

Waters' best Broadway performances. Shot in gorgeous sepia tones, the film relies on strong musical talent and superlative acting by Waters, Anderson, and Horne. It was one of the best Hollywood musicals of the wartime era.[4]

Harold Arlen followed in Vernon Duke's footsteps some years later with his first black-performed musical, *St. Louis Woman* (1946). Although the production was relatively late in Arlen's career, the songwriter had been known for his "Negro songs" since the early 1930s, when he composed music for several of the Cotton Club revues. Roger Edens, later a musical director for MGM, recalled watching Arlen at work during rehearsal at the club: "He was really one of them. He had absorbed so much from them—their idioms, their tonalities, their phrasing, their rhythms—he was able to establish a warming rapport with them. The Negroes in New York at that time . . . had a fierce insularity and dignity within themselves that resented the so-called 'professional Southernism' that was rampant in New York in those days. I was always amazed that they had completely accepted Harold and his super-minstrel-show antics." During this period Arlen composed such hits as "As Long As I Live," "Ill Wind," and the perennial favorite "Stormy Weather," sung by Ethel Waters. Waters later claimed that "Stormy Weather" was "the perfect expression of [her] mood," and she found release in singing it each evening: "When I got out there in the middle of the Cotton Club floor, I was telling things I couldn't frame in words. I was singing the story of my misery and confusion, of the misunderstandings in my life I couldn't straighten out, the story of the wrongs and outrages done to me by people I had loved and trusted." Soon the latest Cotton Club production became known as the Stormy Weather Show.[5]

During the 1940s, Arlen brought black entertainers into previously white shows such as *Bloomer Girl* (1944), which examined the life of Amelia Bloomer (Celeste Holm), a mid-nineteenth-century suffragist and reformer. One of her interests (at least onstage) was the problem of black rights in the pre–Civil War era. Arlen and lyricist E. Y. ("Yip") Harburg explored this theme in "The Eagle and Me," sung by *Cabin in the Sky* and *Casablanca* veteran Dooley Wilson. This musical with an

4. Woll, *The Hollywood Musical Goes to War,* Chap. 10. There were, of course, earlier all-black musical films, such as King Vidor's *Hallelujah!* (1929), but they were not based on Broadway originals. White musicals fared considerably better—sixteen of the 1930s offerings were made into films during that decade.

5. Haskins, *The Cotton Club,* 77; Waters, *His Eye Is on the Sparrow,* 219.

Harold Nicholas, Ruby Hill, Fayard Nicholas, and Pearl Bailey in *St. Louis Woman*
Courtesy Billy Rose Theatre Collection, New York Public Library

integrated cast (generally a rarity prior to 1940) celebrated the heroine's interest in black rights in such songs as "Man for Sale," a historical number with contemporary allusions.

St. Louis Woman, Arlen's postwar venture into black musical drama, differed strongly from the *Cabin in the Sky* and *Porgy and Bess* tradition by its reliance on black writers. Arna Bontemps adapted his 1931 novel *God Sends Sunday* with the assistance of Countee Cullen, who died shortly before the show's premiere. Rouben Mamoulian, of *Porgy and Bess* fame, was also brought in to direct the show. The St. Louis woman is Della Green (Ruby Hill), girlfriend of local bar owner Bigelow Brown (Rex Ingram). Little Augie (Harold Nicholas), a successful jockey, desires Della and is upset by Brown's harsh treatment of her. In a tense barroom scene, Brown is shot. Believing Augie has killed him, Brown curses the jockey with his dying breath, but his former mistress Lila has actually done the foul deed. Augie's luck goes from bad to worse and he continues losing his races. Since Della believes that she has been jinxing Augie, she leaves him. Augie finally begins to win at the track again, but he wants to win Della back as well. Augie vows to rest his case on the outcome of his next race. If he wins, Della will return since she no longer jinxes him; if he loses, he will also lose Della forever. As this is musical comedy, Augie wins and jumps into Della's arms, singing "Ridin' on the Moon."

St. Louis Woman was noted for its remarkable cast. Pearl Bailey made her Broadway debut and sang the top comedy numbers, "Legalize My Name" and "It's a Woman's Prerogative (To Change Her Mind)." Bailey had first received critical acclaim for her nightclub work at the Village Vanguard in New York. Later she undertook a lengthy USO tour before appearing in Paramount's 1947 film *Variety Girl* in a cameo that showcased her talents. Singing "Tired" by Doris Fisher and Allan Roberts, Bailey revealed her wicked way with a comic lyric. Despite the popularity of that novelty number, the singer later regretted that she had allowed it to become her trademark in the 1940s: "I've been so typed. . . . Once I sang a song called 'Tired,' and they began to associate it with me. I became a lazy-moving, tired, slow-dragger. Nobody ever pictured me kissing the leading man. I didn't want to be Lena Horne or Hedy Lamarr, but I was a human being with a capacity." After her *St. Louis Woman* debut, Bailey had supporting roles in the all-white musical comedies *Arms and the Girl* and *Bless You All* (1950).[6]

6. See Pearl Bailey, *The Raw Pearl* (New York, 1968); and *Newsweek,* December 4, 1967, p. 110.

St. Louis Woman also offered an unusual portent for white-created black musicals. For the first time in recent memory, members of the cast stopped the rehearsals to protest the offensive stereotypes in the show. Generally, black actors hesitated to complain publicly about these concerns. Alain Locke suggested that because of a "precarious employment situation . . . [they accept] before the public the yoke of the Broadway stereotypes." Here, however, several cast members objected to the bawdy character and loose morals of the female leads. Mamoulian could not understand the criticisms and responded that "there were many stage dramas which included bawdy characters but he knew of no objection voiced by those casts or audiences." On another occasion the cast objected to Mamoulian's staging of a funeral sequence. Bailey recalled: "When June Hawkins killed her lover . . . she was to fall on her knees and raise her hands to heaven. That, in turn, was to make everyone else sad enough to do the same. Well, sir, that gesture only served to make the cast angry. They felt it was too Negroid." While the cast was reluctant to discuss the matter with Mamoulian, Bailey became a negotiator and smoothed the differences. Although rehearsals continued amiably, this episode suggested that some changes might be coming in black-performed Broadway musicals. Stereotypical roles or images, which had been tolerated as a means to appear on Broadway, might not be accepted so willingly in the future.[7]

Arlen and his frequent collaborator Harburg both continued with either black-performed or black-themed musicals during the next decade. Harburg and Burton Lane created a musical fable, *Finian's Rainbow* (1947). Although the plot concerned a search for gold at the end of the rainbow in a land populated by leprechauns, there was a humorous subplot about a bigoted southern senator who accidentally turns black when he mangles one of his magic wishes. In the midst of this musical comedy never-never land, Miles Jefferson of *Phylon* discovered "a real treat": "For the first time in this reviewer's memory intolerance in the Deep South has been subjected to light, but peppery, spoofing in a musical show, and this has been accomplished in the best of taste and with great style."[8]

After working in Hollywood for a few years, Arlen joined with

7. *Variety*, April 3, 1946, p. 57; *Time*, April 8, 1946; Bailey, *The Raw Pearl*, 106; Locke, "Broadway and the Negro Drama," 746.

8. Miles Jefferson, "The Negro on Broadway, 1946–1947," *Phylon*, VIII (1947), 147–49.

Truman Capote for his second all-black musical, *House of Flowers* (1954). Young southern author Truman Capote, who had only recently begun his writing career with such novels as *Other Voices, Other Rooms* (1948) and *The Grass Harp* (1951), became enchanted with the Caribbean on a trip to Haiti. Work on *House of Flowers*, a tale of two rival bordellos in the West Indies, began soon after. Novice lyricist Capote helped write the songs as well as his first Broadway libretto. In the lead role of Madame Fleur, Pearl Bailey continued her lengthy association with Arlen, and the formidable Juanita Hall (*South Pacific*'s Bloody Mary) portrayed Madame Tango. Among these considerable talents, young Diahann Carroll in her Broadway debut stole the show with her rendition of a lullabye, "A Sleepin' Bee." But *House of Flowers* received only modest reviews. Capote's libretto took the critical heat—many found that it failed to capture a true West Indian spirit. The show closed after only 165 performances. There was a 1968 Off-Broadway revival of the show, but it did not last long.[9]

Arlen returned to Caribbean territory once again with *Jamaica* (1957). Joining him were Harburg and one of Hollywood's greatest talents, Lena Horne. Although primarily known for her screen work, Horne actually began her career in a familiar 1920s pattern as one of Lew Leslie's *Blackbirds* discoveries. Leslie noticed Horne in the Cotton Club chorus in 1936 and promoted her to stardom for his last unsuccessful *Blackbirds* fling in 1939. The show survived only nine performances, with Brooks Atkinson providing only the limpest of leads for his review: "Lew Leslie Gets His 'Blackbirds of 1939' Onto the Stage of the Hudson Theatre." Other critics, such as Robert Coleman, were not impressed by the latest Leslie discovery: "The Rialto's wisest lads have been prophesying great things for Lena Horne, a songstress who graduated from the chorus of the Cotton Club. Miss Horne is pretty, has a pleasing personality, dances well and should develop into a first rate revue artiste with experience. She excelled with 'You're So Indifferent.' But we couldn't help thinking of Florence Mills, Ethel Waters, Aida Ward, and Adelaide Hall, 'Blackbirds' greats of the past."[10]

After the expiration of *Blackbirds of 1939*, Horne moved to Hollywood. She appeared in many films during the 1940s, mostly at MGM. Except for *Cabin in the Sky* and *Stormy Weather*, in which she played leading character parts, most of her roles were small bits in the popular

9. *Variety*, January 12, 1955; New York *Times*, December 31, 1954.
10. New York *Times*, February 13, 1939; New York *Daily Mirror*, February 13, 1939.

MGM musicals of the period. She performed such classics as "Taking a Chance on Love" in *I Dood It* (1943), "Honeysuckle Rose" in *Thousands Cheer* (1943), "Somebody Loves Me" in *Broadway Rhythm* (1944), "Paper Doll" in *Two Girls and a Sailor* (1944), and "Love" in *Ziegfeld Follies* (1945).

All these screen appearances were strikingly similar. Usually Horne appeared almost out of nowhere, sang a magnificent song, and disappeared. Most of these numbers were bracketed by applause so cinematic magic could excise her performances when these films played in the Deep South. As the most extraneous of MGM's musical performers during this period, Horne deserves credit for establishing such a name for herself under such difficult cinematic conditions. Horne finally received the important role of the mulatto Julie in the film of Jerome Kern's life, *Till the Clouds Roll By* (1946), and her rendition of "Can't Help Lovin' Dat Man" from *Show Boat* was excellent. But in the 1951 film version of *Show Boat,* Ava Gardner won the part of Julie. Horne's indirect contribution to the film was her specially developed film makeup (Light Egyptian), which converted Gardner to the appropriate color. Hollywood casting decisions are often a mystery, but Horne's relation with studio bigwigs took a turn for the worse after the Kern commemorative. First, she refused to star in the Broadway version of *St. Louis Woman,* which MGM had optioned as a future screen vehicle for her. Her reason was the stereotypes prevalent in the libretto. The following year she married MGM's talented musical director Lennie Hayton, a white. This first major interracial romance in postwar Hollywood became fodder for the daily newspapers. Horne worked less and less, and it seemed that studio head L. B. Mayer had placed her under embargo. Not only was she not appearing in new MGM films, but the studio was increasingly reluctant to let her perform in concerts or in nightclubs. Ultimately, a Broadway role would rescue her from the limitations and difficulties of a fading film career.[11]

11. See Lena Horne and Richard Schickel, *Lena* (London, 1966). See also Seymour Peck, "Calling on Lena Horne," New York *Times,* October 27, 1957; Joan Barthel, "Now I Feel Good About Being Me," New York *Times,* July 28, 1968; *Liberty Magazine,* April 7, 1945, 52–53; and James Haskins, with Kathleen Benson, *Lena* (New York, 1984), 102–106. Writer Samuel Marx, an MGM producer under Arthur Freed during Horne's tenure, argued that Horne's reasons for being bypassed as Julie, which are often given in interviews, are incorrect. He said that a Lena Horne "Julie" would have been monumental miscasting, since the plot required that the audience receive the surprising news that Julie was a mulatto. Horne was well known as a black performer, and so this key plot element would have been undermined. See "Lena at MGM—Take Two," Los Angeles *Times,* December 5, 1982, p. 54.

Ricardo Montalban and Lena Horne in *Jamaica*
Courtesy Billy Rose Theatre Collection, New York Public Library

When *Jamaica* opened in November, 1957, Brooks Atkinson lamented Horne's relative absence from the entertainment scene, noting that she had been "hiding her talent in supper clubs." But the new Arlen and Harburg musical seemed tailored for her. Songs dominated the evening, with Horne onstage for six solo numbers and five duets (excluding reprises), an unusually heavy performance load. Consequently, the libretto was at a minimum, and most critics objected that it was a series of song cues. But that seemed not to matter, as an elegantly dressed Horne carried the evening in a sprightly tale of Jamaican-American relations. Ballads and torch songs dominated, but Harburg inserted his inevitable topical songs. The lyricist questioned American consumerism ("Napoleon") and nuclear weaponry ("Leave the Atom Alone"), but not race relations. Nevertheless, the race issue was not unnoticed by the critics, some of whom seemed unnerved by the daring casting of Horne and Ricardo Montalban in the leading roles. Although *Variety*'s critic raved about the show, he also sounded a note of caution:

> There may be various reactions to the racial aspects of the show. Although most northern urbanites aren't likely to be concerned (most New Yorkers probably could care less), there may be raised eyebrows and perhaps increased blood pressure among Dixiecrats because of the love scenes between Horne and Montalban, even though the latter appears to have been sun-lamped considerably. This won't hurt the box office draw, however, and should involve no problem for the eventual screen edition of the musical as the dialog and the lyrics are utterly non-committal on the race and color of the hero, and he can be cast any way the studios prefer.[12]

Interestingly, *Jamaica* was one of the few of producer David Merrick's hits of the 1950s that did not become a film. Furthermore, though *Jamaica* revived Lena Horne's mainstream career, Broadway was unable to find another vehicle that displayed her talents so brilliantly. Horne's return to Broadway was not to take place for twenty-four years. She appeared in *Lena Horne—The Lady and Her Music,* which won a special Tony Award in 1981.

Jamaica was the last of Arlen's black musical series. He returned to the Broadway stage only briefly in 1959 with *Saratoga,* a musical version of the Gable and Harlow film, *Saratoga Trunk* (1937), based on the Edna Ferber novel, with lyrics by Johnny Mercer. While the show

12. *Variety,* November 6, 1957.

abandoned the black themes of his earlier shows, it was an integrated endeavor, with an exceptional performance by black cast member Carol Brice. It proved to be Arlen's last Broadway venture.

Arlen's black trilogy proved a boon for black musical talent over the years, but his shows treated issues of race relations somewhat sparingly. Although Harburg often utilized social criticism in his lyrics, he tended to bypass race as a topic in the 1950s in favor of attacks on America's consumer society. This was particularly noticeable in his contributions to *Flahooley,* a 1951 flop, for which he wrote most of the libretto as well as the lyrics. What was true for Arlen and Harburg was generally true for other white composers of black-performed musicals during most of the 1940s and 1950s. In general, these white-created musicals used black characters as a form of exotica, and Caribbean locales often allowed librettists and songwriters to escape the tremendous problems of American race relations. These difficulties seemed absent in the West Indies of Harold Arlen or in the Caribbean of William Archibald and Baldwin Bergersen's *Carib Song* (1945). The recourse to Caribbeana as a popular setting for black musical efforts in the postwar era symbolized a retreat from the complexities of refurbishing the black musical form in response to the changing social context.

Arlen capitalized on the interest in West Indian exotica in his book musicals, but Katherine Dunham had presented it earlier on Broadway in a new form of black revue. Dunham first achieved notice for her performance as Georgia Brown in *Cabin in the Sky,* a role Lena Horne later had in the film. Dunham's road to the Great White Way was remarkably uncharacteristic for the late 1930s. The daughter of a Joliet, Illinois, dry cleaner, Dunham studied anthropology at the University of Chicago. The recipient of a grant from the Julius Rosenwald Fund, she studied patterns of dance in the Caribbean. On her return to the States, she formed her own dance company, which emphasized West Indian and African dance. After *Cabin in the Sky,* she had the fame and the income to further her choreographic desires. She appeared with her own company on Broadway in a series of dance revues, including *Tropical Revue* (1944) and *Bal Negre* (1946). Her dance company also appeared in the "all-Negro variety show," *Blue Holiday* (1945), which featured "Voodoo in Haiti" and "Fiji Island" segments, and in *Caribbean Carnival* (1947).

In 1945, Dunham appeared in William Archibald and Baldwin Bergersen's musical, *Carib Song,* which she choreographed. Another former University of Chicago anthropology student and a friend of Dunham's, Mary Hunter, was the director. As a result, the show presented the most accurate renditions of Caribbean dances. Dunham drew particularly on her experiences and observations in Jamaica, Trinidad, Haiti, and Martinique. She received praise both for her choreography and for her performance as The Woman, yet another unfaithful-female role. But most critics thought the libretto intrusive. Although Dunham returned to Broadway with her dance company in several revues during the next few decades, *Carib Song* was her last effort in a book musical. Nevertheless, her virtually single-handed presentation of Caribbeana in the 1940s ultimately inspired white composers to take up similar subjects in the 1950s. In musicals and dramas in the 1950s, Caribbean black characters seemed to have a greater representation in the world of Broadway than did American black characters.[13]

Most white composers of black musicals in the postwar decade avoided references to racial problems or topical issues. There was, however, one prominent exception, as Kurt Weill and Maxwell Anderson wrote the musical version of Alan Paton's *Cry, The Beloved Country* in 1949. Weill and Anderson had first considered writing a black musical comedy as early as 1939. They were particularly impressed by Harry Stillwell's novel, *Eneas Africanus*. Eneas, a slave, is sent with the master's family silver into hiding during the Civil War. Unable to find his way back to the plantation, he experiences a wide variety of adventures. He becomes prosperous, but he maintains his loyalty to his former master and ultimately returns the silver. Paul Robeson was approached, but he refused to play the role of the loyal slave. Bill Robinson finally agreed to play Eneas, but was held up by contractual obligations to *Hot Mikado*. Weill and Anderson wrote a song entitled "Lost in the Stars," but when Robinson took to the road in *Hot Mikado*, they placed it in their trunk for the future, and delayed the show indefinitely. When Weill and Anderson came together again in the late 1940s, they explored other novels about black life that might be made into musicals. Richard Wright and Paul Green's *Native Son*, which had been a successful 1941 play, seemed a possibility, but, as Weill's biographer Ronald Sanders suggests, "it was not material for a play by Maxwell Anderson, who was far less able than Paul Green was to gaze

13. Marjory Adams, "Star and Director of *Carib Song* Students of Anthropology," unidentified clipping, in "*Carib Song*" File, TC/PFL. For Dunham's autobiography, see *A Touch of Innocence* (New York, 1959).

upon grim truths. *Cry, The Beloved Country* had for Anderson the double advantage of being gentler than works like *Native Son* and further away from home."[14]

Lost in the Stars reunited Broadway's top black musical talents in this "musical tragedy" about the search of Stephen Kumalo (Todd Duncan) for his son Absalom (Julian Mayfield) in racially tense South Africa. Rouben Mamoulian returned to Broadway to stage the controversial story. He used a Greek chorus to comment on events and placed the action of the novel in the foreground. The critics were mixed in their reactions to the Weill-Anderson effort. They all praised the performances of Duncan, Mayfield, and *Porgy and Bess* veterans Warren Coleman and Georgette Harvey, but many found the book heavy-handed. The New York *Times*, however, gave it a rave review, helping the show to a 273-performance run. Atkinson found the show a "memorable musical drama" with "deep, dramatic, and beautiful music." However, the critique of race relations in South Africa rarely caused reviewers to muse about race relations at home, though William Hawkins of the New York *World-Telegram* noted that "racial difficulties in South Africa are probably as severe as they are anywhere in the world." Such commentary seemed acceptable for black musicals with foreign themes and settings, but strong social criticism managed to be avoided by white-created black musicals throughout the 1950s.[15]

With white songwriters and librettists monopolizing the black musical during the postwar era, black songwriters generally turned elsewhere. Although famed composers such as Fats Waller and Duke Ellington did attempt Broadway musicals, their influence was fleeting. Shortly before his death, Waller completed the score for a mostly white musical comedy, *Early to Bed* (1943). Ellington prepared scores for Broadway only twice in a twenty-year period. First, *Beggar's Holiday,* a modernization of *The Beggar's Opera,* reached Broadway in 1946 with an integrated cast featuring Alfred Drake, late of *Oklahoma* fame. It enjoyed a brief run, with modest praise for the Ellington–John LaTouche score. Ellington returned to Broadway in 1966 with a musical version of the

14. Ronald Sanders, *The Days Grow Short: The Life and Music of Kurt Weill* (New York, 1980), 285–87, 373–88 (quotation on 379).

15. William Hawkins, "*Lost in the Stars* Has Zulu Theme," New York *World-Telegram,* October 31, 1949, in "*Lost in the Stars*" Scrapbook, TC/PFL. See also Maxwell Anderson, "Assembling the Parts for a Musical Play," New York *Herald Tribune,* October 30, 1949.

classic film *The Blue Angel. Pousse Cafe* quickly closed, and the Duke's score has faded from memory. Ellington did, however, compose musicals that enjoyed healthy runs in other cities. *Jump for Joy,* a wartime hit in Los Angeles, had a lengthy run, and *My People,* Ellington's look in the 1960s at black history, was popular in Chicago. Ironically, Ellington's significant contribution to Broadway musicals came after his death, when *Sophisticated Ladies* (1981) provided a cavalcade of the composer's classic hits. With Gregory Hines and Judith Jameson as the leads, the show presented effective dance renditions of Ellington's musical creations. After a 767-performance run, the show became a pay-television production.[16]

As black creative artists went elsewhere, New York theatres experienced only a few dim reflections of the golden age of black musical theatre. A 1942 production, *Harlem Cavalcade,* reunited some of the greats of the early 1920s, Noble Sissle, Flournoy Miller, and Tim Moore, in what most critics dismissed as a second-rate vaudeville show. Co-produced by Ed Sullivan, the show paraded current and past Harlem talents before a supportive audience. While the show maintained the flavor of 1920s vaudeville performances, the writers attempted to update the enterprise for the war effort. Tim Moore and Joe Byrd appeared as air-raid wardens, but were stationed in a cemetery, and Flournoy Miller devoted his malaprop routines to trying to fill out a draft board questionnaire. John Mason Brown dismissed the endeavor as old-fashioned in the *World-Telegram*: "What got me down was the simple fact that all the new numbers I was seeing finally seemed old, regardless of their merits. I began to realize that I had seen them or their equivalents not only in the first half, but in every other Negro show that I had ever sat [through] before. By the time the evening was nearly over, I had too much of an old thing." As a result of the harsh reviews, the *Cavalcade* lasted only forty-nine performances.[17]

Blue Holiday attempted a similar approach in 1945, with such talents as Ethel Waters, Josh White, and Josephine Premice. Waters, praised so

16. Ellington's Broadway experience is generally ignored by his biographers. Derek Jewell mentions it briefly in *Duke: A Portrait of Duke Ellington* (New York, 1977), 106. Ellington passes over *Beggar's Holiday* in his autobiography, *Music Is My Mistress* (New York, 1973), but provides information on *Jump for Joy* (1941), a "Sun-Tanned Revu-sical," starring Dorothy Dandridge, Ivy Anderson, and Herb Jeffries (pp. 175–80). Ellington first appeared on Broadway with his band in George Gershwin's *Show Girl* (1929). An unproduced Ellington musical, *Queenie Pie,* was presented by the Philadelphia Music Theatre Festival in 1986.

17. New York *Times,* May 4, 1942; New York *Sun,* May 2, 1942; New York *World-Telegram,* May 4, 1942.

heartily for *Mamba's Daughters* and *Cabin in the Sky,* seemed peripheral here—she was panned by most of the critics. Newcomer Josh White, however, received the best reviews for his performance of folk songs and contemporary numbers, such as "Hard Time Blues," "Evil-Hearted Man," "The House I Live In," and "Free and Equal Blues." The show gave White's career a boost, but *Blue Holiday* disappeared within the week.[18]

Sissle and Blake tried one last time to return to Broadway with a new version of *Shuffle Along* that they had been planning since 1943. This modernization finally came to fruition as *Shuffle Along of 1952,* and it seemed doomed from the start. Although the authors changed the setting from Jimtown in the 1920s to Italy during World War II, original star Pearl Bailey left when she saw the state of the new script. Noble Sissle was injured during rehearsals and was unable to help with the final plans for the show. Finally, just before the show opened, a fire destroyed much of the scenery. Some of the older critics warmly welcomed the Sissle and Blake show, particularly the reprises of "I'm Just Wild About Harry" and "Love Will Find a Way." Most reviewers, however, dismissed the latest *Shuffle Along* as woefully out of date. Black critic Miles Jefferson of *Phylon* also thought the comedy was in poor taste: "The *Shuffle Along* brand of humor has long since been happily buried—the humor of two shambling comedians murdering the English language and indulging in 'Negroisms' is painfully embarrassing in a much more enlightened 1952." Critic Richard Watts, Jr., of the New York *Post,* agreed: "It would have been wiser to let the sleeping dog lie unmolested in the happy dream of its original success." The new Sissle and Blake show faded after just four performances, leading to a lengthy and somewhat early retirement from Broadway musicals for two of the brightest lights of black musical theatre in the 1920s. Their departure symbolized the absence of black talent in the creation of new black or white musical comedies in the postwar world.[19]

18. New York *Times,* May 23, 1945.

19. *Variety,* May 14, 1952; New York *Herald Tribune,* May 9, 1952; New York *Times,* May 9, 1952; Miles Jefferson, "The Negro on Broadway, 1951–1952," *Phylon,* XIII (1952), 109–11; New York *Post,* May 9, 1952. For an account of the changes that had to be made in the original conception and script, see "Three Men Busy Tailoring the '21 *Shuffle Along* to '52," New York *Herald Tribune,* February 10, 1952. "One of the big guffaws in the original *Shuffle Along* was about a Negro who was elected mayor in a mythical town and couldn't spell C-A-T. Nowadays, when most colored people can read even in the deep country, the joke would fall flat."

XIII

DEMOCRACY IN ACTION

Although the black musical had definitively passed into white hands during the postwar era, another development caused black theatrical veterans to take heart. As all-black entertainments dwindled new employment opportunities opened in the hitherto white world of the Broadway musical. For the first time in recent memory, Broadway musicals began to use black performers in impressive numbers during World War II. By the late 1940s, integrated casts and chorus lines evoked hardly any surprise from critics or audiences. As a result, the few remaining black musicals, which had been the primary employers of black singers, dancers, and actors for several generations, now had a potent rival on the Great White Way. With increasing opportunities for black entertainers in Broadway's top musicals, the slow decline in the traditional black musical hardly seemed cause for alarm.

By the early 1950s, Langston Hughes, who had written the longest-running play by a black author to that date (*Mulatto* [1935]), began to celebrate the new look of the "black" theatre in the pages of the New York *Age*:

> The results were seen in the mixed dancing chorus of *On the Town*, the colored and white ensembles of *Finian's Rainbow* and *My Darlin' Aida*, and the complete integration of singers, dancers, and actors in the interracially written and interracially produced *Beggar's Holiday*, the Duke Ellington–John LaTouche novelty co-produced by Negro Perry Watkins and white John R. Sheppard, Jr. In the drama, an interracial producing team, Canada Lee and Mark Marvin, presented *On Whitman Avenue* with a mixed cast. In Gian-Carlo Menotti's *The Medium*, the gypsy boy was

> played by a Katherine Dunham dancer, Leo Coleman, who made love to a white girl.[1]

Even the Metropolitan Opera, which had been "unable" to find black talent in the 1930s, now had Janet Collins, a ballet dancer, performing on its stage, much to Hughes's surprise. As the bastions of segregation were being assaulted both onstage and off, new examples of integrated theatre garnered praise from black critics in a variety of journals. The heyday of the black musical came to represent a segregated past, and the integrated musical became the way of the future. In this atmosphere the all-black musical became a footnote to history rather than a contemporary creative form.

The integrated theatre hailed by Hughes and others may have been novel, but it was not unprecedented. As early as 1904, Will Marion Cook's *The Southerners* presented Broadway with an integrated cast in a musical. Despite threats of walkouts and violence, the show finished its New York run without incident and traveled to several major northern U.S. cities. In addition, backstage talent in this early era swiftly came to be integrated. Cole and the Johnsons, for example, wrote songs for white-performed shows. In the early 1920s, Sissle and Blake provided music for a white musical, *Elsie*, and Creamer and Layton composed the score for *Three Showers* (1920). Similarly, orchestrators, choreographers, conductors, and writers of black musicals often found their talents in demand elsewhere. As the profitability of these newly popular black musicals peaked in the mid-1920s, white creative and financial talents slowly began to assume control backstage, leaving the black talent onstage. Even though the sharp distinctions between "black" and "white" musicals solidified throughout the decade, musicals might still be integrated. Black stars, such as Miller and Lyles, might appear in predominantly white shows, like *Great Temptations* (1926), which featured Jack Benny. Musicals such as *Show Boat* (1927) and Vincent Youmans' *Great Day* (1929) went still further by mixing black and white talent in both leading roles and in the chorus.

By the mid-1930s, a new, and somewhat surprising, segregation seemed common. Although a major star such as Ethel Waters might appear in the cast of *As Thousands Cheer* (1933), her routines were clearly separate from those of the other stars, Clifton Webb, Helen

1. Langston Hughes, "Federal Theatre Led the Way to Plenty of Integration on Broadway," New York *Age*, May 2, 1953, p. 10.

Broderick, and Marilyn Miller. During the same year *Strike Me Pink* included "Home to Harlem," a moving song about a black criminal (George Dewey Washington) who longs for his Harlem home. After a few minutes, Washington vanished, and Lupe Velez and Jimmy Durante performed their usual musical comedy antics. On the whole, the existing but often limited notion of theatrical integration disappeared during the early years of the Great Depression, as black employment opportunities remained relegated to the black musicals of the decade.[2]

While Broadway itself remained segregated throughout the 1930s, American theatre did not. Working counter to Broadway's new racial consciousness was the Federal Theatre Project. This might seem somewhat surprising, since the FTP, with the formation of its Negro Units, clearly played a major role in encouraging black dramatic theatre. Nevertheless, at the same time this government organization also supported a new integration in theatrical life. The creative process, which in the 1920s had slowly been removed from black control, now brought whites and blacks together in all aspects of theatrical planning from costume and scenic design to lighting and electrical work. The advances were apparent onstage as well, for black performers were no longer limited to roles as menials or to roles specifically designed for black characters. Interracial casting became commonplace as the FTP program flowered, and black actors performed in dramas, comedies, and musicals.

Although offical policy encouraged integration in all divisions of the FTP, the actual process was not always smooth. Some individuals occasionally defied directives. The *Daily Worker* featured a stream of articles during 1937 that revealed that black actors and backstage technicians were still facing prejudice within the FTP. Black members noted the use of racial epithets, and some found that they were discriminated against in casting decisions. The source of the stories might be questioned, but it is noteworthy that director Flanagan saved these articles in her scrapbooks, which often detailed just the FTP's triumphs. Nevertheless, follow-up articles often revealed that offenders were either fired or forced to resign.[3] Although prejudice continued to exist in the ranks of the FTP, the organization generally acted upon the complaints of black participants within a short period of time. In this fashion, Flanagan forcefully indicated that prejudice would not be

2. Green, *Ring Bells! Sing Songs!*, 80–81.

3. "Hallie Flanagan" Scrapbook, 1937, in TC/NYPL. See, for example, *Daily Worker*, August 1, 23, September 5, 1937.

tolerated within the Federal Theatre Project. As a result, one of the FTP's major legacies, according to Langston Hughes and other critics, was the eventual breakdown of segregation onstage and behind the scenes as well: "With few previous exceptions, it was the Federal Theatre that dared to cast Negro actors in non-Negro roles, not only on Broadway, but in its units elsewhere as well. The Federal Theatre broke down not only the old taboos against colored Americans as backstage technicians, but the bars against colored actors playing other than racial roles."[4]

As a result of the extensive FTP training program for black actors and backstage technicians, Broadway tended to welcome the newly trained black talent along with the theatrical veterans in the dramas and the musicals of the 1940s. Although there were few new black musicals in this period, black performers appeared in the many integrated white musicals opening after 1945. Harold Rome's *Call Me Mister* (1946), a revue about the returning GI's, seemed the first to signal this new trend. An open call requested former GI's or USO performers. Several actors wanted to know "what type" of performers (that is, were blacks invited to audition?), and the management replied that color did not matter. Almost twelve hundred responded to the call, and sixty were chosen, including three blacks, Bruce Howard, Alvis Tinnin, and Laurence Winters. These three actors, who had lengthy theatrical as well as military careers, were not confined to minor roles in the chorus of the new show, but were given the responsibility of explaining the problems of the black GI in postwar society. Winters, for example, assumed center stage in the "Red Ball Express" number, which was about black war heroes being denied access to jobs on their return home. The success of this long-running show seemed to encourage others, as theatrical integration blossomed in the postwar era.

Along with music and dance, the musical theatre suddenly seemed to be selling democracy. The playbill for Ellington's 1946 *Beggar's Holiday* touted its advanced attitude toward race:

> *Beggar's Holiday,* though thoroughly American, like its English forerunner has opened new vistas in our theatre. The entire artistic endeavor was bi-racial from the start. . . . The production is the first wherein actors, singers, and dancers were hired on the basis of talent and not complexion. The orchestra, under the direction of Max Meth, uses both White and Negro musicians. The harmonious relationships among all concerned

4. Hughes, "Federal Theatre," 10.

Alfred Drake and Avon Long in Duke Ellington's *Beggar's Holiday*
Courtesy Billy Rose Theatre Collection, New York Public Library

> and the success of the venture prove that intelligent Americans can regard color as no barrier to artistic collaboration and it points the way to collaboration along more general lines for the common good of all Americans.[5]

Later the same season, *Finian's Rainbow* offered similar vistas. Miles Jefferson found that it displayed "democracy in its casting" to a greater extent than did *Beggar's Holiday*: "There are no star roles for the Negroes in the cast . . . , but so completely a part of the show are the Negro performers, who compose more than one-third of the company, that it demonstrates an object lesson in race goodwill. The mixed dancing chorus performs terpsichorean tricks in the friendliest race diffusion." Jefferson further saluted the authors for the "courage and imagination to break down restricting color barriers which, alas, have spilled over into the theatre from the outside world of reality."[6]

Two seasons later, Jefferson thought that the perspective still seemed bright. Despite the absence of all-black musicals in the 1948–1949 season, black performers were well represented in the year's top musical hits. Cole Porter's longest-running show, *Kiss Me Kate,* featured several black performers in supporting roles. Lorenzo Fuller performed the showstopper "Too Darn Hot," and Annabelle Hill led the cast in "Another Op'nin', Another Show." Once again, black dancers were a central part of the ensemble. The season's other major musical hit, Rodgers and Hammerstein's *South Pacific,* provided a leading role for Juanita Hall, a former member of the Hall Johnson Choir, who performed the memorable "Bali Ha'i." Although the subplot concerned the problem of miscegenation in the South Pacific, the song "Carefully Taught" was a forceful lecture on prejudice that could be directed to American situations as well. Lieutenant Joseph Cable explained to the audience that "you've got to be taught, before it's too late . . . to hate all the people your relatives hate."[7]

John Lovell, Jr., a professor of English at Howard University and drama critic for the *Crisis,* noticed the same trends. He attempted to quantify the increased participation of black performers in Broadway plays. The numbers indeed confirmed that black employment in major roles was indeed on the upswing.

5. *Beggar's Holiday* playbill, in TC/NYPL.

6. Miles Jefferson, "The Negro on Broadway, 1946–1947," *Phylon,* VIII (1947), 147–49.

7. Miles Jefferson, "The Negro on Broadway, 1948–1949," *Phylon,* X (1949), 109–11.

YEAR	SHOWS WITH BLACK PERFORMERS	TOTAL BLACK PERFORMERS
1940	3	52
1941	3	12
1942	12	117
1943	16	146
1944	20	115
1945	20	219
1946	28	279

Lovell found the quality of the employment almost as important as the quantity. These were not trivial roles in most cases, but secondary or starring roles. Second, most of the black performers were in integrated shows, rather than in all-black shows, as had been the case during the 1920s, when such shows dominated Broadway. The prognosis seemed clear. Broadway's onstage segregation seemed destined to disappear: "Integration is obviously not only good business, but smart business. It probably means that the old Negro show of delightful memory is on the way out, along with the old 'lily-white' show. American drama is learning that restricted themes have been pretty well exhausted; it is turning to the great field of melting-pot drama, to the Whitmanesque land of numerous peoples and cultures and wonderful interblendings. It is at last grasping the notoriously open truth that this field was inexhaustible from the start."[8]

Despite such optimistic statistics and rhetoric, the musical's fling with democracy began to seem transitory. Jefferson entitled his review of the 1950–1951 season "the empty season." The following year became "another transparent season," and he feared that the postwar advances were fading. Actors Equity also took note of this trend and, in 1951, appointed Frederick O'Neal to head a committee to investigate possible cures for the declining employment of black performers on Broadway. O'Neal seemed an appropriate choice. He had organized and performed with several black theatre groups, the Aldridge Players in St. Louis from 1927 to 1937, for example, and the American Negro

8. John Lovell, Jr., "Roundup: The Negro in the American Theatre (1940–1947)," *Crisis* (July, 1947), 212–17. See also Lovell, "Democracy in a Hit Revue," *ibid.* (March, 1947), 76, for comments on *Call Me Mister;* and Lovell, "Singing in the Streets," *ibid.* (June, 1947), 174, for Langston Hughes's *Street Scene.* "Roundup" and "Singing" have banner headlines—"On the Stage Social Significance" and "The Stage Teaches Democracy."

Theatre (ANT, which he co-founded with Abram Hill) in the 1940s. His most successful work with the ANT, *Anna Lucasta,* ultimately moved to Broadway for a successful run, and O'Neal received the Clarence Derwent Award for the best supporting performance on Broadway in the 1944–1945 season. Despite such growing renown, O'Neal experienced the difficulties typical for many black actors. Jobs remained few and far between, and he was forced to prove himself repeatedly with each new audition. In an attempt to rectify these problems, O'Neal worked with the Negro Actors Guild and became chairman of the executive board. He undertook similar tasks with Actors Equity, becoming the union's first black vice-president and, in 1964, its eighth president.[9]

O'Neal was clearly alarmed by the data concerning black employment on Broadway. He reported to Equity that only thirteen blacks had parts in Broadway plays between September 1, 1951, and March 15, 1952. Only three had supporting roles; the rest had bit parts or were extras. Of the forty-nine plays that opened during the season, only seven employed blacks. *The Shrike* employed four, and two were brought from Britain as extras in the Laurence Olivier troupe. Unfortunately, most of the plays had short runs, so by March only *The Shrike* was still employing black performers. Backstage statistics were even worse. As of March 15, 1952, there were no black directors, stage managers, authors, composers, choreographers, musical directors, publicity men, advance agents, casting agents, or company managers. Nor were there any stagehands, theatrical photographers, ticket agents, or theatre party agents in the Broadway theatre, "despite the fact that there were qualified persons able to fill most or all of the above positions," many of whom had been trained by the FTP.[10] There seemed to be some hope for later in the season, with the arrival of the new *Shuffle Along,* but that short-lived and ill-fated production hardly dented the statistics.

What was the solution? Actors Equity joined with a variety of theatrical organizations in order to solve the problem. The League of New York Theatres, the Dramatists' Guild, the Negro Actors Guild, and the

9. Ethel Pitts Walker, "The American Negro Theatre," in Hill (ed.), *The Theater of Black Americans,* II, 49–62. For information on O'Neal, see his file in SCCF/NYPL, which documents his curious attempt in 1958 to become president of Equity. Although O'Neal was unopposed for the office, two-term president Ralph Bellamy suddenly decided to run. Bellamy denied that a "racial issue" was involved. New York *Post,* May 26, 1958. See also "Man in the News," New York *Times,* May 6, 1954.

10. Miles Jefferson, "The Negro on Broadway, 1951–1952," *Phylon,* XIII (1952), 109–11; "Integration," *Equity,* XXXVII (June, 1952), 19–20.

NAACP appointed a committee to investigate the situation. Its members included Cornelia Otis Skinner, Joseph James, Frederick O'Neal, and Alfred Drake; Langston Hughes and playwright Sidney Kingsley drafted the report. The committee urged "the portrayal of the Negro as a more general part of the scheme of our society, for example, as postmen, policemen, clerks, secretaries, government workers, doctors, and teachers, without the necessity of emphasis on race." Indeed, this had often been done earlier in such musicals as *On the Town* (1944), *Inside U.S.A.* (1948), *Out of This World* (1950), and *South Pacific.* Recently, however, those advances had faded, as an "ill-directed sensitivity to this problem has worked inadvertent harm to the Negro artist." Hughes and Kingsley suggested that white authors, afraid of accidentally offending black performers with stereotypical roles, had tended to eliminate them from scripts. As a result, black employment on Broadway had dwindled. The solution, according to the report, was "not [to] eliminate the Negro artist, but [to enlarge] his scope and participation in all types of roles and in all forms of entertainment—just as in American life, the Negro citizen's role now extends from the kitchen to the United Nations."[11]

Despite the efforts of these organizations, democracy continued to dwindle in both the drama and the musical on Broadway during the 1950s. Instead of the mixed casts that emerged in the postwar era, Broadway substituted an integration from the top. Renowned entertainers from nightclubs, films, and popular recordings took center stage as proof of theatre's new racial tolerance. As a result, jobs for black secondary players, chorus members, and dancers faded as the decade progressed. Nevertheless, talents such as Lena Horne (*Jamaica*), Eartha Kitt (*Mrs. Patterson,* 1954), Harry Belafonte (*John Murray Anderson's Almanac,* 1953, and *3 For Tonight,* 1955), and Sammy Davis, Jr. (*Mr. Wonderful,* 1956), could still obtain a theatrical berth in either a revue or a musical comedy.[12]

Of these four performers, only Eartha Kitt found her career shaped by her Broadway experience. Although born in the United States, Kitt earned a modest reputation in Paris, where she had performed with the Katherine Dunham Dancers. Theatre and motion picture im-

11. Jefferson, "The Negro on Broadway, 1951–1952," 109–11.

12. The New York *Times* reported on April 23, 1957, that the five-year effort to improve black employment on Broadway had been a failure. The committee placed the blame on "insufficient information." For Davis' account of the production of *Mr. Wonderful,* see Davis and Jane Boyer and Burt Boyer, *Yes I Can* (New York, 1965), 288–325.

presario Orson Welles saw Kitt's performance in a Parisian nightclub and offered her a co-starring role in his 1951 production of *Faust.* Kitt first received notice in America with this dramatic role, and she gained wider attention for her musical revue debut in Leonard Sillman's *New Faces of 1952,* where she showcased her talents in a sultry rendition of "Monotonous," which revealed her as a bored jet-set sophisticate. Kitt promptly earned stardom in a show that included such future stars as Paul Lynde, Alice Ghostley, and Carol Lawrence. Her rise was rapid, and she appeared both on Broadway and in Hollywood throughout the 1950s.

Kitt moved to Hollywood for the film version of *New Faces* at Twentieth Century-Fox, and then she returned to Broadway to star in *Mrs. Patterson,* a vehicle written for her by Charles Sebree and Greer Johnson. One of the few presentations during the 1950s that was written by a black author (Sebree), *Mrs. Patterson* featured Kitt as a young poverty-stricken teenager who lives in a world of fantasy. One of her dreams is to grow up and be a white lady like Mrs. Patterson, the snobbish woman who employs her mother as a domestic. While the authors had written what was ostensibly a drama, they built on Kitt's talents by interpolating five songs during her dream sequences. Although most critics found the play somewhat lacking in interest, almost all applauded Kitt's ample talents, with Brooks Atkinson finding the new star "an incandescent young woman with lively intelligence, a darting sense of movement, keen eyes and an instinct for the stage." Only George Jean Nathan, critic for the New York *Journal American,* demurred. Long hostile to black productions and performers, he found Kitt "a Negro topsy who made something of a hit, for no discernible reason other than that she was colored. Miss Kitt still doesn't indicate any particular talent in this new medium but seems to get away with the lack of it with many theatre-goers and the reviewers on account of her race, since it has become sufficiently known that whereas a white actress in the same situation would be given the works, a colored one is given a good break."[13]

Since the opinion of the majority of critics reigned, Kitt continued to work in theatre, films, television, and nightclubs during the 1950s. She appeared in one more Broadway musical, *Shinbone Alley* (1957), and a short-lived drama, *Jolly's Progress* (1959). As the decade ended, Kitt

13. New York *Times,* December 3, 1954; *Variety,* December 8, 1954; Nathan quoted in Miles Jefferson, "The Negro on Broadway, 1954–1955," *Phylon,* XVI (1955), 303, 312.

spent more of her time in Hollywood, appearing in such films as *The Mark of the Hawk* and *St. Louis Blues* (1958) and *Anna Lucasta* (1959). During the 1960s, however, Kitt found that obtaining new roles was increasingly difficult. Some attributed that to her being difficult to work with; others blamed her marriage to white businessman William McDonald. By the mid-1960s, the former Broadway queen had become Cat Woman on the camp-crazed "Batman" television show. Kitt's faltering career received a virtual death blow in 1968, when she attended a White House luncheon given by Lady Bird Johnson. Kitt avoided pleasantries that afternoon and spoke of the most important issues of the day, explaining that "the nation's youths were rebelling because they were being snatched off to be shot in Vietnam." The outburst earned the president's immediate scorn. More important, Kitt discovered that job prospects were fading still faster. CIA documents revealed in 1975 that the agency had been collecting data on Kitt since 1956 for her outspoken opinions, and had played a role in discouraging individuals from hiring the singer. Kitt's career ground to a halt until her triumphant return to Broadway in *Timbuktu!,* a modernized version of *Kismet,* in 1978.[14]

Although some integration may have occurred among a few leading roles in white musicals, the postwar advances for featured players and chorus members were short-lived. Drama maintained a few roles for prominent black actors, but they were often fairly minor portrayals of what Miles Jefferson called "the Eternal Menial." Performers who had distinguished themselves in leading roles in plays during the early 1950s found themselves clinging to Broadway as the maids, butlers, and workers during the latter part of the decade. Musicals rarely made use of such characters, and even these smaller parts for black performers disappeared by the late 1950s. Lena Horne noted this trend while she was appearing on Broadway in *Jamaica.* When asked during a 1958 interview whether "the tendency toward the stereotype [in Broadway show roles was] as inflexible as it has always been," Horne observed that a subtle change had occurred during the 1950s:

> I don't think it is as inflexible, but they have gone the other way and not made a niche for Negro performers. We have discontinued the use of the stereotype, but we have opened up nothing else. I think that a good role, whether it's a maid or a laundress, is to be desired if it's a good role. But in

14. New York *Times,* January 3, 1975. For Kitt's autobiography, see *Alone with Me* (Chicago, 1976).

> the past they have never varied the stereotype, so by cutting it out completely it has hurt the Negro performer economically. You have the desire to play other things beyond the stereotype, but you can't even play that anymore.[15]

Backstage life also maintained its virtually all-white character, despite efforts in 1952 to integrate the theatrical world. Although the first black stagehands were finally admitted to the Theatrical Stage Employees Union in 1955, few were available for jobs when producer David Merrick began hiring for *Jamaica.* When an all-white staff greeted Merrick, he asked the union to provide five black stagehands. Told that was impossible, Merrick threatened the union with publicizing its delaying tactics, and, suddenly, the leaders found the requested workers. Little changed for Merrick's future productions, and on one occasion, the head of the union suggested to Merrick that he find the stagehands himself.[16]

Although the entire musical comedy cast and crew had been integrated during the late 1940s, just ten years later only the top parts remained open to black performers. This situation certainly boosted the careers of a few black superstars, but it also brought tough times for the secondary black players who had only recently entered the world of the white musical comedy.

Actors Equity ultimately played a major role in destroying the institutional barriers to theatrical integration during the late 1950s and 1960s. During the early 1950s, the actors' union focused on studying and documenting the phenomenon of black underemployment in the legitimate theatre. Once the analysis appeared complete, the union, particularly under the new leadership of President Frederick O'Neal, concentrated on the means of increasing black employment in the theatre, thus reversing the slow disappearance of "theatrical democracy," the hallmark of the postwar era. The complete integration of the legitimate theatre became the goal of Actors Equity during this period.

Equity established "integration showcases" in the late 1950s in order to demonstrate to theatrical producers and general audiences as well that black performers could be successful in any type of role. For example, a 1959 showcase allowed newcomers Diahann Carroll and

15. "Interview—Lena Horne," *Equity,* XLIII (April, 1958), 4–7.
16. New York *Times,* April 25, 1968.

Louis Gossett to display their considerable and diverse talents. Lloyd Richards, who would become a noted Broadway director in the 1960s and head of the Yale Drama School, guided the effort, attempting to prove that black directors could perform the same tasks their white cohorts did. The afternoon's selections proved varied, with excerpts from Ben Jonson's comedy, *Volpone*; Robert Anderson's *Tea and Sympathy*; Leonard Sillman's *New Faces*; and John Murray and Allen Boretz's frenetic farce, *Room Service*. Diahann Carroll provided the introductions, singing "Love Makes the Stage Go Round," a paean to integration that Jerry Bock and Sheldon Harnick had written especially for the event.[17]

The notion that black theatrical talent had to "prove" that they could perform the same tasks as whites reveals the extent to which black theatrical history had been erased in the late 1950s. Most producers hesitated to cast black performers in so-called white roles, arguing that audiences would never accept it and that it was impractical. One producer, who preferred not to be named by the New York *Times*, explained: "I think it is completely naive to assume Negroes can play white parts indiscriminately, because the essence of theatre is casting discrimination. You don't just cast anybody for any part. If the part calls for a short, fat man, you don't cast a tall thin man. When a man's color is a factor in the characterization, you have to consider it. You have to discriminate."[18]

Although white artists had no problems performing black roles, thanks to the minstrel tradition of "blacking up," the reverse notion continued to cause difficulty on the Broadway stage in the 1950s and 1960s. "Whiting up" did occur, such as in Canada Lee's performance in *The Duchess of Malfi* in 1946 with Elisabeth Bergner. Elliot Norton of the Boston *Post* declared that Lee had made "stage history": "Using a special makeup, the base of which is a white paste that women use to conceal skin imperfections, and wearing a thick brown wig, he looked like a white man. Except for the shape of his nose, which is flat and broad, there was nothing in his appearance to suggest his race, and nothing in his performance. Perhaps this was the most striking thing about the whole performance, there were some scenes in which you forgot entirely that he was a colored man in makeup." Some years later, another form of "whiting up" was used in Jean Genêt's long-

17. Windsor Lewis, "Integration Showcase," *Equity*, XLIV (June, 1959), 20–21; program, in "Theatre—Discrimination" File, SCCF/NYPL.

18. New York *Times*, June 15, 1964.

running *The Blacks* (1961), which used stylized masks to create the white characters. Nevertheless, casting a black performer in a traditional white role continued to provoke comment until well into the 1960s. Even when Diana Sands received the role of Saint Joan in 1967, the New York *Times* devoted three columns to the casting choice. Sands explained her selection to Sam Zolotow in words that echoed Frederick O'Neal: "I think it's about time—and it is correct—that an American Negro actor should be cast in all types of roles that he or she is qualified for. It will reach the point, if we continue this way, that such casting will not be considered unusual."[19]

In an attempt to lessen the producers' resistance, Equity contracts signed during the 1960s provided for open casting for all parts, instead of the standard practice of calling for "Negro performers" only for specific roles. The 1962 contract established that "there shall be no discrimination against any actor or applicant for a part or position by reason of race, creed, color or national origin."[20]

Equity also assaulted the practice of audience segregation, which had lingered into the 1950s throughout the country, despite virtually constant protest. This effort did yield some temporary success during the 1940s, but it was estimated that nearly 40 percent of the road theatres still practiced segregation or barred black patrons altogether by the early 1950s. Particularly galling was the fact that the National Theatre in the nation's capital was one of the most ardent proponents of restricting black patrons. After the brouhaha over *The Green Pastures* in the early 1930s, the management temporarily relented and allowed blacks to attend performances of the touring *Porgy and Bess* and *At Home Abroad* in 1936. After box office receipts were tallied, the management declared that blacks in the National's audience chased away potential white patrons and hurt revenues, so they were barred from the National for the next decade. In 1946, Robert E. Sherwood, whose production of Maxwell Anderson's *Joan of Lorraine* was playing in Washington, proposed a boycott of Jim Crow theatres by actors, playwrights, and producers. Sherwood's notion was not entirely unprecedented. Billy Rose had recently closed a touring production of *Carmen Jones,* since Washington's Uline Arena had prohibited black patrons. Sherwood urged fellow writers to participate in the boycott, and by January, 1947, some thirty-three playwrights joined the protest, in-

19. Boston *Post,* September 26, 1946; Stanley Kauffmann, "En Route to the Future," New York *Times,* July 31, 1966, Sec. II, p. 1; New York *Times,* August 14, 1967.

20. New York *Times,* March 19, 1967, p. 30.

cluding Thornton Wilder, S. N. Behrman, and Donald Ogden Stewart.

Equity attempted quiet negotiations with the National manager, Marcus Heiman, on the matter, but he remained adamant. Why should he be a "guinea pig" for social change when virtually every institution in the nation's capital, from schools to motion picture theatres, was segregated? As a result of Heiman's continuing refusals, Equity proposed that after a one-year negotiating period, none of its actors could appear on the National's stage. This 1947 contractual requirement, which the League of New York Theatres at first resisted, was to be implemented in June, 1948. Heiman stalled and then closed the National, converting it into a movie house, which was free from any threats from Actors Equity. The boycott eventually had its intended effect. After four years of paltry revenues as a movie theatre, the National reopened in 1952 as a legitimate theatre with Ethel Merman in *Call Me Madam*. The new management allowed blacks to attend any performance of any future shows.[21]

Once the National Theatre had been integrated, similar tactics were employed to complete the task throughout the United States. A series of contracts signed during the 1950s prohibited Equity members from working before a segregated audience in most types of public performances. A 1961 contract completed this effort by extending these Equity rules to industrial shows and to the one geographical holdout, Washington, D.C., which had claimed exceptions in earlier contracts. This campaign proved the most successful of any on the Equity agenda, finally ending the practice of segregated or restrictive seating in professional theatres in the United States.[22]

Despite Equity's active campaign for integration onstage as well, progress seemed markedly slow to the union's Committee on Integration. This committee, which was chaired by O'Neal, assembled statistics on black employment both on and Off-Broadway over a ten-year period in an attempt to chart its progress and devise possible remedies to any problem that might be discovered. By 1966, the committee was dismayed to learn, there was no clear trend of improvement in any area.

The employment figures revealed great swings in black employment

21. For an account of the Equity campaign, see "Theatre—Discrimination" File, SCCF/NYPL. See also *PM*, October 30, 1946; New York *Times*, August 3, 6, 1947; *Theatre Arts* (May, 1947), 3; *Equity*, XXXII (May, 1947), 7, 14; *Business Week*, May 3, 1947, p. 87; and the articles by Washington *Post* drama critic Richard L. Coe, reprinted in New York *Times*, June 20, 1948, April 27, 1952.

22. *Equity*, XLVI (August, 1961), 3; New York *Herald Tribune*, October 9, 1961.

BLACK EMPLOYMENT, ON AND OFF-BROADWAY, 1955–1966

SEASON	TOTAL JOBS AVAILABLE FOR BLACKS		TOTAL SHOWS EMPLOYING BLACKS		SHOWS USING INTEGRATED CASTING	
	ON	OFF	ON	OFF	ON	OFF
1955–56	142	25	20	8	7	4
1956–57	75	47	11	11	2	2
1957–58	182	26	24	6	10	3
1958–59	24	21	9	9	5	3
1959–60	135	46	15	13	4	3
1960–61	126	29	18	9	8	4
1961–62	123	50	14	20	10	11
1962–63	51	26	21	12	13	7
1963–64	168	116	24	27	16	11
1964–65	74	32	22	20	15	11
1965–66	54	25	16	10	9	5

SOURCE: *Equity*, 1955–66.

from year to year. The 1955–1956 Broadway season provided 142 jobs for black performers, but the following season found the number of roles cut virtually in half. The season of *Jamaica* (1957–1958) offered a bonanza of 182 roles; the next season saw a cut to one-ninth of that level. Off-Broadway experienced similar fluctuations, offering, for example, 116 jobs in 1963–1964, but only 32 the following season. It seemed that Equity had been able to do little to ensure steady employment for black performers either on or Off-Broadway.

Ironically, the only factor that increased black employment in the theatre was not more integration (as Equity had hoped) but, instead, the presence of predominantly black shows. In the 1956–1957 season, two musical shows—the integrated *Shinbone Alley* and a *Show Boat* revival—offered 66 percent of the jobs. In the following season, four musicals—*Jamaica, Simply Heavenly,* and revivals of *Show Boat* and *Lost in the Stars*—provided 74 percent of the jobs for black performers. In the 1961–1962 season, three shows—*Kwamina, Purlie Victorious,* and *Kicks and Company*—gave black actors 90 of the 123 available roles. The message was clear to Actors Equity by the early 1960s. Their recent efforts had done very little to increase theatrical integration. Instead, black shows, and often musicals, continued to supply the majority of employment opportunities for black performers.

Frederick O'Neal became increasingly dismayed by the seeming failure of Equity's program and policies. In 1967, Equity formally admitted that discrimination still existed in the theatre. The seventy-two-member governing body endorsed President O'Neal's statement and sent a missive to producers and casting directors. When asked by the New York *Times* for his opinions on the matter, O'Neal wondered, "How long does one wait for voluntary compliance with these things?" Contemplating the failure of Actors Equity's plans, he mused that "those outside the theatre are going to force the issue." He envisioned theatres picketed by civil rights groups protesting the poor treatment of black actors. In fact, CORE had already picketed the all-white musicals *How to Succeed in Business Without Really Trying* and *Subways Are for Sleeping* in 1962. The settings, an office and the New York City subway system, could logically have had black cast members, but neither show moved in this direction.[23]

The New York State Commission for Human Rights investigated theatrical hiring policies the following year, and its conclusions were

23. New York *Times*, April 1, 1962, p. 61.

similar to those of Equity's study. Of the 523 actors in 22 Broadway shows in March, 1968, only 57 were black, 7 Hispanic, and 1 of Asian origin. Backstage statistics were equally dismal. Of 664 production employees on Broadway that season, only 14 were black. Although the stagehands' union had been integrated in 1955, only 2 of the 381 working on Broadway that season were black. Most producers denied that discrimination existed in the theatre and that they could do anything about it anyway. David Merrick stood virtually alone in his revelation of the effects of theatrical prejudice. Merrick, a noted Broadway producer who began his career in the 1950s, had presented such black shows as *Jamaica* and the Pearl Bailey–Cab Calloway *Hello Dolly.* He claimed that he sponsored the "black Dolly" in order to prove that "a white man's story about the upper class could be done with an all-Negro company. Well, as you know," said Merrick, "it did work." Few solutions were offered at the hearings, and the Commission for Human Rights suggested the possibility of affirmative action guidelines in the future.[24]

Merrick's mention of the "all-Negro" *Dolly* as a point of pride reveals a major controversy over goals for black entertainers in the theatre in the 1960s. On one hand, the new *Dolly* possessed remarkable symbolic value for the age. It answered a long-expressed desire of Actors Equity in its demonstration that blacks could portray "white" roles without the slightest harm or distortion occurring to the theatrical property. Indeed, Bailey and Calloway brought a new charm to a show that had borne Carol Channing's personal stamp since its 1964 opening. Successors Betty Grable, Martha Raye, Dorothy Lamour, and Ginger Rogers had performed the role admirably, but only Bailey started to redefine it. *Hello Dolly* also fulfilled Merrick's desire to increase black employment on Broadway, both onstage and behind the scenes. Indeed, his firm commitment to these goals remained remarkable, as others still tended to waver on the commitment to affirmative action on the Broadway stage.

The notion of *Dolly* as a new symbol of race relations in the 1960s was embraced by both Lyndon and Lady Bird Johnson, who greeted Bailey when she brought the show to Washington, D.C. The Johnsons, who had been fond of the show since the Democrats adapted its title song as "Hello Lyndon" in 1964, joined in the high spirits created by Bailey's rendition. She beckoned to the Johnsons in their box seats,

24. *Ibid.*, April 25, 1968.

and they joined Dolly Levi for a march around the promenade that encircled the orchestra. The Johnsons took up the new *Dolly* much as Eleanor Roosevelt had prominently attended *Swing Mikado* and *Mamba's Daughters*. They were not merely going to the theatre; they were making a statement. The Johnsons saw the all-black *Dolly* as a symbol of the fulfillment of black aspirations: Dolly Levi could be performed by a black or a white in a color-blind America.[25]

Despite Bailey and the Johnsons' pride in the "all-Negro" *Dolly,* the star was somewhat surprised and distressed to hear criticism of the project. When informed that several black artists argued that the show should have an integrated rather than an all-black cast, Bailey responded, "Why do they have to talk racial into everything? . . . Is everybody looking to separate the whole world? I love everybody and I don't want to see anybody hurt." Frederick O'Neal, once again, led the criticism. While he rejoiced that the Merrick show would vastly increase black employment on Broadway that season, he wondered whether actors "were sacrificing [their] principles for a few bucks." O'Neal contended that the show subverted Equity policy, which was that producers cast "according to ability" and not color. Therefore, the new *Dolly* hardly heralded a new age, but, instead, harked back to the black *Mikado*s of 1939. Nevertheless, O'Neal was hesitant to lodge a formal protest with David Merrick. The show *did* supply jobs for the union members, though it did seem contrary to Equity rules.[26]

Amid the dismal litany of black employment statistics for the theatre in the late 1950s and 1960s, there was one element of hope. Actors Equity, like most institutions of the 1950s, envisioned an integrated future. O'Neal explained to the press, "We gauge progress in this area by the number of Negroes engaged for roles not racially designated." Yet the statistics seemed to foster hope in another direction. Black shows, and particularly musicals, remained the most important force for determining black employment on Broadway. Rather than ignore this success in favor of an integrationist dream, perhaps this fact could help improve black employment in the legitimate theatre.

25. *Ibid.*, November 5, 1967.
26. *Ibid.*, July 29, 1967.

XIV

LANGSTON HUGHES AND THE NEW BLACK MUSICAL

While most black authors avoided the musical theatre during the 1950s, only Langston Hughes struggled to revise a once-popular form for a new era. Hughes, better known as a poet and a dramatist, had been interested in the musical theatre since his days at Columbia University in the 1920s. He was one of the ardent devotees of *Shuffle Along* in the early days of the Harlem Renaissance. Although Hughes never contributed to any of the successful black musicals of the 1920s, he did work briefly on an unproduced effort, *O Blues!*, which was to have starred Paul Robeson. He also collaborated with J. Rosamond Johnson during this period in an attempt to set some of his poems to music.[1]

When Hughes finally achieved a Broadway showing, it was for a drama *Mulatto*, rather than for a musical. This 1935 dramatic effort, which played 373 performances, remained the longest-running show by a black author until Lorraine Hansberry's *A Raisin in the Sun* in 1960. The title of Hansberry's play provides an indirect homage to her theatrical predecessor, since the phrase derives from a Hughes poem, "Lenox Avenue Mural": "What happens to a dream deferred / Does it dry up / Like a raisin in the sun?"

Mulatto, like several dramas of the period, focused on the problems of miscegenation on a large plantation in Georgia. Colonel Norwood (Stuart Beebe) allows his black mistress, Cora (Rose McClendon), to move into the house after his frail wife's death. Norwood sires four children with Cora, and he treats them modestly well as long as they

1. Hughes, *The Big Sea*, 223–24; Faith Berry, *Langston Hughes: Before and Beyond Harlem* (Westport, Conn., 1983), 77; Arnold Rampersad, *The Life of Langston Hughes: I, Too, Sing America*, Vol. I, 1902–1941 (New York, 1986), 133–135.

understand their place within the southern system of race relations. The youngest son, Robert (Hurst Amyx), however, has inherited his father's pride and refuses to play the anonymous mulatto child. After some time at college, he returns home to challenge the Colonel and the ways of the South. The Colonel is unable to accept Robert's unusual independence and is tempted to shoot his rebellious scion. As Norwood reaches for a gun during an argument Robert attempts to stop him. In the ensuing battle Robert strangles his father. When the Colonel's friends arrive and discover the murder, they begin to search for the youth in the nearby swamps. Cora attempts to hide her son from southern justice, but ultimately she realizes that Robert will be discovered. She then gives Robert the Colonel's gun, and he shoots himself. Cora, who for so long was subservient to the Colonel's whims, now stands fast as she is slapped by the evil overseer Talbot. The curtain descends as Cora remains immobile, perhaps mad. Hughes notes that "it is as though no human hand can touch her again."[2]

While *Mulatto* emerged as a success in the theatrical record books, it seemed a far less satisfying enterprise for Hughes. He recounts in his autobiography that he was unaware that his 1931 play was being prepared for a Broadway production in a somewhat rewritten form by Martin Jones, the white producer of the show. When Hughes attended a preview, he was somewhat surprised that Robert's sister (who leaves for school in Act I of the written version of the play) remained on the plantation during the succeeding acts. Jones explained that sex sells, so he allowed the beautiful young lady to miss her train. Hughes was less than welcome at rehearsals, and he received no complimentary seats for the opening. Neither he nor the black members of the cast were invited to an opening-night buffet dinner. Hughes then bought tickets for relatives and friends: "At first at the Vanderbilt, the box office tried not to sell Negroes seats in the orchestra. When I learned of this, I not only protested, but I bought as many orchestra seats myself as I could afford in the very center of the theatre. These I gave to the darkest Negroes I knew, including Claude McKay."[3]

Hughes's experiences with musical theatre were similarly dispiriting. In the waning days of the great black musical revues, Hughes was hired to contribute to a West Coast show, *Negro Revue*, in 1939 for the

2. Langston Hughes, *Five Plays by Langston Hughes*, ed. Webster Smalley (Bloomington, Ind., 1963).

3. Langston Hughes, *I Wonder As I Wander* (New York, 1956), 307–14. For Hughes's recollections about *Mulatto*, see also Langston Hughes interview, May 6–7, 1961, in Hatch-Billops Oral History Collection, New York City.

Hollywood Theatre Alliance. One of the few black writers involved in the project, Hughes was stunned and embarrassed by the white writers' attempts to evoke black humor. Too often, the material resembled "Amos 'n' Andy" scripts, in which black dialect on its own was assumed to be hilarious.[4] Hughes eventually left the production. He recorded his experiences in "Note on Commercial Art," a poem that encapsulates the history of black musical theatre and black culture in general:

> You've done taken my blues and gone—
> You sing 'em in Paris
> And you sing 'em in Hollywood Bowl,
> And you mixed 'em up with symphonies
> And you fixed 'em
> So they don't sound like me.
>
> Yep, you done taken my blues and gone.
>
> You also done took my spirituals and gone.
> You put me in Macbeth
> And all kinds of Swing Mikados
> And in everything but what's about me—
> But someday somebody'll
> Stand up and talk about me,
> And write about me,
> Black and beautiful—
> And sing about me,
> And put on plays about me!
>
> I reckon it'll be
> Me myself![5]

Hughes and fellow author Arna Bontemps attempted to rectify the new white domination of black musical theatre with their own black revue, *Cavalcade of the Negro Theatre,* which would tell the true story of the Afro-American contribution to American entertainment. In 1940, Hughes and Bontemps signed an agreement to collaborate and began an intensive study of the history of black musical theatre. Researchers hunted minstrel music; Florence Mills's niece supplied song material; ASCAP furnished lists of "Negro hit songs"; and the writers endeav-

4. Berry, *Langston Hughes,* 293–94.

5. Langston Hughes, "Note on Commercial Art," in *Crisis* (March, 1940), 79. A revised version refers to *Carmen Jones* and substitutes "Broadway" for "Paris." See *Selected Poems of Langston Hughes* (New York, 1970), 190.

ored to locate the stars of the early black theatre, such as Abbie Mitchell, who had disappeared from public view. With the conviction that the finished work would be "authentic and correct," the collaborators sought a New York producer in the summer of 1940, after an abortive Chicago production. Unfortunately, the Hughes-Bontemps show received many promises but few guarantees. After passing from agent to agent, and producer to producer, for several months, the true story of the black theatre remained without a Broadway berth, and Hughes and Bontemps abandoned the project.[6]

In the postwar period, Hughes's opinion of the musical theatre seemed to mellow. As he witnessed the "boom in democracy" on New York's stages he began to see the results of the Federal Theatre Project's efforts at integration. Hughes himself participated, writing the lyrics for Kurt Weill's music in *Street Scene* (1947). While Hughes's collaboration with some of Broadway's top creative talents resulted in favorable critical comment for his lyrical efforts, the writing process was somewhat harried. Hughes attempted to include a strong black figure in the "street scene," but the character was whittled down in importance as the play progressed. Ultimately, Hughes's black voice became the second janitor in the apartment house. Initially, the character was the sole janitor, but Elmer Rice, author of the original play, refused to remove the Swedish janitor from the new libretto. From three major songs, the black janitor ended up with one, "I Got a Marble and a Star," which Hughes described as "more in the tradition of Broadway shows." Somewhat dismayed by the experience, Hughes confided to Bontemps that "the only way for colored to do much down on that street without outside influences diluting their product will be for the race to open a theatre of its own."[7]

Street Scene was the first of many new musical projects by Hughes of which only a few ultimately enjoyed a theatrical premiere. Hughes worked on several musical comedies during this period, such as *Just Around the Corner,* a musical concerning a group of "genteel hoboes who arrive in New York City on a box car on the fateful day in 1933 when Roosevelt closed the banks." This show, which featured black musical veteran Avon Long, enjoyed a tryout in Ogonquit, Maine, in 1950, but shuttered prior to a New York move.[8]

6. Charles H. Nichols (ed.), *Arna Bontemps–Langston Hughes Letters, 1925–1967* (New York, 1980), 57–75.

7. *Ibid.*, 210. See also Sanders, *The Days Grow Short,* 342–59.

8. *Variety,* August 2, 1950.

At the same time, Hughes was working on several operas. Two were musical versions of dramas. *Troubled Island,* a 1949 opera with music by William Grant Still, revived a play about Jean Jacques Dessalines and the Haitian Revolution, which had been performed by the Roxanne Players in Detroit and the Gilpin Players at Cleveland's Karamu House in 1936. Shortly afterwards, William Grant Still, who had set several of Hughes's poems to music, contacted the author and asked if he would prepare an opera libretto. Still read *Troubled Island* and soon began work. Although the opera was completed in the late 1930s, a production was not to appear until 1949. Hughes explained: "Plays are hard enough to get produced, but operas are 10 times as difficult." Leopold Stokowski admired the work and promised to conduct it at the New York City Center. But the conductor left the City Center after his marriage to Gloria Vanderbilt, and the project was delayed. The New York City Opera management re-optioned Hughes's work in 1946 for a 1949 production. This, according to Hughes, was "the first time that any opera written entirely by Negroes has been given a major production by any organized opera company in the United States."[9]

The following year Hughes collaborated with composer Jan Meyerowitz on *The Barrier,* an operatic version of *Mulatto.* Here, with Hughes providing the libretto, the ultimate work proved closer to the author's intentions than did the original 1935 production. Unlike Langston Hughes's other operatic efforts of the period, *The Barrier* enjoyed a brief Broadway run in November, 1950. After successful performances at the University of Michigan and Columbia University, the show received a Broadway option. *The Barrier* embarked on a tryout tour to Washington, where it played the small New Gayety, a former burlesque house that had switched to legitimate plays shortly after the National closed. In Baltimore, it was learned that the seating at Ford's Theatre would be segregated. Star Muriel Rahn and Langston Hughes had rigid contractual obligations, so they could neither refuse to perform in nor attempt to withdraw *The Barrier.* They both said, however, that they intended to picket the show along with the Baltimore NAACP and the Committee Against Segregation in Baltimore Theatres. In the face of mounting negative publicity, the Ford's Theatre management cancelled the showing of the opera. *The Barrier* attempted to move to New York City ahead of schedule. As a result it

9. *Ibid.*, November 25, 1936; Langston Hughes, "*Troubled Island*: The Story of How an Opera Was Created," Chicago *Defender,* March 26, 1949; Verna Arvey, "Still Opera Points the Way," *Music Forum and Digest* (August, 1949), 9–11.

opened in an inadequate theatre with little advance publicity. Most critics were lukewarm; George Jean Nathan, historically unresponsive to shows by black authors, left after the first act. Some, though, found much to praise. Edith Oliver of *The New Yorker* noted: "The Messrs. Hughes and Meyerowitz have tackled in *The Barrier* the most virulent and debilitating of all social diseases, prejudice, and they have done so in an uncompromising, even brutal manner. Their exposition of the hideous effects that prejudice leaves upon all segments of a society exposed to it . . . spares no one—neither the persecuted, the persecutors, the audience, nor the authors themselves." Miles Jefferson agreed with Oliver, finding that the Hughes and Meyerowitz opera compared favorably with Broadway's other operatic hit of recent days, Gian-Carlo Menotti's *The Consul* (1950), which ran eight months and received the New York Drama Critics' Award for best musical of the season. Nevertheless, *The Barrier* expired after a four-performance run.[10]

The mixed results of Hughes's varied theatrical efforts seemed to revive his cynicism about the Broadway theatre that had shown itself after his work on *Negro Revue.* Although he had originally lauded the postwar democratic boom in the theatre, he began to take a much more caustic look in his columns for the Chicago *Defender.* By 1953, his earlier opinions resurfaced: "White Americans control commercial entertainment for *white* Americans. There will be no complete revelation of Negro talent in entertainment in America until some areas of it are controlled completely by Negroes providing entertainment for their own racial group first, and only incidentally for others who wish to enjoy it." Privately, he also expressed concern about the different treatment of white and black authors in the Broadway theatre. After attending a performance of Albert Hague's new musical, *Plain and Fancy* (1955), about life among the Amish, he confided to Bontemps: "MGM already signing up Hague, and sent a car and chauffeur for his use opening night. See what happens to white! In US about as long as Meyerowitz. Culled here all their days and—!"[11]

Hughes endeavored to transform the current state of black entertainment on Broadway virtually on his own. While most "black"

10. *New Yorker,* January 28, 1950; New York *Times,* January 19, 1950; "No JC [*sic*] Dates for *Barrier,*" unidentified article, in "Theatre—*The Barrier*" File, SCCF/NYPL. Hughes's letter to the head of the Baltimore NAACP is also located in this file.

11. Langston Hughes, "Writer Laments Non-Existence of Permanent Negro Theatre in America," Chicago *Defender,* April 11, 1953; Nichols (ed.), *Arna Bontemps–Langston Hughes Letters,* 329.

musicals of the 1950s featured a few prominent black performers in shows created by whites, Hughes attempted to forge a new black musical entertainment based on black sources with black casts and for black audiences. *Simply Heavenly* (1957) was the first of a series of Langston Hughes musicals that attempted to revive black musical theatre from its lethargy of recent years. This new musical utilized familiar Hughes characters, Jesse Semple (Simple) and the patrons of Harlem's Paddy's Bar.

Simple and company had their origins in the Chicago *Defender* in 1942. Hughes initially used them as "a mouthpiece for the negativism prevalent among many ordinary Harlemites toward the war effort—a 'this is a white folk's war' feeling—based on discrimination in the Armed Forces and the most Hitler-like insult of all to colored peoples, the segregated blood banks the white folks had set up." As time passed, Simple mellowed and extended his barroom conversations beyond issues concerning racism and war. Simple finally was immortalized in book form in 1950, when Simon and Schuster published *Simple Speaks His Mind,* and later in *Simple Takes a Wife* (1953). *Simple Strikes a Claim* followed shortly afterward. The books were so successful, Hughes began to write a dramatic version of Simple's life. The first producers Hughes signed with desired a musical, so he collaborated on twenty songs for the show with composer David Martin. Unfortunately, the producers went bankrupt, and Hughes's new management team wanted a straight play. *Simply Heavenly* combined the early scripts and emerged officially as a "comedy with music."[12]

Simply Heavenly opened in a small theatre on West Eighty-fifth Street, somewhat far from the sites of earlier black musical triumphs. Although the reviews were favorable and business was hearty, the Fire Department noticed several violations and closed the theatre. The show attempted to move Off-Broadway, but no theatres were available. When a Broadway showcase became available, producer Stella Holt booked the Playhouse Theatre. The use of a Broadway stage demanded a few changes, especially the introduction of orchestrations for a full orchestra, a union requirement. As a result, this formerly intimate and somewhat modest show was, according to Hughes, "kicked right square to Broadway [by the Fire Department]."[13]

The critics greeted *Simply Heavenly* in a somewhat bewildering fash-

12. Langston Hughes, "The Happy Journey of *Simply Heavenly,*" New York *Herald Tribune,* August 18, 1957.

13. *Variety,* August 28, 1957.

ion. All agreed that it differed greatly from such current showcases for black performers as *Mr. Wonderful* and *Jamaica.* Critics went back to their history textbooks to search for theatrical antecedents. Lee Silver of the *Daily News* observed that it was the "first time in twenty-five years that a Negro musical of Negro authorship will be seen on Broadway." *Women's Wear Daily* harked back still farther, noting that this was "the first all-Negro musical to reach the Times Square area since the early 1920s when such works as *Shuffle Along, Liza,* and *Runnin' Wild* held forth." Such inaccurate comments reveal the extent to which the history of black musical theatre had been lost (or mangled) by the late 1950s. Additionally, some critics claimed that they were unable to understand the show, since it eschewed the traditions of these earlier black musicals. Gone were the tap-dancing, the graveyard sequences, and the Miller and Lyles malaprop humor. One critic asked why the show was such a disappointment, and a black woman sitting next to him explained, "We get things in this show you couldn't possibly react to." *Simply Heavenly,* as Hughes argued earlier, was written first for black audiences, and only secondarily for those whites who wished to attend.[14]

Simply Heavenly also differed from recent shows about black characters in that it allowed the protagonists to retain their culture rather than avoid it. The black musical characters in musicals created by whites tended to forget their heritage and way of life unless they resided on some Caribbean island. The fear of charges of stereotyping or prejudice often caused white authors to remove the blackness of their creations, so that these roles could almost as easily have been played by white performers. Here, such fears were dismissed, as revealed when Character comes to visit Paddy's Bar and dismisses Miss Mamie, the domestic, as a stereotype. Mamie is infuriated and replies:

> Why, it's getting so colored folks can't do nothing no more without some other Negro calling you a stereotype. Stereotype, hah! If you like a little gin, you're a stereotype. You got to drink Scotch. If you wear a red dress, you're a stereotype. You got to wear beige or chartreuse. Lord have mercy, honey, do-don't like no black-eyed peas and rice! Then you're a down-home Negro for true—which I is—and proud of it! I didn't come here to Harlem to get away from my people. I come here because there's more of 'em. I loves my race. I loves my people. Stereotype![15]

14. New York *Daily News,* August 8, 1957; *Women's Wear Daily,* August 22, 1957; New York *World-Telegram and Sun,* August 21, 1957.

15. Langston Hughes, *Simply Heavenly,* in *Five Plays,* 125–26.

Boyd, Simple's neighbor, is writing a book about the inhabitants of the bar. When he is asked whether the people in Paddy's Bar are stereotypes, Boyd explains: "In the book I'm writing they're just folks." These "folks" retained their culture, heritage, and personality in the age of Broadway integration.

The arrival and production of *Simply Heavenly* implicitly challenged Equity's solution for integration. Those involved in the presentation of the show hoped that "it will achieve a success on Broadway that will open the way for a new theatrical cycle in which more Negro writers and actors will be benefitted." While the goals resembled those of Equity, the means were to be different. In 1957, Broadway musicals still were stubbornly refusing to become integrated. Perhaps, then, integration was not to be the solution for black creative artists and performers. Instead, as O'Neal's yearly statistics revealed, the key factor affecting black participation in the Broadway theatre was not necessarily integration, but the creation of a new black theatre.[16]

Hughes worked virtually alone for the next several years to revive the black musical for the age of the civil rights movement. During the early 1960s, a Hughes musical appeared almost yearly on or Off-Broadway, and each caused a varying degree of controversy as they veered away from accepted patterns of black musical theatre. *Black Nativity* (1961), a black version of the Christmas story, attempted to integrate gospel music into the story of the birth of Jesus. When the initial title, *Wasn't It a Mighty Day?,* was changed during rehearsals, cast members Carmen de Lavallade and Alvin Ailey resigned, since they found the new title in "bad taste." Some suggested that the title was "racist" in the context of Broadway's new hopes for racial harmony and integration. One of the producers, Mike Santangelo, wrote the executive director of the SCLC to determine if the title was indeed racist and whether it should be altered. Wyatt Walker, a former assistant to Martin Luther King, Jr., replied: "As involved as I am here in the deep south, the word *black* is inoffensive to me; in fact, one of the wholesome results of the rising colored nations in the world is the new attitude for the use of the word *black* without a derogatory connotation." Rehearsals continued, and the new title was retained.[17]

When *Black Nativity* opened, the initial controversy was forgotten as critics warmly welcomed Hughes's new version of the Christmas story,

16. New York *Daily News,* August 8, 1957.

17. New York *Post,* December 3, 1961; Wyatt Walker to Mike Santangelo, n.d., in "*Simply Heavenly*" File, TC/NYPL. An unsigned handwritten comment casts doubt on letter's authenticity.

especially its strong emphasis on gospel music provided by Alex Bradford, Marion Williams, and Princess Stewart. Howard Taubman in the New York *Times* led the raves: "How these singers can belt out a religious tune! They sing with the afflatus of jazzmen in a frenzy of improvisation. The rhythms are so vibrant that they seem to lead an independent existence. The voices plunge into sudden dark growls like muted trombones and soar into ecstatic squeals like frantic clarinets." With such strong approval, *Black Nativity* had a successful New York run and then embarked on a European tour, which climaxed triumphantly at the Spoleto Festival. Back in America, *Black Nativity* appeared once again in New York and then toured twenty-two cities. The show had a major role in legitimizing gospel and (actual) black music in general on Broadway.[18]

Hughes followed his triumph with another musical that had gospel themes. *Tambourines to Glory* (1963), based on his 1958 novel, had been planned for several years. At one point, the Theatre Guild's Lawrence Langner had expressed interest in the project and had encouraged a 1960 tryout in Westport, Connecticut. When Langner died, the project was aborted. The surprise success of *Black Nativity* led producer Joel Schencker to try to revive interest in the show. Despite Schencker's optimism, the company found it difficult to attract backers for an all-black production. Several were dubious because the show would have been one of the few non-integrated shows on Broadway in that year. In a bizarre reversal, some potential investors even expressed the fear that whites denied jobs as actors in the show would picket the theatre. The whimsical Hughes offered to "let a white actor play the role of chauffeur," should there be pickets against the show's unusual form of reverse discrimination. The author later explained the absurdity of such complaints: "In the field of art, there is such a thing as a regional theatre, an ethnic theatre. I hope one day there will be a Negro theatre up in Harlem. There are both a place and a need for it. But in a play about Harlem—well, if you're doing *The Playboy of the Western World,* Negroes shouldn't go to picket the Irish either."[19]

Tambourines, like *Black Nativity,* used gospel songs. Some were traditional, and some had been written years earlier with gospel singer Jobe

18. New York *Times,* December 12, 1961. Between *Black Nativity* and *Tambourines to Glory,* a Hughes musical, *Gospel Glow,* received a brief presentation at Brooklyn's Washington Temple. Described as the "first Negro passion play," it strongly resembled *Black Nativity* in its structure and reliance on gospel music. For a brief description, see New York *Times,* October 28, 1962.

19. Lewis Nichols, "Poems To Play," New York *Times,* October 27, 1963.

Huntley, who had set Hughes's words to music. Initial attempts to record the songs were not successful, despite Mahalia Jackson's strong interest. Hughes later wrote a play centered on these gospel songs, but since no one expressed an interest over a three-year period, he produced a novel that evoked the spirit of the music. With the show's rebirth as a musical in the wake of *Black Nativity,* Hughes hoped to use the gospel sound before it became "so commercial [that] Mitch [Miller] will have it."[20]

Hughes first became fascinated with gospel music when he moved to Chicago as a teenager. When he heard the music of the local Holiness or Sanctified church, he was "entranced by their stepped-up rhythms, tambourines, hand-clapping, and uninhibited dynamics, rivalled only by Ma Rainey singing the blues at the old Monogram Theater." Gospel singing in the poorer black churches excited Hughes for its spontaneity and its improvisation. He marveled that no gospel music seemed to be sung in the same manner twice in a row. Hughes once overheard Mahalia Jackson's pianist ask her, "Why don't you sing it like you did the last time?" Jackson replied, "Because I don't want to, that's why." Each evening, whether in church or later in the theatre, gospel maintained that capacity to surprise Hughes, and he discovered new meaning in these songs each time he heard them.[21]

Although *Black Nativity* had incorporated gospel music in the telling of the story of Christ, Hughes argued that *Tambourines to Glory* was the first musical to use gospel music "as an actual part of the play itself." The former show simulated a church service, while Hughes's new creation integrated gospel music into its dramatic structure. The new play focused on the black storefront churches that had given birth to gospel. Here, a little true religion and a little phony evangelism combine as a small storefront church in Harlem becomes the luxurious Tambourine Temple. *Tambourines* refers to their use in gospel music and as collection plates at revival meetings. Most of the plot is more secular than that of *Black Nativity,* for example, but Hughes provides a new villain, Big-Eyes Buddy Lomax (Louis Gossett), who is actually the Devil in disguise. In this Harlem tale, God and the Devil fight for the souls of the founders of the new church, Laura Wright Reed (Hilda Simms) and Essie Belle Johnson (Rosetta LeNoire).

Critics greeted the gospel music of *Tambourines* with the same enthu-

20. *Ibid.*

21. Langston Hughes, "Gospel Singing: When the Spirit Really Moves," *New York Herald Tribune Magazine,* October 27, 1963, pp. 12–13.

siasm they had offered *Black Nativity.* Howard Taubman again found that "its gospel singing has the beat and feeling of hallelujah time," and on occasion he felt like participating in the proceedings. Nevertheless, a few other critics noticed a disturbing trend in these new black musicals, which, they complained, were no longer totally accessible to white audiences. Martin Gottfried of *Women's Wear Daily* noted that the musical was "deeply rooted in the ethnic patterns of the Harlem Negro. And in that may lie the drawback of this musical for many non-Negroes. The attitudes, humor, and physical flavor of a particular group hold an enormous amount of warmth and affection for its members. These very familiar things, which go to make up the individuality of a group, often become uninteresting and foolish to outsiders. There is a great deal in *Tambourines to Glory* that will appeal to Negroes much more than to white people."[22]

Hughes's final major musical offering, *Jerico-Jim Crow* (1964), differed from his recent works. Although these shows explored black cultural heritage, they were somewhat reticent about the current state of race relations in America. While the mere act of utilizing all-black casts and traditional black music while Broadway accentuated integration was in itself both a challenge and a comment. Nevertheless, the author's recent plays had hitherto avoided any contemporary criticism of American life. *Jerico-Jim Crow* abandoned Hughes's recent caution, by offering a history of black life in America from the time of slavery to the 1960s. Jim Crow, portrayed by white actor William Cain, reappears from generation to generation, much like the Devil in *Tambourines to Glory,* in a variety of guises. On some occasions he is a slaveholder, a white policeman, and a modern white southerner who sings "Better Leave Segregation Alone." Jim Crow continually harasses two young blacks, Gilbert Price and Hilda Harris, and two older blacks, Joseph Attles and Rosalie King. The music, both traditional and new, evoked the emotions and spirit of black history and culture.[23]

Although Langston Hughes appeared virtually alone in his attempt to revive the heritage of black musical comedy in the late 1950s, he was

22. *Women's Wear Daily,* November 4, 1963. See also New York *Morning Telegram,* November 5, 1963; New York *Journal American,* November 7, 1963; Langston Hughes, *Tambourines to Glory,* in *Five Plays.*

23. New York *Post,* January 13, 1964; *Village Voice,* January 23, 1964; New York *Times,* January 13, 1964; New York *Herald Tribune,* January 14, 1964; *Jerico-Jim Crow* typescript, in TC/NYPL. Hughes's autographed copy uses two hyphens in the title, but most publicity releases and reviews use only one, between *Jerico* and *Jim.*

soon joined by others in the early 1960s. The black musical, which had been shunned by most black creative artists during the previous decade, became a newly acceptable vehicle for expressing black themes and ideals. *Fly Blackbird* (1962) was the first in this new generation of black musicals. The show combined the talents of Dr. James Hatch, a white, and Clarence Jackson, a black, of the UCLA Theatre Arts Department. The authors claimed that their inspiration for *Fly Blackbird* was a speech by Martin Luther King, Jr., on the West Coast. A one-act play in its first formulation, the show was billed as "a new satirical musical about the Freedom Riders." After a successful run at the Metro Theatre in Los Angeles, producer Helen Jacobson moved the show to Off-Broadway. *Fly Blackbird* presented the conflict between two philosophies of civil rights. William Piper (Avon Long) and his daughter, a Sarah Lawrence graduate, believe "Everything Comes to Those Who Wait." On the other hand, the daughter's boyfriend Carl (Robert Guillaume) notes in song that things have to be changed "Now." Ultimately, Piper sees that Carl's notion is correct, and in a poignant final scene, he sings "Who's the Fool?" as he considers the error of his ways.

The Hatch and Jackson musical traveled to New York via Toronto and took influential critic Nathan Cohen by surprise. He saw that it differed profoundly from other black musicals that had visited the Canadian city over the years. Cohen argued that "there is something quite revolutionary about *Fly Blackbird.* It is not a play about Negroes for white people, but about Negroes for Negroes, to help the latter see themselves with more clarity and in a more significant context, to share a common body of traditions, trials, and thoughts unknown to the Caucasian in that sense, although a Caucasian was a co-author." Although Cohen was geographically distant from the titular center of the new black theatre, he sensed a change in new black musicals and dramas that were targeted for Broadway. Formerly, these shows, whether by black or white authors, were primarily for white audiences. By the early 1960s, black authors were returning to the genre, but were beginning to use musical comedy to speak primarily to black audience members. As co-author Jackson explained, "We're attempting to capture a mood, a sense . . . of what's going on."[24]

Ballad for Bimshire (1963) also directed its message to black theatregoers. This Irving Burgie–Loften Mitchell musical was a potent response to the white-created musicals about Caribbean life. Instead of

24. Toronto *Daily Star,* May 3, 1961; New York *Post,* March 22, 1962.

the "isn't life exotic?" vision offered by its Broadway progenitors, the show instead asked satiric questions about the nature of colonialism and underdevelopment in Bimshire (a nickname for Barbados). The creators hoped to ensure that black audiences would flock to the show. Instead of waiting for blacks to discover *Ballad for Bimshire,* Sylvester Leaks, who had specialized in black theatre parties (a relatively tiny phenomenon at this time), was hired to encourage blacks to attend this show. Before the opening, fifty theatre parties were waiting in the wings, an unprecedented number for a black-performed show. These "parties," unlike the traditional groups in the 1950s, brought in new black theatregoers, many of whom were attending an Off-Broadway show for the first time.[25]

Trumpets of the Lord, which opened just before Christmas, 1963, followed in the footsteps of *Black Nativity* and *Tambourines to Glory.* Author Vinnette Carroll adapted James Weldon Johnson's *God's Trombones: Seven Negro Sermons in Verse,* which was published in 1927. Johnson's work celebrated the black preachers he recalled from his youth in the South and as a young man in New York City. Although these preachers had often been depicted as comic figures in American popular culture, Johnson hoped to give them "the niche in which [they] properly belong: It was the old-time preacher who for generations was the mainspring of hope and inspiration for the Negro in America. . . . This power of the old-time preacher, somewhat lessened and changed in his successors, is still a vital force; in fact, it is still the greatest single influence among the colored people of the United States." What Johnson had succeeded in doing in 1927, Vinnette Carroll, director Donald McKayle, and stars Theresa Merritt, Cicely Tyson, and Al Freeman, Jr., accomplished in 1963. The electric gospel singing again captured the New York critics, and gave the show a healthy initial run, as well as a Broadway revival in 1969.[26]

Author Vinnette Carroll returned to the theatre with a work in a similar vein in 1965. Expanding her talents, she directed Langston Hughes's one-act *The Prodigal Son,* which joined Bertolt Brecht's *The*

25. New York *Herald Tribune,* September 10, 1963.

26. James Weldon Johnson, *God's Trombones: Seven Negro Sermons in Verse* (New York, 1969), 2–3; New York *Times,* December 23, 1963. Carroll's is actually the second musical adaptation of *God's Trombones.* A one-act version, with music by Robert Cobert and featuring Frederick O'Neal, enjoyed a brief run at the 41st Street Theatre in February, 1960. Also on the bill was another one-act play, *Shakespeare in Harlem,* "written" and directed by Robert Glenn, which adapted several of Langston Hughes's poems for the stage. See New York *Times,* February 10, 1960; New York *Post,* February 10, 1960.

Exception and the Rule on a double bill at the Greenwich Village Mews Theatre. Announced as a "gospel song-play," the work continued in the genre Hughes initiated in *Black Nativity.* Featuring Glory Van Scott, Philip A. Stamps, and Dorothy Drake, the new show, which joyously welcomed the prodigal son, proved to be Hughes's last theatrical work. He died in 1967 as the new black musical, which he had helped to foster, was beginning to flower once again.[27]

While Langston Hughes and others were reshaping the world of the black musical Off-Broadway, the Broadway musical moved only grudgingly into the 1960s. Although 1950s black musicals by white authors had ignored the question of race, it seemed that some slight changes were occurring in the new decade. The fall season of 1961 promised two relative oddities: musicals about miscegenation. How indeed could race be avoided by either Richard Adler's *Kwamina* or Richard Rodgers' *No Strings*?

Richard Adler had composed *Pajama Game* and *Damn Yankees* in the early 1950s, each of which ran for more than one thousand performances. When his able lyricist, Jerry Ross, died in 1955, Adler's career seemed to falter. *Kwamina,* a tale of the modern and the traditional in Africa, seemed to be his hope for a return to Broadway and yet another success. Robert Alan Aurthur's libretto focused on the conflict between British-educated physician Kwamina (Terry Carter) and his chieftain father. It also told of an interracial love affair between Kwamina and Eve (Sally Ann Howes), a British doctor visiting his African homeland.

The musical's themes were noble and generally unprecedented in Broadway musical history, but librettist Aurthur seemed unable to deal with the implications of his plot. Fearing to be too daring for Broadway audiences, Aurthur treated this love relationship with such restraint that critics barely noticed the subplot as *Kwamina* traveled on its tryout to Toronto and Boston. Indeed, that proved to be the show's undoing on the road. Critics lambasted Aurthur for ignoring the obvious questions the musical raised. Like many others, Nathan Cohen panned the show: "Mr. Aurthur fears the miscegenation theme. Whatever the reason he never allows their physical intimacy to extend beyond Eve flinging herself into Kwamina's arms at the Act I curtain

27. New York *Herald Tribune,* May 21, 1965. For the script of *The Prodigal Son,* see Langston Hughes, *Materials From the Vertical Files of the Schomburg Collection, 1926–1967,* Box 5, Microfilm, NYPL.

and walking hand-in-hand at the final curtain. The dialogue is discretion itself." Cohen then suggested that the authors were so successful avoiding the issues of race, they might as well make both leads white and forget about it altogether.[28]

Facing the Toronto reviews the next morning, director Robert Lewis replied, "What the hell! We're never going to play Montgomery, Alabama. We might as well say what's on our minds." Despite Lewis' bravado, the show changed little while on the road. It was still tentative in its approach to the major issues. While several New York critics welcomed Aurthur's ambition, Richard Adler's music, and Agnes De Mille's choreography, most dismissed the libretto. Howard Taubman, in particular, deplored the "tendency for some of the characters to become mouthpieces for a viewpoint rather than human beings." Critics still faulted the tentative presentation of the interracial romance, but white audiences in New York in 1961 found it somewhat daring. Norman Nadel of the New York *World-Telegram and Sun,* standing in the 54th Street Theatre lobby heard murmurs about the immorality of miscegenation. He devoted a special column to refuting that charge.[29]

One month later, Broadway welcomed another musical that had miscegenation as its theme. *No Strings,* the new Richard Rodgers musical, offered a variety of firsts. Here, the composer who had experienced fruitful partnerships with Lorenz Hart and Oscar Hammerstein II, was now going to supply his own lyrics for the first time on Broadway. Diahann Carroll, whom Richard Rodgers had admired since her days in Harold Arlen's *House of Flowers* (1954), would star as a Paris-based fashion model who falls in love with American photographer Richard Kiley. Rodgers had hoped to star Carroll in a show for many years. He attempted to utilize her in *Flower Drum Song* (1958), but the makeup artists "could not make her look sufficiently Oriental." Rodgers and Hammerstein chose Pat Suzuki in their musical version of life in San Francisco's Chinatown.[30]

Although *No Strings* focused on Kiley and Carroll's romance, Rodgers went to great lengths in the pre-opening public relations interviews to stress that "the musical . . . has absolutely nothing to do with any racist angle. 'We are not dealing with race relations. One of the

28. Toronto *Daily Star,* September 5, 1961.

29. Toronto *Daily Star,* September 7, 1961; New York *Times,* October 25, 1961; New York *World-Telegram and Sun,* November 7, 1961. The musical was financed by John Schlesinger, a South African industrialist with interests in mining, shipping, and real estate.

30. Lewis Funke, "Man Running Scared," New York *Times,* March 11, 1962.

reasons the setting is France is because such a situation is completely acceptable there. In our show the point never comes up. The role could be played by a white girl without a line being changed. We chose Miss Carroll because we've wished for a long time to see her in something on the stage.' " As a result of *No Strings*'s avoidance of obvious issues, the show received reviews similar to *Kwamina*'s (especially since Rodgers' show followed Adler's show within a month in both Toronto and New York). Norman Nadel took veteran Broadway playwright and *No Strings* librettist Samuel Taylor to task for his "timid story" when an audience clearly expected "forthright penetrating developments." Even the word usage muffled any questions about race. The words *white* and *Negro* were avoided, as was any mention of Harlem, the model's implied birthplace. Instead, model Carroll was born and bred "north of Central Park."[31]

It might be argued that the mere casting of an interracial couple as romantic leads in both *Kwamina* and *No Strings* was in itself a political statement for the Broadway of the early 1960s. Such a move seemed to validate Actors Equity's vision of an integrated Broadway in which blacks might portray roles intended originally for whites. Indeed, in *No Strings,* race appeared irrevelant, for, as Rodgers claimed, the fashion model might "be played by a white girl." Yet, as early as 1961, this vision of the mid-1950s seemed to be outdated by the quickening pace of the civil rights movement. In this context, the avoidance of issues concerning race at a time when race was being continually debated in government, in the courts, and in the mass media, a race-less image for the Broadway musical was clearly becoming irrelevant.

Miscegenation moved to center stage once again in Broadway's next white-written black musical, *Golden Boy* (1964), with Sammy Davis as its powerhouse star. As is often the case when a potent box office draw is signed for Broadway, thoughts of the script become secondary. Producer Hillard Elkins signed Clifford Odets to revise his 1937 play about a boxer's struggle to reach the top. British director Peter Coe, whose *Oliver!* had been both a London and a Broadway hit in 1960, was hired to repeat his magic. Coe hesitated at first, explaining that he "knew nothing of Harlem and its people." "Ah well," the producer replied, "we want you because you *don't* know anything about Harlem." Coe gamely took the reins of what would prove to be an extremely troubled show. Odets clearly found it difficult to update the lead character,

31. New York *Times,* November 26, 1961; New York *World-Telegram and Sun,* March 24, 1962.

Joe Wellington, for the 1960s. During the tryout, Joe evolved from a boxer to a violinist, a pianist, and, ultimately, a medical student. Odets died in the midst of this turmoil, and a former student, William Gibson, the author of *Two for the Seesaw* (1958), was brought in to save the libretto. He returned Joe to the world of boxing and gave him a white girlfriend, Lorna Moon (Paula Wayne). In the interim, Coe was fired because he "didn't know anything about Harlem," and film director Arthur Penn was brought in to rescue the enterprise.[32]

Normally such difficulties make the show an inevitable catastrophe, but Penn and Gibson doctored it into reasonable shape for the opening. Unlike earlier black shows written by whites, *Golden Boy* attempted to address issues that had been avoided. Joe's brother, a union organizer in the play, was converted into a civil rights leader. Wellington, rather than ignoring his origins, makes a trip to Harlem—yes, the word was actually uttered onstage—to visit his old friends. The visit becomes a production number, "127th Street," a satiric glance at the problems modern Harlemites were facing. Only in the subplot about miscegenation did librettist Gibson have trouble giving words to his protagonists, and evasion once again supplanted meaning. Nonetheless, *Golden Boy* received favorable reviews: there were accolades for the entire cast, especially veteran singer Billy Daniels. Shortly after its premiere the New York *Times* asked, "Are Inter-racial Stage Romances on the Rise?," and responded that "a trend could be in the making."[33]

Hallelujah, Baby! (1967), Broadway's last major white-written black musical in the 1960s, seemed to be the most ambitious. This new show by Arthur Laurents (libretto) and Jule Styne, Betty Comden, and Adolph Green (score) attempted to provide the history of the civil rights movement from the turn of the century to the present as seen in the lives of two black characters, Georgina (Leslie Uggams) and Clem (Robert Hooks), and Harvey (Alan Case), a white, all of whom remain ageless throughout the musical. The plot perhaps seems familiar—Langston Hughes used a similar technique in *Jerico-Jim Crow* a few years earlier. There is one key difference in *Hallelujah, Baby!*: the white character is not the Jim Crow figure, but Georgina's confidant, helper, and potential suitor. Laurents' historical survey as seen through Georgina is represented by her striving to be a popular entertainer in white society. Only in the last few moments of the evening does Georgina

32. London *Daily Mail*, July 24, 1965.
33. New York *Times*, November 8, 1964.

recognize the emptiness of efforts to pass into white society and embraces the civil rights movement. For most of the critics, though, the show was buried in the past, representative of the white dramas of the 1930s and 1940s, which seemed woefully outdated in the aftermath of Watts. Walter Kerr, now the major critic for the New York *Times,* may have approved of Uggams' performance, but in general he looked on the evening in sheer embarrassment: "The musical that . . . [has] been put together with the best intentions in the world is a course in Civics One when everyone else in the world has already got to Civics Six." In a follow-up review, Kerr added that "we sense the belatedness, the abstraction, the irrelevance to Now."[34]

Hallelujah, Baby! did have a few defenders among black theatregoers. Ralph Bunche wrote to the New York *Times,* arguing that it "was good enough for [him] that 'the problem' was dealt with forthrightly, and, here and there, by Broadway's standards, even a bit daringly." But several black critics agreed with Kerr's assessment. Lindsay Patterson, a playwright and a historian of black theatre, said: "He [Kerr] is to be congratulated, along with Lena Horne [who turned down a role in the show], for his rejection of a show that is 100 years too late."[35]

As onstage integration faded during the late 1950s, a similar phenomenon occurred in the creative arena as well. For the most part, white- and black-created musicals evolved separately. White musicals in the Broadway mainstream tended to avoid questions about race. Often the predominant reaction was a flight to exotic themes and foreign shores. New black musicals, particularly those by Langston Hughes, remained firmly ensconced in Afro-American life and culture. Rather than ignoring the real problems of race relations in the 1950s and 1960s, Hughes, Hatch, and Jackson addressed those concerns for American blacks in musical comedy form. While the white-created musicals might have provided a blissful escape from the growing civil rights movement of the 1950s, by the 1960s these shows became increasingly anachronistic. As a result, the works of such Broadway masters as Richard Rodgers, Richard Adler, and Jule Styne were unable to please the critics with their renditions of black musicals while lesser-known theatrical artists, such as Hughes, Hatch and Jackson, and Vinnette Carroll, to name a few, began to surprise both critics and audiences with a new form of black musical that responded to the dominant issues of the age. Additionally, these new musicals avoided

34. *Ibid.,* April 20, 1967, April 14, 1968.
35. *Ibid.,* May 14, 1967.

didacticism as they also provided a vibrant entertainment that white-designed black musicals had lacked in the previous decade. While Hughes provided the impetus, it was clearly only the beginning, as a new black musical was about to dominate Broadway in a manner comparable to the Golden Age of the 1920s, when critics began to speak of a new Black White Way.

XV

REVIVAL

In the years after Langston Hughes's death in 1967, the black musical was transformed from a marginal theatrical genre to a Broadway success story. A flood of awards greeted such new black musicals as *Purlie, Ain't Misbehavin', Raisin, Eubie!,* and *Dreamgirls.* The lead performers in these shows—Nell Carter, Robert Guillaume, Cleavon Little, and Gregory Hines—graduated to film, theatre, and television stardom. Behind the scenes, a younger generation of black writers, directors, choreographers, and scenic designers began to assume greater control over these ventures. White-created black musicals, such as *1600 Pennsylvania Avenue* and *A Broadway Musical,* continued to flail about desperately for an audience. The success of the black musicals also contributed to a black theatrical employment boom, swelling the paltry numbers of the 1950s and early 1960s. Although film versions remained the exception for most of these new black musicals, network and cable television partially filled the gap by supplying vast audiences. Additionally, while audiences for these shows had traditionally been predominantly white, a black Broadway audience began to grow in the 1970s. It was relatively small at first, but this new generation of black theatregoers ultimately helped to provide the economic boost necessary for the development of black dramatic and musical theatre.

The causes of this reversal in the fate of black musical theatre are many, but they are all tied to the growing irrelevance of the black musical by the early 1960s. This white cultural construct began to be perceived as increasingly out of step with the times not only by black critics and audiences but by whites as well. Kerr's review of *Hallelujah, Baby!* in the New York *Times* clearly stated this growing dissatisfaction.

New black musicals could no longer hope to ignore the major problems of the age or view them in a rosy light. The optimistic vision of *Hallelujah, Baby!* in the wake of Watts heightened the incongruity. Langston Hughes and others in the late 1950s and the 1960s foresaw a change of direction. In order to revive the forms of the 1920s for a new age, a black musical would have to address contemporary black concerns. Since whites had for years been increasingly unable, or unwilling, to treat such issues, black creative artists would once again have to shape a theatrical genre that had slowly been removed from their control since the early part of the Jazz Age. Not only would the writing and the style of the musical have to change, but its fundamental nature as well. Black Broadway musicals, whether written by white or black authors, had always been designed for white audiences. Questions and fears of their acceptance had shaped the black musical since its inception. Cole and the Johnson brothers worried about it, as did Sissle and Blake. Hughes and others argued that the new black musical had to free itself from the demands and prejudices of predominantly white audiences. Instead of writing shows for whites, authors of black musicals had to write for black viewers. And if black audiences were not there for these new productions (as many producers argued during the 1950s), then it became the responsibility of the shows' creators to search them out and foster a new generation of theatregoers.

The first hint of revival of the black musical was noticed in the caldrons of Off-Broadway, which experienced a boom during the late 1950s and early 1960s. Off-Broadway not only sheltered new and experimental forms of theatre from the high costs of Broadway, but it also had traditionally offered greater freedom of political expression than did its mainstream counterpart. Tiny Greenwich Village theatres with fewer than three hundred seats (which provided lower labor costs according to union contracts) became the haven for many black musicals in the late 1960s, much as the 1920s black musicals began in the less desirable and often more economical theatres. While Harold Arlen, Jule Styne, and Leonard Bernstein could command the huge sums necessary for a Broadway musical production, new talents found an economic refuge Off-Broadway where they could experiment with new theatrical formats for a select audience. Even Langston Hughes, the most prominent of the artists interested in black musical theatre, sought Off-Broadway houses for most of his new offerings. *Simply Heavenly,* as noted earlier, reached Broadway only by accident. With minimal costs for these shows, black artists were able to weather their period of exile and prove the black musical in a new environment.[1]

Also furthering the interest in black musical theatre was the concomitant revival of black drama in the early 1960s. With the surprise success of Jean Genêt's *The Blacks,* which opened in 1961 and ran for an unprecedented 1,408 performances, producers began to look more favorably on financing black-performed or black-created dramas. The conventional wisdom, that black dramas were inevitable flops, no longer seemed valid. *The Blacks* also introduced a new generation to several top black performers such as Cicely Tyson, James Earl Jones, Louis Gossett, Godfrey Cambridge, and Roscoe Lee Brown. Charles Gordone, who later won a Pulitzer Prize for *No Place To Be Somebody,* was also in the cast. Although Genêt was white, he set the tone for future offerings by asking the question that concerned many black dramatists in the 1960s: "But what exactly is a black?" He answered the question with such perceptiveness that Lorraine Hansberry later called him a "white Negro." The revival in black drama, which was certainly aided by the success of Genêt's play, ultimately gave the American stage classic works by LeRoi Jones (Amiri Baraka), Douglas Turner Ward, Ed Bullins, Charles Gordone, James Baldwin, Joseph A. Walker, and Charles Fuller, to name a few.[2]

Private funds supported most black productions during this period, but grants from public and private foundations encouraged black theatre throughout the United States. The most enduring institution, the Negro Ensemble Company (NEC), began producing plays of interest to black audiences in 1968 and continues to the present day. Its origins can be traced back to 1966, when Douglas Turner Ward, author of the successful double bill *Happy Ending* and *Day of Absence* (1965), wrote an article for the New York *Times* on black theatre organizations. Ward argued that the emphasis on such promising playwrights as Louis Peterson, Lorraine Hansberry, Ossie Davis, James Baldwin, and LeRoi Jones had obscured the true situation of blacks in the modern theatre: "Despite an eminent handful, Negro dramatists remain sparse in number, productions sporadic at most, and scripts too few to indicate discernible trends. (Last year, during a forum on 'What Negro Play-

1. Stuart W. Little, *Off-Broadway: The Prophetic Theater* (New York, 1972), 100–36.

2. Jean Genêt, *The Blacks: A Clown Show,* trans. Bernard Frechtman (New York, 1960); Little, *Off-Broadway,* 121–29; Mance Williams, *Black Theatre in the 1960s and 1970s: A Historical-Critical Analysis of the Movement* (Westport, Conn., 1985), 11–13.

wrights Are Saying,' not even panel members could cite enough plays to make the plural subject matter viable)." Ward suggested a "theatre concentrating primarily on themes of Negro life, but also resilient enough to incorporate and interpret the best of world drama—whatever the source."[3]

After the article's publication, the Ford Foundation invited Ward to develop a proposal for a new black theatre group. The foundation ultimately provided generous funding for the organization, which has trained many black performers, directors, writers, and backstage technicians. Although several critics initially argued that the NEC, by accepting the foundation grants, was creating a new form of dependence on white institutions, the theatrical company survived its first few difficult years and its search for an identity. Recently, however, the NEC has produced a host of successful presentations, such as *The River Niger* (1973), *Home* (1979), and *A Soldier's Play* (1981). Many have received major theatrical awards, and some have moved on to Broadway and have been televised or filmed.

While the NEC has primarily produced dramas and comedies during the past twenty years, other companies, such as the Urban Arts Corps, under the direction of Vinnette Carroll, have propelled several musicals from its workshops to Broadway. Harlem-born Carroll was originally trained as a psychologist before she turned to acting. She studied drama at the New School at the same time as future talents Marlon Brando and Rod Steiger, and she began teaching at the High School of the Performing Arts. Her students have included Cicely Tyson, Sherman Hemsley, Calvin Lockhart, and Jonelle Allen. During the 1960s she applied to the New York State Council on the Arts for the establishment of a theatre where "a black actor could have a place to learn his art and not have to rely on just being black to get a job." The Urban Arts Corps was founded in the late 1960s on West Twentieth Street, where it staged a variety of dramas and musicals by black artists with minority casts. The Urban Arts Corps became remarkably successful in the production of musical comedies—*Dont Bother Me, I Cant Cope* (1972) and *Your Arms Too Short to Box With God* (1976) became Broadway hits. Carroll's triumph with these musicals rather than dramas was partially unintentional. She explained that the chief reason she did musicals

3. Ellen Foreman, "The Negro Ensemble Company: A Transcendent Vision," in Hill (ed.), *The Theater of Black Americans*, II, 72–84; Clayton Riley, "We Will Not Be 'a New Form of White Art in Blackface,' " New York *Times*, June 14, 1970; Douglas Turner Ward, "American Theater: For Whites Only?" New York *Times*, August 14, 1966.

was that "white producers won't pick up anything intellectual by us, no matter how good it is. They only want the singing and dancing. It's where the quick money is."[4]

While many black artists utilized dramatic forms for their theatrical works throughout the 1960s, others turned to the newly refurbished black musical to explore black life and culture in the 1960s and 1970s. In doing so, they repudiated the sunny optimism of the white-created black musical, creating instead works that sought to understand the dynamic of Afro-American life in the United States. These changes in black musical theatre were clearly evident by 1971. Charles Gordone's *No Place To Be Somebody* featured a curious exchange that underscored this development. One character enters a bar and asks his friend: "How'd you make out at that audition?" The aspiring actor responds: "It was a musical. Musical about slavery!" Dramatic productions, such as *In White America* (1963), had discussed the importance of slavery, but black musicals often ignored this major and controversial issue in Afro-American history—unless it was in the context of dancing sunflowers in the good old South, as in the Lew Leslie revues. By the late 1960s, however, controversy was becoming the keynote of new black musical shows.[5]

The Believers (1968), written by Josephine Jackson and Joseph A. Walker, clearly signaled the transition to a new generation of black musicals. It opened just one year after *Hallelujah, Baby!*, but the twelve months seemed a millennium. Subtitled *The Black Experience in Song, The Believers* musically addressed issues that recent white-created musicals had avoided. If, indeed, these shows had any sense of history, they tended to view black life in America as beginning only after emancipation. *The Believers*, however, focused virtually the entire first act on the era prior to reconstruction. Here, black history began in Africa, where people were entrapped by white slavers and brought to America. Although slaves, blacks developed a new American culture from their African background, as revealed by their musical heritage. The second half of the show brought the history to the present day, asking tougher questions than did its Broadway counterpart *Hallelujah, Baby!*. Its contemporary numbers revealed the many possible directions the civil rights movement might take from "Burn This Town"

4. New York *Times*, December 19, 1976.

5. Charles Gordone, *No Place To Be Somebody*, reprinted in Lindsay Patterson (ed.), *Black Theater: A 20th Century Collection of the Work of Its Best Playwrights* (New York, 1971), 644.

to "Learn to Love." The New York *Times* noted the great change in the black musical on opening night: "*The Believers* has something to say about being a Negro in the United States that its predecessors (How quickly they have dated!) did not say. Instead of ending with a whimper of pain, or a cheerful (or threatening) plea for racial togetherness, *The Believers* ends with the crisp, jaunty rattle of an African drum."[6]

Despite several favorable reviews, *The Believers* faced many of the economic problems its predecessors had also confronted. Although rental for the Off-Broadway Garrick Theatre (and later the Cherry Lane) was minimal, and there were few expenses for costumes, lighting, and sets, audiences were slow to discover the show. In order to encourage attendance, the management supplied discount tickets to school groups and offered weekly discussions of the show after the performance. The audience was often half white and half black, a rather high ratio of black patrons for this period.[7]

Although the proliferation of black drama during the 1968–1969 Broadway season has led critic Dan Isaac to designate it the "moment in American cultural history when Black Theater came of age," the following season also saw a surge in the production of black musicals. Although these shows were of varying quality, almost all expressed strong opinions on the current state of race relations in the United States. *Buck White* was Broadway's first look at the new black musical. This show was based on an Off-Broadway hit, *Big Time, Buck White* (1968), which originated in Budd Schulberg's Watts Writers' Workshop. The original version features the preparations for a black militant leader, Buck White, who is to give a speech at a local hall. Buck finally arrives in Act II and answers questions from the audience (some real, some planted) about the current state of Black America. Most critics thought that the play, by white author Joseph Dolan Tuotti, provided a witty and knowing analysis of the recent black experience, and the show managed a moderate run. Black composer Oscar Brown, Jr., revised and directed the musical version and wrote the songs as well.[8]

Producer Zev Bufman's casting coup was his selecting one of the most controversial black figures of the age, Muhammad Ali (then known as Cassius Clay). That no doubt created extensive publicity for the show, but Ali may not have been the best choice for such a de-

6. New York *Times*, May 10, 1968.
7. *Ibid.*, July 15, 1968.
8. *Ibid.*, July 20, October 30, November 23, December 3, 7, 1969.

manding role. The show received favorable reviews for those portions that remained close to the earlier version. But the songs and Ali's performance failed to distinguish the musical version. The New York *Times* critic noticed that the audience nevertheless enjoyed the show. In an effort to emphasize this fact, the management asked Clive Barnes to attend a preview performance. Barnes witnessed the show with a "completely integrated audience," which, as he realized, was "a considerable remove from the usual first-night crowd." Barnes was accustomed to all-white opening nights, and so he was somewhat surprised by the "great time" the audience had. Nonetheless, word of mouth, that traditional theatrical savior, failed to work its magic, and *Buck White* disappeared within the week.[9]

Sambo opened two weeks later at Joseph Papp's New York Shakespeare Festival Public Theater, which had been receptive to works by black playwrights. Papp was still basking in the glow of the Pulitzer Prize for the previous season's *No Place To Be Somebody* when the theatre offered Ron Steward's "black opera with white spots," *Sambo*. The show received mostly unfavorable reviews because it abandoned several of the expectations of the musical comedy in its structure. There was no plot or book, according to the critics. Instead, the various characters presented their feelings in song, and Sambo was variously a "militant, drug addict, nationalist, spiritualist, entertainer, Son of Africa, child." The show, which faded quickly from Broadway, toured the city's parks during the summer months.[10]

Before *Sambo* closed, the New York *Times* printed a scathing review by black playwright Larry Neal. The show was, he said, "stale Papp" and a distant copy of that other Public Theater hit, *Hair*. What is significant about Neal's review is its signal that the *Times*, the prime source of theatrical opinion, had opened its pages to black writers. Neal's commentary was one of a series of follow-up reviews. Nikki Giovanni, Clayton Riley, and Peter Bailey attempted to explain the new black theatre movement to the newspaper's readers at a time when the regular reviewers Mel Gussow and Clive Barnes (a native of Britain) seemed slightly bewildered by these developments. The critiques revealed a wide variety of opinion, often surprising the white producers who assumed that all black critics would enjoy all black shows. When these expectations were confounded, angry letters to the *Times* objected to this new practice of double reviews. Despite the

9. *Ibid.*, December 4, 1969.
10. *Ibid.*, December 23, 1969; *Village Voice*, January 1, 1970.

diversity of opinion, these reviews (whether positive or negative) placed the shows in a historical context for the readers. At the same time, the practice also gave the best new black shows additional publicity and encouraged ticket sales.[11]

Billy Noname, Off-Broadway's first black musical in the 1970s, recounts the problems of growing up black in America from 1937, when Joe Louis became world heavyweight champion, to the evening of King's assassination. Black author William Wellington Mackey presents Billy Noname (Donny Burks) as a young man without a sense of identity in Act I. But in Act II, Billy Someone ponders whether to be a playwright or a militant or a nonviolent integrationist. Amid the philosophical discourse were several exciting songs, and dramatic choreography by Talley Beatty. The music received favorable reviews, but critics panned the book. *Billy Noname* had only a brief run.[12]

Purlie, the first black musical to reach Broadway during the 1970s, might at first have seemed a throwback to the white-created shows of the previous decade. While the producer and director (Philip Rose), the composer (Gary Geld), and the lyricist (Peter Udell) were white, the source of the show was Ossie Davis' 1961 comedy hit, *Purlie Victorious.* The inspiration for the Purlie tales was, strangely, *The World of Sholom Aleichem* (1953), a Broadway play for which Ossie Davis had been the stage manager. Davis was impressed by the vivid characters "with their gaiety, their fecklessness, the unembarrassed exhibition of their frailties, and their unity under terrible, sometimes terrifying conditions." Davis later hoped that *Purlie Victorious* would be the counterpart to Aleichem's Jewish characterizations. Davis starred as Purlie, who returns to his plantation home with the hope of buying an old house and converting it into a church. When his funds for the project disappear, he attempts to outwit the staunch segregationist Cap'n Cotchipee and obtain the money. *Purlie Victorious* was clearly a comedy, but Howard Taubman noted in the New York *Times* that "it unrelentingly forces you to feel how it is to inhabit a dark skin in a hostile, or at best, grudgingly benevolent world." Some ten years later, the creators of the musical *Purlie* hoped that it would have the same effect on modern audiences. In order to ensure the success of the new ven-

11. Larry Neal, "A Black View of *Sambo*: A Pitiful Answer to Doris Day," New York *Times,* January 11, 1970. For criticism of "black views," see New York *Times,* March 30, 1969, and July 12, 1970.

12. New York *Times,* March 4, 1970; *New Yorker,* March 14, 1970.

ture, Ossie Davis was hired as co-librettist (with Rose and Udell), and much of the original script was retained.[13]

Clive Barnes found the new *Purlie* "victorious," as did most of the other critics. Particular praise was given to the strong cast, which swept Broadway's major awards that season. Leads Cleavon Little and Melba Moore both won Tony and Drama Desk awards for their performances, and both topped *Variety*'s critics' poll. Moore also won a Theatre World Award, and Little received a New York Drama Critics Circle Award. Supporting cast members Sherman Hemsley (later CBS television's George Jefferson), Linda Hopkins, and Novella Nelson gave the evening a comic and a musical flair.

Despite widespread mainstream approval, *Purlie* had some difficult times at the box office. Producer Philip Rose hired Sylvester Leaks, the public relations director of the Bedford Stuyvesant Restoration Corporation, to attempt to increase ticket sales among black patrons. Leaks had attempted a similar task years earlier for Rose during the run of *Purlie Victorious*. He had extensive contacts with church, fraternal, and social organizations, and such groups might be encouraged to attend performances of shows like *Purlie*. Leaks, unlike all other ticket brokers, aimed for black theatre parties, which most Broadway agents had previously ignored. This effort ultimately aided *Purlie* and helped to extend its run to 688 performances. While Leaks's work cannot be considered the only reason for *Purlie*'s success, it put Broadway producers on notice that a potent source of ticket sales had been underutilized. Rather than ignore black audiences, producers might start to consider them as a part of the ultimate profit picture. *Purlie*'s efforts in this direction started a new push in the 1970s to bring a formerly invisible black audience to the Great White Way.[14]

Purlie introduced Broadway audiences to a new black musical that had a social message beneath the comedy. But it hardly prepared them for the most controversial shows of the 1971–1972 season, the musicals *Aint Supposed to Die a Natural Death* (1971) and *Don't Play Us Cheap!* (1972), by Melvin Van Peebles. Van Peebles had startled the film industry with *Sweet Sweetback's Baadasssss Song* (1971), which movie mavens and mainstream critics had dismissed as a bomb. Yet the movie sur-

13. New York *Times*, March 17, 1970; Ossie Davis, "I Kept Asking Myself What a Real Black Father Would Say About It," Philadelphia *Bulletin*, October 8, 1972; *Variety*, September 13, 1972.

14. *Variety*, August 19, 1970.

vived by word of mouth and turned a healthy profit due to the high revenues from black movie audiences that Hollywood had written off as nonexistent. *Sweet Sweetback* indicated to Hollywood that blacks were looking for films that might be of interest to them. Van Peebles thus indirectly started the "blaxploitation" film trend of the early 1970s, which specifically targeted black audiences. To a certain extent, *Aint Supposed to Die a Natural Death* attempted to do the same thing on Broadway.[15]

Aint Supposed was a far cry from the cheery plantation life of *Purlie*. Van Peebles focused on the populace of the slums of Harlem: the whore, the pimp, the corrupt black policeman, the beggar, the militant rifleman, the bag lady, and the homosexual queen, all of whom express their feelings in Van Peebles' songs. Clive Barnes commented on the abrupt departure from the past in this new musical: "Black is coming to Broadway these days, and I mean real black, not just someone singing 'Ol' Man River.' " Barnes continued, damning the new show with strong praise: "Whites can only treat *Aint Supposed to Die a Natural Death* as a journey to a foreign country, and on those terms it has the power to shock and excite. It is by no means a comfortable evening, and many Broadway theatregoers will not understand what it is saying." Clayton Riley, the entertainment editor of the *Amsterdam News* and one of the *Times*'s back-up critics, later tried to rescue the show from Barnes's confusion. Riley found that Van Peebles wove "a new black magic" and he hoped that theatregoers would have "the guts" to see *Aint Supposed to Die a Natural Death.*[16]

Most reviews were "mixed," which, George S. Kaufman once noted, meant "good and lousy." Some, such as George Oppenheimer of *Newsday,* found it an abomination, "a conundrum of ugliness, violence, tastelessness, and fury," while Brendan Gill of *The New Yorker* wished it a long run. Henry Hewes of *Saturday Review* wrote a curious appraisal, suggesting that the show was so good, it ought to leave Broadway: "*Aint* represents a new departure in musical theatre and in black drama and should be kept alive. How? It could move to Harlem's New Lafayette Theatre, where it probably could play many months to black audiences, and white theatregoers interested enough to make the journey uptown. Or it could move to the Negro Ensemble Company, where it would be supported by audiences that are mixed evenly between blacks and non-blacks." Marilyn Stasio of *Cue,* who found

15. "Melvin Van Peebles" files, in TC/NYPL and TC/PFL.
16. New York *Times,* October 21, November 7, 1971.

the new show "innovative and thoroughly original," attempted to explain the harshness of even the favorable reviews: "Embedded in the criticism was a keen sense of outrage that Van Peebles had dared break open the locked closet door of the ghetto and expose that gruesome skeleton for all the world to see. White critics particularly resented what they interpreted as Van Peebles' condemnation of *them*, as whites, for their causal role in the real-life creation of these human indignities." As a result of the tone of the reviews, Stasio found, "black and white theatregoers were united in their disinclination to look on poverty, despair, and suffering made bare."[17]

After the first reviews appeared, attendance dropped precipitously, but Van Peebles, no doubt remembering *Sweet Sweetback*, refused to let the show die. He tried a variety of ways to increase publicity and, consequently, attendance for the show. Van Peebles called on black entertainers such as Bill Cosby, Ossie Davis, Diana Sands, and Nipsey Russell to perform bits or songs in the show. Although these guest shots were announced, they were unable to stem the decline in sales. Despite Cosby's presence, for example, the house was only half full. Van Peebles also attempted to use the media to increase knowledge about his shows. White performers were often invited to appear on talk shows to discuss their latest theatrical triumphs and perform musical numbers, but television was hesitant about dealing with Van Peebles and his cast. Van Peebles noted that his appearances had been confined to "prime time black shows," which Cosby explained: "You know, they're on at 4 A.M." Van Peebles' continued complaints to the press did bring some action, however—and "Today" extended to Van Peebles its traditional invitation to Broadway performers and writers.

Van Peebles also relied on techniques that seemed to have helped *Purlie* (and certainly *Sweet Sweetback* as well), by attempting to increase the number of black theatregoers. Initially the audiences for *Aint Supposed* were evenly mixed, but as attendance dropped off, the white portion of the audience seemed to disappear. Within a short period, members of the company called churches, schools, and civil rights organizations, encouraging benefits or theatre parties. Discussions were held after matinees in order to create enthusiasm for the production and improve word of mouth. Congresswoman Shirley Chisholm led one of these discussion meetings and ultimately decided to announce her 1972 presidential bid from the stage of *Aint Supposed to Die*

17. *Newsday*, October 21, 1971; *New Yorker*, October 30, 1971; *Newsweek*, November 1, 1971; *Saturday Review*, November 13, 1971; *Cue*, November 27, 1971.

a Natural Death. These new marketing techniques helped Van Peebles' show survive for 325 performances, mostly on the strength of increased black turnout.[18]

Melvin Van Peebles was one of the few creators of musicals, whether black or white, to have two shows open on Broadway in the same season. Seven months after the premiere of *Aint Supposed,* Van Peebles returned to the boards with another black musical, *Don't Play Us Cheap!,* which received sparkling reviews. Part of the reason for the warm reception was that the show differed greatly from his previous venture. *Variety* explained the difference in a remarkably straightforward fashion: "Unlike *Aint,* this new show does not seem to be infused with hate, and it offers what appears to be a racial attitude without foul language, deliberate squalor, or snarling ugliness. The points are made with humor rather than rage and they are probably more palatable and persuasive for general audiences."[19]

Van Peebles told a joyous tale of a Saturday night rent party in Harlem and a mysterious encounter with two demons who assume human form in order to wreck the festivities. One demon ultimately relents when he falls in love with the lady of the house. The high spirits of the evening led to critical praise from a variety of quarters, from Clive Barnes to Nikki Giovanni, author of *Gemini,* who found it a sheer pleasure to see herself on stage: "I take a certain pride that someone could put a set on Broadway of a Harlem apartment with a door that has five locks on it, a mirror in the living room that frames photographs of Martin Luther King, Malcolm X, Adam Clayton Powell and John Kennedy, with Aretha Franklin peeping through. Not that my life is a stage but that someone can say " 'Hey, it's all right to be joyful about it.' " Magnificent performances highlighted the evening, especially by Avon Long, Rhetta Hughes, and Esther Rolle (later the star of Norman Lear's CBS television show "Good Times"). *Don't Play Us Cheap!* failed to match the run of Van Peebles' earlier show, though it survived the summer of 1972 and continued into the fall. Nonetheless, the show was one of the few modern black musicals to be filmed, though the motion picture, which was produced by the multitalented Van Peebles, was completed prior to the Broadway production.[20]

18. New York *Daily News,* September 24, 1971, January 7, 1972; New York *Post,* February 5, 1972.

19. *Variety,* May 24, 1972.

20. New York *Times,* May 18, 28, 1972; *New Yorker,* May 27, 1972; Nikki Giovanni, "I Get a Charge From Seeing Myself On Stage," New York *Times,* May 28, 1972.

Van Peebles was not the only dynamo of the 1971–1972 season. *Dont Bother Me, I Cant Cope* (1972) also brought to the fore people who might also restructure the new black musical theatre. Vinnette Carroll, the author of *Trumpets of the Lord* and the director of *The Prodigal Son,* also directed the first major success of the Urban Arts Corps, *Dont Bother Me, I Cant Cope.* Written by and starring Micki Grant, who had starred in earlier Off-Broadway productions such as *Fly Blackbird* and *Jerico-Jim Crow,* the new musical had a more optimistic stance than had Van Peebles' works. Grant explained: "I believe there is room for all kinds of theatre; it doesn't have to be one or the other. There's room for angry Black theatre and there's room for a show like ours, a show that has pride and dignity and music that is indigenous to our background. The show is *us,* and we hope we are communicating to everyone. We are not doing this show to be *separate.*" Grant also said that "this is considered sacrilege by some people today." Indeed, the show received harsh words from black critics for its deviation from the current problem-oriented goals of the black musical. Additionally, she noted that she was writing for the whole community, not just black audiences. Her positive description of Afro-American life attracted wider audiences than had earlier black musicals, and it ran for 1,065 performances.[21]

Raisin (1973), to a great extent, resembled *Purlie* (1970). Although white talent dominated the creative aspects of the production, with Judd Woldin and Robert Brittan writing the songs, the show maintained strong links to its earlier incarnation, *A Raisin in the Sun* (1959) by Lorraine Hansberry. Robert Nemiroff, Hansberry's husband for a time, co-authored the libretto (which relied closely on the original) and produced the show. Hansberry, however, never saw the musical production of her work. She died of cancer in 1965.

Hansberry's *A Raisin in the Sun* was a Broadway landmark in 1959. The first work by a black female dramatist to appear on Broadway, the show defied all naysayers and had a successful run. Hansberry won the New York Drama Critics Circle Award against such formidable competition as Tennessee Williams (*Sweet Bird of Youth*), Archibald MacLeish (*J.B.*), and Eugene O'Neill (*A Touch of the Poet*), and she was the first black dramatist to receive such an honor. The play examined the

21. New York *Sunday News,* April 20, 1972; *Variety,* April 26, 1972; *Amsterdam News,* July 22, 1972. For information on Micki Grant, see *Essence* (November, 1972), 32; and New York *Times,* May 7, 1972.

life of the Younger family, who wished to leave the slums of Chicago and move to the suburbs. Lena Younger, the matriarch, nursed this dream for her family after her husband's death. Hindering the Younger family's plans, however, is the all-white suburban association, which is willing to pay the family not to move into their neighborhood. Son Walter Lee Younger (Sidney Poitier) is tempted by the offer, but Lena refuses to let her dream die, and the move to the suburb continues. The play provided juicy roles for the theatre's most talented black performers: Claudia McNeil, Ruby Dee, Sidney Poitier, Diana Sands, Ivan Dixon, and Louis Gossett. Even future dramatists Lonne Elder III and Douglas Turner Ward appeared in minor roles. The play remained on Broadway for 530 performances, surpassing the record for a black dramatist set by Langston Hughes's *Mulatto*. Hollywood beckoned, and the property was soon filmed by Columbia Pictures, with several cast members reprising their original roles.[22]

The musical version of *Raisin* began its theatrical life at the Arena Theatre in Washington, D.C., far from Broadway's commercial glare and high expenses. Initial critical response was favorable, so Nemiroff was able to raise $500,000 for a Broadway showcase. (The Washington production had only cost $60,000.) After a lengthy tour, the new *Raisin* received as warm a welcome as its progenitor. Clive Barnes found the show's strengths in its ability to retain the best of Hansberry along with the new musical staging and performances. As a result, noted Barnes, "it became a show with a heartbeat very much of its own." *Raisin* did admirably during the yearly awards. Virginia Capers won a Tony for the best performance by an actress in a musical. The show itself won the Tony for best musical, and co-stars Joe Morton, Ralph Carter, and Ernestine Jackson earned Theatre World Awards for their contributions.[23]

Much of the credit for the new *Raisin* must be given to director-choreographer Donald McKayle, who helped convert the new show into a musical. A friend of Hansberry's from her teenage years, McKayle began dancing as a youth, and within a short time he founded his own dance company. He had directed or choreographed theatrical works earlier, such as *Trumpets of the Lord*, but *Raisin* was his first Broadway assignment. His key was to work on choreography and music first, allowing the libretto, which had already proven itself, to

22. See Robert Nemiroff, *To Be Young, Gifted, and Black: Lorraine Hansberry in Her Own Words* (Englewood Cliffs, N.J., 1969); Ernest Kaiser and Robert Nemiroff, "A Lorraine Hansberry Bibliography," *Freedomways*, XIX (1979), 285–304.

23. New York *Times*, May 31, 1973.

follow. As a result, *Raisin* excelled in both its dramatic and musical elements, and the show ran for 847 performances.[24]

The social relevance of early 1970s black musicals admittedly remained stronger Off-Broadway than on, with the sole exception of Van Peebles' shows. Nevertheless, both *Purlie* and *Raisin* combined entertainment and a message. *Purlie* did it with humor; *Raisin* with its family drama. *The Wiz* (1975), however, the next major black musical, seemingly dismissed the worries of the age. This musical found its inspiration in L. Frank Baum's tales from the turn of the century and in the succeeding plays and films that had rendered the saga of Dorothy familiar to all. Admittedly, the most difficult task for the creators of the new show would be challenging the most enduring version, the 1939 MGM film that starred Judy Garland, Bert Lahr, Jack Haley, and Ray Bolger. The formula for *The Wiz* involved placing Dorothy and company in a different context. The music, the choreography, the sets, and the costumes would all reflect contemporary black life rather than the mythical Kansas barnyard on MGM's back lot.

Ken Harper, a black producer, sponsored the show with the help of $1.2 million from Twentieth Century-Fox, and Gilbert Moses and George Faison were hired as director and choreographer. *The Wiz* ran into trouble during its tryout run, and a variety of doctors were summoned to help the ailing show. Costume designer Geoffrey Holder, who had originally been contacted to direct the show, assumed control for the Philadelphia and Detroit tryouts, and he gave the show a coherent vision. Reviews were mixed after *The Wiz* arrived in New York, but the negative notice in the *Times* was a sure death knell for the production. Nevertheless, Twentieth Century-Fox pumped additional money into an advertising campaign in an attempt to save the show. The money, instead of going to newspaper advertisements, was channeled into a television commercial that emphasized the colorful choreography and contemporary music of *The Wiz.* Although a relatively new method of theatrical advertising, it had been successful in recent years in breathing life into struggling shows. *Pippin,* which co-starred Ben Vereen, was acknowledged as one of the most recent beneficiaries. The television spots attracted more business soon after their showing.[25]

24. Donald McKayle, "*Raisin* as Life: An Inside View," *Amsterdam News,* October 20, 1973; New York *Times,* October 28, November 4, 1973.

25. *Encore,* April 21, 1975; *Variety,* February 26, 1976; Williams, *Black Theatre in the 1960s and 1970s,* 101–104. For information on Geoffrey Holder, see New York *Times,* May 25, 1965.

Tiger Haynes, Hinton Battle, Stephanie Mills, and Ted Ross in *The Wiz*
Courtesy Martha Swope

There was also a campaign in the black community to counter the major critics. The *Amsterdam News* led the way with a "special editorial" entitled "Now It's the Drama Critics." The paper attacked their ambivalence and recommended "this most unusual satire highly": "The play is one which should be supported by the black community since its demise may come as a result of the inability of the 'mainstream play killers' to respond to a white story satirized by Blacks, produced by Blacks, sung by Blacks, and seen predominantly by Blacks on opening night. The audience welcomed *The Wiz* with open arms (seven curtain calls)." The word *satire* appeared often in this editorial, underlining the notion that the white critics for the major newspapers and weekly magazines were unable to understand this modernized tale of a black Oz. Even the New York *Times* admitted this in a follow-up review, which argued that *The Wiz* may "say something extra to blacks." Bryant Rollins found that *The Wiz* was "full of symbols and associations, obvious and obscure, that relate to crucial aspects of the black experience and culture. The main themes running through the show are slavery and emancipation, the black church and religion, the great black migration from rural south to urban north." In this context the Emerald City became a revised vision of Harlem through the fantasies of such films as *Shaft* or *Superfly.* This black vision, which white audiences could not decipher, apparently brought black organizations and theatre parties to *The Wiz.* There were often black majorities for the weekend matinees, though the Wednesday matinee, long a white theatre party bastion, remained 60 percent white.[26]

After a shaky beginning, *The Wiz* began to approach sell-out status and ultimately won seven Tony Awards, including best show and best director. In its continuing attraction for both black and white audiences, *The Wiz* seemed to be the ideal nominee for a "crossover" hit. Perhaps for this reason, and the financial backing of Twentieth Century-Fox, *The Wiz* was the only black musical of the 1970s to be filmed by a major studio. Nevertheless, the motion picture, which featured Diana Ross and Lena Horne, failed to duplicate the show's magic at the box office.

With the financial success of *The Wiz,* new black musicals retreated from the "problem" shows of the early 1970s. Racism, segregation, lynchings, and discrimination, issues emphasized in previous years, were now avoided. Clearly, musicals that attracted blacks but refused

26. *Amsterdam News,* January 11, 1975; Bryant Rollins, "Does *The Wiz* Say Something Extra to Blacks?" New York *Times,* December 28, 1975.

to alienate whites were most likely to be profitable. Some might argue that *The Wiz* ignored contemporary black life, but it still drew on Afro-American culture in its music, choreography, design, and libretto. This seemed to be one of the lessons of *The Wiz*. Instead of addressing solely the difficulties of black life in America, a new musical might draw on positive aspects of black culture and history for inspiration and style. That notion became the hallmark of a string of highly successful black musicals that emerged in the late 1970s. Their source was the rich heritage of Afro-American popular entertainment, a celebration of black history and life. Historical figures and eras that had been neglected or ignored now became the source for post-Bicentennial black musicals that looked to new, and less controversial, directions in Afro-American history.

The 1975–1976 season offered two new black musicals that explored different aspects of black entertainment. The first, *Me and Bessie* (1975), featured Linda Hopkins, who had recently won a Tony for her performance in *Inner City* (1971), in a historical evocation of the life and music of Bessie Smith. Hopkins walked to center stage and admitted to the audience: "I ain't Bessie. But, you know there's a lot of Bessie in me." Then in a combination of anecdotes, reminiscences, and songs, Hopkins brought the legend of Bessie Smith back to life. The shows hits included renditions of "Romance in the Dark," "There'll Be a Hot Time in the Old Town Tonight," and "Empty Bed Blues." The show enjoyed almost a year-long run at Broadway's Ambassador and Edison theatres.[27]

Bubbling Brown Sugar (1976) provided a historical tour of black entertainment on Broadway and in Harlem from the turn of the century through the 1940s. This cavalcade offered glimpses into the performances of Bert Williams, Billie Holiday, Duke Ellington, and others from the heyday of Harlem night life. The show originated at the AMAS repertory theatre as a tribute to the music of Sissle and Blake; the director was Rosetta LeNoire. An attempted move to Broadway was stalled when legal problems arose about presenting their songs. As a result, writer Loften Mitchell helped to expand the show's concept to include many of the great black entertainers and their music. Mitchell was criticized, however, for moving toward escapism and away from the social relevance of the black musicals of the early 1970s. Mitchell, however, disputed this notion, finding a new relevance in his resurrec-

27. New York *Times*, March 19, 1976.

tion of black entertainment history: "I would hope that this play would cause a rethinking in terms of the black community. I would hope that it would have some kind of contagious effect, a chain reaction that would make folks say, 'look a here, we ain't all that poor. We may be broke, but we're not poor.'" For Mitchell, also a noted historian of black theatre, an exploration of the black past could be a source of identity and pride for the black community.[28]

While *Bubbling Brown Sugar* triumphed at the ANTA Theatre, Broadway saw one of the last all-white-created "black musicals" founder at the Mark Hellinger. Once again, top talents were involved in the creation of *1600 Pennsylvania Avenue.* Alan Jay Lerner joined with Leonard Bernstein to create this new Bicentennial musical. On the surface, the show recounted a musical history of several major presidents and their wives. Yet Lerner's true interest was the domestic staff of the White House, the black servants who represented the marked contrast between the ideals and the reality of the American Constitution. This musical "Upstairs, Downstairs" was born out of Lerner's increased frustration over the slow pace of change in race relations in the United States. Conceiving the musical as a source of social change through education (as Langston Hughes had earlier), Lerner and Bernstein hoped the musical would ultimately improve racial harmony. Despite these high ideals, the show failed in some of its characterizations of black characters. For example, according to Gilbert Moses, the original libretto underestimated the intelligence of the White House servants. At a picnic, a magician's tricks terrify the black onlookers, who had supposedly never seen such awe-inspiring legerdemain. The sequence was jettisoned from the final version of the show.

The response of Lerner and Bernstein to the growing theatrical disaster was to fire director Frank Corsaro. This, in itself, was not unusual. What was, however, was the recruiting of Gilbert Moses and George Faison as co-directors. Moses had directed plays by Baraka and Bullins, as well as Van Peebles' *Aint Supposed to Die a Natural Death*; Faison had recently won plaudits for his choreography of *The Wiz.* By turning control over to a black production team, Lerner and Bernstein seemingly admitted that only black creative talent could save a show

28. Loften Mitchell is the author of *Black Drama: The Story of the American Negro in the Theatre* (New York, 1967), which certainly provided a historical framework for *Bubbling Brown Sugar.* See also *Ebony* (February, 1976), 125; *Amsterdam News,* March 6, 1976; and New York *Times,* March 25, 1977.

that was about black life. A white vision was once again out of place in the context of the 1970s. Ultimately, Moses and Faison could not save *1600*—it was too late to totally restructure the show. However, they did remove several embarrassing sequences and strengthen the motivations of the black characters. They also created a harmony among black and white cast members that had been missing from the beginning. For example, Moses noticed that rehearsals for black and white cast members had been held separately, thus increasing a sense of segregation. Black cast members were more willing to accept direction from Moses than from Corsaro. Nonetheless, the triumph of Moses and Faison was largely symbolic, for white creators would clearly have increasing difficulties in presenting the spirit, feelings, and desires of blacks within the context of the old-style black musical. One later attempt, *A Broadway Musical* (1978), with music and lyrics by *Bye, Bye, Birdie*'s Charles Strouse and Lee Adams, attempted to spoof these white-created black musicals, but it, too, faded quickly from Broadway.[29]

Midsummer greeted a new black production of *Guys and Dolls.* This 1950 Pulitzer Prize musical owed its revival to the recent success of *Bubbling Brown Sugar.* Producer Moe Septee turned to that show's choreographer and asked Billy Wilson what he wanted to do next. Wilson had directed a traditional version of the show some years earlier at Brandeis University, where he was the head of the dance program, and he was taken by the similarities between the Damon Runyon characters and the modern black experience. He later attempted to reconceive the original show in black terms. This was somewhat difficult, as original librettist Abe Burrows had approval over the new script and was somewhat hesitant to change the dialogue. As a result, Wilson's changes were primarily in the tempo of the music and the style of choreography. The show received generally favorable reviews, but it was trapped between old and new. Despite the performances of Robert Guillaume, Ernestine Jackson, Norma Donaldson, and Ken Page, *Guys and Dolls* had only a modest run.[30]

Vinnette Carroll returned to Broadway at Christmas with a gospel version of the Book of Matthew. While the last days of Christ were clearly central to the musical, Carroll later admitted that she saw Christ as a Martin Luther King, Jr., figure, a "man who was saying things that people didn't want to hear." *Your Arms Too Short to Box With God* had

29. New York *Times*, May 2, 1976.
30. *Ibid.*, July 18, 23, 1976.

initially been commissioned by the Italian government for the Spoleto Festival in 1975. Once again this Carroll production found its beginnings in the Urban Arts Corps. Alex Bradford (of the Bradford Singers) provided the music, with additional songs by *Dont Bother Me, I Cant Cope* veteran Micki Grant. The show harked back to gospel traditions within the black church and also, in a theatrical sense, to Langston Hughes's gospel musicals. From the opening number, "We're Gonna Have a Good Time," which set the tone for the evening, critics and audiences welcomed the show. Critics were particularly dazzled by the voices of William Hardy, Jr., Salome Bey, Clinton Derricks-Carroll, and Delores Hall, who had been singing gospel music since she was a child. Hall was honored with a Tony Award for her electrifying singing talents. After a year-long run, *Your Arms Too Short* toured sixty-six American cities, returning to Broadway in June, 1980, to the Ambassador Theatre.[31]

The following season's *Timbuktu!* (1978) seemed yet another black musical caught between past and present. The source was a white musical, *Kismet* (1953), with music by Alexander Borodin, adapted by George Forrest and Robert Wright. The original librettist, Luther Davis, also returned to revise the script and produce the show. Davis decided to give *Kismet* a black setting and move the story to Timbuktu in the fourteenth century. He explained that "there were many sophisticated cultures in Africa, and I thought it was important for people to know that and not put the Africans down in the primitive book all the time." Geoffrey Holder, who had shaped *The Wiz,* was hired to perform similar magic with *Timbuktu!,* and Eartha Kitt was lured out of semi and somewhat enforced retirement to play the siren Sahleem-La-Lume. Once again, the performers (particularly Kitt) received high praise for their efforts, but the outdated libretto caused interest in *Timbuktu!* to flag. Its 221-performance run barely lasted through the summer of 1978.[32]

Ain't Misbehavin' returned the black musical to center stage in May, 1978, with another survey of the history of black musical theatre. The show provided a look at the songs of Fats Waller, performed by Ken Page, Armelia McQueen, Charlaine Woodward, Andre De Shields, and Nell Carter. The show originated in the tiny Manhattan Theatre Club.

31. *Amsterdam News,* March 19, 1977; New York *Sunday News,* December 19, 1976; New York *Times,* January 23, 1977.

32. Luther Davis, "Rewriting *Kismet* Into *Timbuktu,*" *Theatre Review* (January, 1978), 58.

where Richard Maltby, Jr., realized that few potential cast members had seen or even heard of Fats Waller. Much of his music had seemingly passed into oblivion, and his publishers were unable to supply copies of the songs. Maltby also hired black choreographer Arthur Faria and orchestrator Luther Henderson to provide the style for the song cavalcade. Faria created an aura of 1930s and 1940s musical entertainments that captured the mood of Waller's compositions. The show's premiere proved a startling success, and it quickly moved to Broadway's Longacre Theatre. After the show won three Tony Awards (for best musical and for Maltby and Carter), it created a new interest in the music and personality of Waller, who had died in 1943 at age thirty-nine.[33]

Eubie! opened the following season with yet another cavalcade of the talent of "Black Broadway." While *Ain't Misbehavin'* continued its tribute to Waller at a nearby theatre, this new show offered homage to the long-forgotten talents of Eubie Blake, who had helped to initiate the golden age of black musical comedy with *Shuffle Along* in 1921. The key to the success of *Eubie!* was the sense of the historical period in the song numbers, as a nostalgic glow suffused the entire evening. Henry LeTang and Billy Wilson capitalized on one of the high points of the 1920s black Broadway—tap-dancing. Leading the cast in this regard were Gregory and Maurice Hines, formerly the child stars of Hines, Hines, and Dad. They had appeared on Broadway only once before, as children in *The Girl in Pink Tights* (1954), but in *Eubie!* they used their tapping feet to propel them to stardom. Their performances, along with the range of Blake's repertory, helped the show to a respectable run, even though it opened in the midst of a newspaper strike, an unforeseen event that has been known to kill many a lesser show.[34]

Eubie! also played a major role in clarifying Eubie Blake's contribution to the history of black musical theatre. After the collapse of *Shuffle Along of 1952,* Blake virtually disappeared from the public eye, and his reputation faded. Blake's resurrection can be traced to two events, the John Hammond recording sessions by Blake for Columbia Records in 1968 and 1969, and Robert Kimball and William Bolcom's biography, *Reminiscing With Sissle and Blake* in 1973, which recalled the earlier triumphs of black musical theatre. *Eubie!* finally returned the hero of

33. New York *Sunday News,* April 23, 1978; *Time,* June 5, 1978; New York *Times,* May 7, 10, 21, 1978.

34. *Village Voice,* November 24, 1978. For information on Gregory Hines, see New York *Times,* November 24, 1978.

the 1920s to the Broadway stage, and introduced new audiences to the songs and piano work of a master. Well into his nineties, Blake continued to perform for audiences throughout the United States and Europe, re-igniting memories of the heyday of black Broadway.

The string of black musical hits led producers to seek new properties for the 1979–1980 season, which featured more black musicals than had any season since the 1920s. As this bandwagon effect accelerated, the quality of each succeeding show varied widely. A few flopped outright. *But Never Jam Today,* a musical version of *Alice in Wonderland,* had long been planned by the Urban Arts Corps, but no version had proved workable. A 1978 effort sponsored by the producers of *Annie* with music by Micki Grant flopped in Philadelphia. The latest attempt reached Broadway in July, 1979, but it lasted only a week. *Comin' Uptown,* a black musical version of *A Christmas Carol,* with Gregory Hines as Scrooge, utilized some of the talents behind *Raisin,* but it expired within the month. *Reggae,* from the producer of *Hair,* hoped to popularize the music of Jamaica for Broadway in the same fashion that his earlier show introduced rock music to the theatrical scene. Critics did admit to enjoying the music, but most lambasted the libretto by Melvin Van Peebles and swiftly sent the show on its way.

The two critical successes of the season considered aspects of the history of black popular entertainment. *One Mo' Time* (1979) returned to the heyday of black vaudeville in the 1920s. Vernel Bagneris, who remembered his grandmother's tales of the famed Lyric Theatre in New Orleans, provided a typical evening for modern audiences. With echoes of Ma Rainey, Bessie Smith, and Ethel Waters, the show provided an ideal historical re-creation of the period in which TOBA (Theatre Owners Booking Agency or "Tough on Black Actors") controlled the destiny of these itinerant talents. The show's success spawned a London production and a touring company as well. As *One Mo' Time* moved from its original berth at the Village Gate Theatre, additional dialogue was added to convey the difficult relationship between the black performers and the white theatre manager. Critics raved about the show, with *Time* magazine noting that "from one minute to the next, *One Mo' Time* is a hot, wild, ribald and rousing delight."[35]

The 1979–1980 season culminated with *Black Broadway,* a cavalcade of black music and entertainers who had graced Broadway

35. New York *Times,* December 7, 1979, August 31, 1980.

since the turn of the century. Originating at the Newport Jazz Festival, this revue reunited some of the greats of black musical history. John W. Bubbles, the original Sportin' Life from *Porgy and Bess,* was now confined to a wheelchair, but he returned undaunted to sing "It Ain't Necessarily So." Edith Wilson, who made her debut on the Town Hall stage in 1921 in *Put and Take,* was also in the production. So was the originator of Broadway's "Charleston" in *Runnin' Wild,* Elisabeth Welch, who had been performing in London during the past few decades. Adelaide Hall also arrived from London to sing "I Can't Give You Anything But Love," the song she premiered with Bill Robinson in *Blackbirds of 1928.* The younger generation of black Broadway talents also lent able support to these veterans: Bobby Short, Gregory Hines, and Nell Carter gave a contemporary turn to several old standards. Although in residence for only a limited run, *Black Broadway* served to reconcile the history of black theatre and the interest in black drama and musical comedy.[36]

Sophisticated Ladies (1981) completed the contemporary reexamination of the major figures of Broadway's black musical heritage. This tribute to Duke Ellington became the most complex of the recent historical revues, since the composer, unlike Blake or Waller, only rarely channeled his talents toward the musical theatre. His few productions, while occasionally provocative, had poor response from both critics and audiences alike. Musical theatre therefore did little to enhance Ellington's growing reputation. *Sophisticated Ladies* faced the most difficult task of the black Broadway revues. It had to adapt orchestral and choral music as well as popular song for the stage. It consequently became the most troubled of the new black musical cavalcades, opening to unanimous pans in its Washington premiere. Donald McKayle, who had worked magic with *Raisin,* failed to bring a coherent vision to the Ellington show. Similarly, stars Gregory Hines and Judith Jameson (of the Alvin Ailey dance troupe) represented wildly diverse traditions of dance and entertainment and often seemed at odds with each other. Play doctors, such as Samm-Art Williams, the author of the NEC hit *Home* (1979), were daunted by a libretto needing to link such a wide variety of musical styles.

Michael Smuin, co-director of the San Francisco Ballet, managed to turn the show around during its tryout, normally an impossible task. Jettisoning the book, Smuin concentrated on the show's strengths, the

36. *Ibid.,* May 2, 1980; *Black Broadway* playbill, in TC/NYPL.

choreography (with the assistance of tap-dance genius Henry LeTang) and the music. Smuin also tried to allow Hines and Jameson to use their diverse talents to best advantage. The new structure for the show allowed the major Ellington works to shine, including "Mood Indigo," "Sophisticated Lady," "Take the 'A' Train," "Caravan," and "Solitude."[37]

The new *Sophisticated Ladies* emerged as a Broadway hit, running almost two years. It also completed the 1970s reevaluation of the contributions of black music to American life in general and to the Broadway stage in particular. What had been both ignored and lost from the historical record suddenly became a major box office force on Broadway. Whether it was the gospel glow of the musicals of Hughes and Carroll, or the Broadway showstoppers of Waller and Blake, the importance of the theatre's black musical heritage could no longer be denied.

37. New York *Times,* March 3, 1981.

EPILOGUE

Into the 1980s

On the evening of June 6, 1982, euphoria swept both the audience and the presenters at the thirty-sixth Antoinette Perry (Tony) Awards as *Dreamgirls* (1981), the latest in a string of successful black musicals, earned the major awards for performers in a musical. This dramatization of the life of the Dreamgirls, a Supremes-like singing group, became both the critical and the box office hit of the season. Frank Rich of the New York *Times,* who had issued few raves during his tenure, declared that the first act finale (Tony Award–winner Jennifer Holliday's performance of "And I Am Telling You I'm Not Going") made "Broadway history." A follow-up review almost a year later revealed that his enthusiasm was undiminished. He praised the show for its daring, which, he found, was preferable even to Charles Fuller's Pulitzer Prize–winning *A Soldier's Play* (1981). The most resoundingly successful black musical in several seasons, it seemed to herald new life for the genre, as, once again, the black musical had begun to rework the Broadway musical in its own image.[1]

While this surface success seemingly portended a new life for the black musical, *Dreamgirls* exhibited a creative contingent that was virtually all white, a division rarely seen since the late 1960s. Michael Bennett, the renowned creator of *A Chorus Line* (1975), joined with author and lyricist Tom Eyen and composer Henry Krieger in bringing this long-evolving show from workshop to Broadway's Imperial Theatre. Several of the cast members from the earliest performances offered suggestions and ideas for the show's final format, but the familiar segregation between creative and performing artists in the black musi-

1. New York *Times,* June 8, 1982.

Jennifer Holliday (*seated*) in *Dreamgirls*
Courtesy Martha Swope

cal reappeared by opening night. An argument concerning the creative contributions surfaced in the pages of the New York *Times*. Cleavant Derricks, who portrayed Jimmy Early, a James Brown figure, in *Dreamgirls*, explained the evolution of his character: "Tom's concept was that the only thing Jimmy Early cares about is singing soul music. . . . Tom knew what he wanted but he needed the words. We'd get up in the workshop and improvise and create the characters. Tom would write down what we were saying." Eyen, who won a Tony for the *Dreamgirls* script, replied with a letter cosigned by Henry Krieger: "The cast worked from a printed script. Improvisations, when they were used, were to find the rhythms and essences of the actors in order to enhance their roles. These improvisations were not used to create the characters, words or music of *Dreamgirls*." In a similar fashion, relations between Bennett and cast members were occasionally less than amicable.[2]

Despite this contradiction, *Dreamgirls* revealed that several of the desires of those who created the black musical had come to fruition. For far too long, white versions of black musicals had created their own vision of Afro-American and Caribbean life. With the black attempt to reclaim this cultural form in the 1960s, it became evident that such stereotypical constructs would no longer be accepted by critics or by audiences. Even when most of the authors were white, the newer black musicals looked to black sources. For example, a month before *Dreamgirls* premiered, *The First* (1981) brought to Broadway a musical version of Jackie Robinson's entry into the white world of baseball. *The Amen Corner* (1983), by several of the creators of *Raisin*, relied on a 1965 James Baldwin play. In a similar fashion, *Dreamgirls* took its inspiration from black musical history during the age of Motown.

The Tony sweep for the *Dreamgirls* cast also indicated the growing participation of black performers in the world of musical comedy. Often, the outstanding performance of a black actor or actress had received media attention primarily because of race, as with, say, Diana Sands's portrayal in *St. Joan* in 1968. By the 1980s, such issues no longer seemed newsworthy. When Debbie Allen, of television's "Fame," appeared in the Gwen Verdon role in the revival of *Sweet Charity*, not a single newspaper article commented that her appearance was yet another advance in Broadway's history of race relations—as

2. *Ibid.*, December 20, 1981, April 4, 11, 1982.

had been the case in the past. The sole question was her performance, and all agreed that she had equaled her talented predecessor.[3]

Ironically, the prospects of the black musical may be threatened as questions of race relations or integration on Broadway seemingly become unimportant or unnoticed. The black musical has tended to thrive in periods in which the legitimate theatre has been less than receptive to the contribution of black artists to its creative endeavors. With doors closed to black performers and artists, alternatives were necessary to allow the participation of black artists. The more white musicals started to open their doors to black performers, as in the late 1940s and early 1950s, prime talent was often drawn away from black productions. As theatrical integration slowed dramatically in the late 1950s and early 1960s, a new black musical, created by black talents, once again came to the fore.

If such a pattern seems destined to repeat itself in the 1980s, the black-created black musical may once again be in jeopardy. *Dreamgirls* and Bob Fosse's *Big Deal* (1985), a black-performed musical based on the ltalian film *Big Deal on Madonna Street* set in Chicago in the 1930s, bracket a period in which few black musicals, whether created by blacks or whites, had a respectable run on Broadway. Only Melvin Van Peebles managed to bring a new black-created musical to Broadway during this five-year period, his short-lived *Waltz of the Stork* (1982). The only financially successful show, *The Tap Dance Kid,* composed by Henry Krieger of *Dreamgirls,* had a healthy run despite lukewarm reviews. The warmhearted tale was of a middle-class youth who shuns the upwardly mobile dreams of his family in order to pursue a career in tap-dancing.

Broadway's renewed acceptance of integration is hardly the only reason for the rather shaky prognosis for the black musical in recent years. With rampant inflation in the 1970s, the costs for any musical have risen considerably. To a certain extent, small workshop-originated productions that relied on music from the past, such as *Eubie!* or *Ain't Misbehavin',* managed to shelter themselves from the vast increase in production costs. However, newly created musicals for a Broadway setting are now in the multimillion-dollar range. As a result, all new American musicals, whether black or white, have been

3. For a survey of black contributions to the Broadway theatre, see Mel Gussow, "Broadway Enjoying Black Talent Boom," New York *Times,* October 15, 1976; and Jon Pareles, "Black Music on Broadway. From Cab Calloway to Prince," New York *Times,* January 26, 1986.

suffering in the late 1980s. Only tried-and-true productions seem economically viable. In particular, London successes such as *Les Misérables, Starlight Express,* and *The Phantom of the Opera* have been making the transatlantic crossing on the strength of favorable reviews, ample funds in the coffers, and the support of major corporate backers. In such a context, the black musical, which has historically been among the first to be hit by economic hardship, may be facing even more difficulties in the future. Or, as in the past, a tactical Off-Broadway retreat may be in the offing. Such recent shows as *Williams and Walker* (1986) and *Mama, I Want to Sing* (1983) have managed to win critical praise and financial success far from the corridors of the Broadway theatre.

Nonetheless, while black musical theatre may once again suffer hard times on Broadway, it may be argued that these shows may have changed the face of American musical theatre as a whole. Black musical theatre, initially a separate and unequal stepchild of American musical theatre, has slowly been integrated into the musical comedy mainstream as it helped to Americanize and modernize the structure, music, and dance of musical theatre between 1898 and the 1920s, and ultimately in the 1960s and 1970s bring important political issues to an art form that had hitherto been dismissed as "escapist." While the socially conscious black musical that existed in the 1970s may have disappeared, the potential for new black contributions to the world of musical comedy remains strong. Despite long droughts in the past, black artists have often returned to this cultural form and in the process changed both the shape and direction of the black musical and American musical theatre as well.

SELECTED BIBLIOGRAPHY

Abramson, Doris E. "The Great White Way: Critics and the First Black Playwrights on Broadway." *Educational Theatre Journal,* XXVIII (March, 1976), 45–55.

———. *Negro Playwrights in the American Theatre, 1925–1959.* New York, 1969.

Adubato, Robert A. "A History of the WPA's Negro Theatre Project in New York City, 1935–1939." Ph.D. dissertation, New York University, 1978.

Alkire, Stephen Robert. "The Development and Treatment of the Negro Character as Presented in the American Musical Theatre, 1927–1968." Ph.D. dissertation, Michigan State University, 1972.

Anderson, Jervis. *This Was Harlem: A Cultural Portrait, 1900–1950.* New York, 1981.

Anderson, Maxwell, and Kurt Weill. *Lost in the Stars.* In *Famous American Plays of the 1940s,* edited by Henry Hewes. New York, 1960.

Applebaum, Stanley, ed. *Show Songs from "The Black Crook" to "The Red Mill."* New York, 1974.

Arata, Esther Spring. *More Black American Playwrights.* Metuchen, N.J., 1978.

Arata, Esther Spring, and Nicholas John Rotoli. *Black American Playwrights, 1800 to the Present.* Metuchen, N.J., 1976.

Archer, Leonard C. *Black Images in the American Theatre: NAACP Protest Campaigns—Stage, Screen, Radio & Television.* Brooklyn, 1973.

Armitage, Merle, ed. *George Gershwin.* New York, 1938.

Bailey, Pearl. *The Raw Pearl.* New York, 1968.

Benchley, Robert. *Benchley at the Theatre: Dramatic Criticism, 1920–1940.* Edited by Charles Getchell. Ipswich, Mass., 1985.

Berry, Faith. *Langston Hughes: Before and Beyond Harlem.* Westport, Conn., 1983.

Bigsby, C. W. E. "Three Black Playwrights: Loften Mitchell, Ossie Davis, Douglas Turner Ward." In Bigsby, *The Black American Writer,* II. Deland, Fla., 1969.

Blesh, Rudi, and Harriet Janis. *They All Played Ragtime.* New York, 1971.

Bogle, Donald. *Brown Sugar.* New York, 1980.

———. *Toms, Coons, Mulattoes, Mammies, and Bucks.* New York, 1973.

Bontemps, Arna, ed. *The Harlem Renaissance Remembered: Essays, Edited with a Memoir.* New York, 1972.

Bontemps, Arna, Countee Cullen, and Johnny Mercer. *St. Louis Woman.* In *Black Theater: A Twentieth Century Collection of the Work of Its Best Playwrights,* ed. Lindsay Patterson. New York, 1971.

Bordman, Gerald. *American Musical Revue: From "The Passing Show" to "Sugar Babies."* New York, 1978.

———. *American Musical Theatre.* New York, 1978.

Boskin, Joseph. *Sambo: The Rise and Demise of an American Jester.* New York, 1986.

Busacca, Basil. "Checklist of Black Playwrights: 1823–1970." *Black Scholar,* V (September, 1973), 48–54.

Capote, Truman. *House of Flowers.* New York, 1968.

———. *The Muses Are Heard.* New York, 1956.

Charters, Ann. *Nobody: The Story of Bert Williams.* New York, 1970.

Cole, Bob. "The Negro and the Stage." *Colored American Magazine* (1902), 301–307.

Cook, Will Marion. "Clorindy, the Origin of the Cakewalk." *Theatre Arts* (September, 1947), 61–65.

Craig, E. Quita. *Black Drama of the Federal Theatre Era.* Amherst, 1980.

Cripps, Thomas E. *Race Films as Genre.* Bloomington, Ind., 1978.

———. *Slow Fade to Black.* New York, 1977.

Cuney-Hare, Maud. *Negro Musicians and Their Music.* New York, 1974.

Cunningham, Virginia. *Paul Laurence Dunbar and His Song.* New York, 1969.

Dance, Stanley. *The World of Duke Ellington.* New York, 1970.

Davin, Tom. "Conversations with James P. Johnson." *Jazz Review* (July, 1959), 10–14.

Davis, Ossie, Philip Rose, and Peter Udell. *Purlie.* New York, 1971.

Davis, Sammy, Jr., Jane Boyer, and Burt Boyer. *Yes I Can.* New York, 1965.

Dennison, Sam. *Scandalize My Name: Black Imagery in American Popular Music.* New York, 1982.

Dunham, Katherine. *A Touch of Innocence.* New York, 1959.

Durham, Frank. *DuBose Heyward, the Man Who Wrote "Porgy."* Columbia, S.C., 1954.

Edmonds, Randolph. "Concerning Negro Drama." *Opportunity* (September, 1931), 284, 288.

———. "Some References on the Negro in American Drama." *Opportunity* (October, 1930), 303–305.

Ellington, Duke. *Music Is My Mistress.* New York, 1973.

Emanuel, James A. *Langston Hughes.* New York, 1967.

Erenberg, Lewis A. *Steppin' Out: New York Nightlife and the Transformation of American Culture, 1890–1930.* Westport, Conn., 1981.

Fabre, Geneviève E. *Drumbeats, Masks, and Metaphor: Contemporary Afro-American Theatre.* Translated by Melvin Dixon. Cambridge, Mass., 1983.

Fabre, Geneviève E. *et al.*, eds. *Afro-American Poetry and Drama, 1760–1975: A Guide to Information Sources.* Detroit, 1979.

Fisher, Rudolph. "The Caucasian Storms Harlem." *American Mercury,* XI (August, 1927), 393–98.

Flanagan, Hallie. *Arena: The Story of the Federal Theatre.* New York, 1985.

Fletcher, Tom. *The Tom Fletcher Story: 100 Years of the Negro in Show Business.* New York, 1954.

Fordin, Hugh. *Getting to Know Him: A Biography of Oscar Hammerstein II.* New York, 1977.

Friedman, Charles. "Toward American Opera." *Theatre Arts* (June, 1953), 33–34.

Genêt, Jean. *The Blacks: A Clown Show.* Translated by Bernard Frechtman. New York, 1960.

Gilliam, Dorothy Butler. *Paul Robeson, All-American.* Washington, D.C., 1976.

Grant, Micki. *Dont Bother Me, I Cant Cope.* New York, 1972.

Green, Jeffrey P. "*In Dahomey* in London in 1903." *Black Perspective in Music,* XI (Spring, 1983), 22–40.

Green, Stanley. *Encyclopaedia of the Musical Theatre.* New York, 1976.

———. *Ring Bells! Sing Songs! Broadway Musicals of the 1930's.* New Rochelle, N.Y., 1971.

Greene, David Mason. *Greene's Biographical Encyclopedia of Composers.* New York, 1985.

Hamilton, Virginia. *Paul Robeson: The Life and Times of a Free Black Man.* New York, 1974.

Hammerstein, Oscar, II. *Carmen Jones.* New York, 1945.

Hammond, John, and Irving Townsend. *John Hammond on Record.* New York, 1977.

Hansberry, Lorraine. "Me Tink Me Hear Sounds in De Night." *Theatre Arts* (October, 1960), 9–11.

Haskins, Jim. *The Cotton Club.* New York, 1977.

Haskins, James, with Kathleen Benson. *Lena.* New York, 1984.

Hatch, James V. *Black Image on the American Stage: A Bibliography of Plays and Musicals, 1770–1970.* New York, 1970.

"Hatch-Billops Archives Interviews with Playwrights." *Negro American Literature Forum,* X (1976), 64–65.

Henriksen, Henry. "Black Patti." *Record Research,* no. 177/8 (November, 1980), 8.

Heyward, DuBose. "*Porgy and Bess* Return on the Wings of Song." *Stage* (October, 1935), 25–29.

Heyward, DuBose, George Gershwin, and Ira Gershwin. *Porgy and Bess.* In *Ten Great Musicals of the American Theatre,* edited by Stanley Richards. Radnor, Pa., 1973.

Hill, Errol, ed. *The Theater of Black Americans.* 2 vols. Englewood Cliffs, N.J., 1980.

Horne, Lena, and Richard Schickel. *Lena.* London, 1966.

Houseman, John. *Run-Through.* New York, 1972.

Huggins, Nathan Irvin. *Harlem Renaissance.* New York, 1971.

———. *Voices From the Harlem Renaissance.* New York, 1976.

Hughes, Langston. *The Big Sea.* New York, 1940.

———. *Five Plays by Langston Hughes.* Edited by Webster Smalley. Bloomington, Ind. 1963.

———. *I Wonder As I Wander.* New York, 1956.

———. *Selected Poems of Langston Hughes.* New York, 1970.

———. "When Harlem Was in Vogue." *Town and Country* (July, 1940), 64.

Hughes, Langston, and Milton Meltzer. *Black Magic: A Pictorial History of the Negro in American Entertainment.* Englewood Cliffs, N.J., 1967.

Isaacs, Edith J. R. *The Negro in the American Theatre.* College Park, Md., 1968.

Jablonski, Edward, and Lawrence D. Stewart. *The Gershwin Years.* New York, 1973.

Jackson, C., and James Hatch. *Fly Blackbird.* In *Black Theater, USA: Forty-five Plays by Black Americans, 1847–1974,* edited by James Hatch and Ted Shine. New York, 1974.

Jewell, Derek. *Duke: A Portrait of Duke Ellington.* New York, 1977.

Johnson, Hall. "*Porgy and Bess*—A Folk Opera." *Theatre Arts Monthly* (January, 1936), 24–28.

Johnson, James Weldon. *Along This Way.* New York, 1968.

———. *Black Manhattan.* New York, 1968.

———. *God's Trombones: Seven Negro Sermons in Verse.* New York, 1969.

Jones, LeRoi. *Blues People: Negro Music in White America.* New York, 1963.

Kaiser, Ernest, and Robert Nemiroff. "A Lorraine Hansberry Bibliography." *Freedomways,* XIX (1979), 285–304.

Kellner, Bruce, ed. *The Harlem Renaissance: A Historical Dictionary for the Era.* Westport, Conn., 1984.

Kimball, Robert, and William Bolcom. *Reminiscing with Sissle and Blake.* New York, 1973.

Kimball, Robert, and Alfred Simon. *The Gershwins.* New York, 1973.

Kinkle, Roger D. *The Complete Encyclopedia of Popular Music and Jazz, 1900–1950.* 4 vols. New Rochelle, N.Y., 1974.

Kirkeby, Ed. *Ain't Misbehavin': The Story of Fats Waller.* New York, 1966.

Kitt, Eartha. *Alone with Me.* Chicago, 1976.

Kreuger, Miles. *Show Boat: The Story of a Classic American Musical.* New York, 1977.

Lawrence, Vera Brodsky. "Scott Joplin and *Treemonisha.*" *Treemonisha* liner notes, Deutsche Grammophon, 2707–083.

Levine, Lawrence W. *Black Culture and Black Consciousness: Afro-American Folk Thought from Slavery to Freedom.* New York, 1977.

Levy, Eugene. *James Weldon Johnson: Black Leader, Black Voice.* Chicago, 1973.

Lewis, David Levering. *When Harlem Was in Vogue.* New York, 1979.

Little, Stuart W. *Off-Broadway: The Prophetic Theater.* New York, 1972.

Locke, Alain. "Broadway and the Negro Drama." *Theatre Arts* (October, 1941), 745–50.

———. "The Negro and the American Stage." *Theatre Arts Monthly* (February, 1926), 112–20.

McArthur, Benjamin. *Actors and American Culture, 1880–1920.* Philadelphia, 1984.

McKay, Claude. *A Long Way From Home.* New York, 1969.

Marshall, Herbert, and Mildred Stock. *Ira Aldridge: The Negro Tragedian.* Carbondale, Ill., 1968.

Mathews, Jane DeHart. *The Federal Theatre, 1935–1939: Plays, Relief, and Politics.* Princeton, 1967.

Mitchell, Loften. *Black Drama: The Story of the American Negro in the Theatre.* New York, 1967.

———. *Voices of the Black Theatre.* Clifton, N.J., 1975.

Nemiroff, Robert. *To Be Young, Gifted, and Black: Lorraine Hansberry in Her Own Words.* Englewood Cliffs, N.J., 1969.

Nichols, Charles H., ed. *Arna Bontemps–Langston Hughes Letters, 1925–1967.* New York, 1980.

O'Connor, John, and Lorraine Brown, eds. *Free, Adult, Uncensored: The Living History of the Federal Theatre Project.* Washington, D.C., 1978.

Odets, Clifford, William Gibson, and Lee Adams. *Golden Boy.* New York, 1965.

Paris, Arthur. "Cruse and the Crisis in Black Culture: The Case of Theatre, 1900–1930." *Journal of Ethnic Studies,* V (1979), 51–68.

Patterson, Lindsay, ed. *Black Theater: A 20th Century Collection of the Work of Its Best Playwrights.* New York, 1971.

Perry, Margaret. *The Harlem Renaissance: An Annotated Bibliography and Commentary.* New York, 1982.

Pitts, Ethel Louise. "The American Negro Theatre: 1940–1949." Ph.D. dissertation, University of Missouri, Columbia, 1975.

Rampersad, Arnold. *The Life of Langston Hughes: I, Too, Sing America.* Vol. I, *1902–1941.* New York, 1986.

Richards, Sandra. "Bert Williams: His Stage Career and Influence on the American Theatre." Ph.D. dissertation, Stanford University, 1973.

Robeson, Susan. *The Whole World in His Hands.* Secaucus, N.J., 1981.

Rose, Al. *Eubie Blake.* New York, 1979.

Ross, Ronald P. *Black Drama in the Federal Theatre, 1935–1939.* Ann Arbor, 1972.

Sampson, Henry T. *Blacks in Blackface.* Metuchen, N.J., 1980.

Sanders, Ronald. *The Days Grow Short: The Life and Music of Kurt Weill.* New York, 1980.

Shafer, Yvonne. "Black Actors in the Nineteenth Century American Theatre." *CLA Journal,* XX (March, 1977), 387–400.

Sherr, Paul C. "*Change Your Luck*: A Negro Satirizes White America." *Phylon,* XXXII (1971), 281–89.

Simmons, R. C. "Europe's Reception to Negro Talent." *Colored American Magazine* (1905), 635–42.

Southern, Eileen. *Biographical Dictionary of Afro-American and African Musicians.* Westport, Conn., 1982.

———. *The Music of Black Americans: A History.* New York, 1971.

Stearns, Marshall, and Jean Stearns. *Jazz Dance: The Story of American Vernacular Dance.* New York, 1968.

Stuckey, Sterling. *Slave Culture, Nationalist Theory, and the Foundations of Black America.* New York, 1987.

Tichenor, George. "Colored Lines." *Theatre Arts Monthly* (June, 1930), 485–90.

Toll, Robert C. *Blacking Up: The Minstrel Show in Nineteenth-Century America.* New York, 1974.

Vacha, J. E. "Black Man on the Great White Way." *Journal of Popular Culture,* VII (1973), 283–301.

Vance, Joel. *Ain't Misbehavin'. Fats Waller: His Life and Times.* New York, 1979.

Van Peebles, Melvin. *Aint Supposed To Die a Natural Death.* New York, 1973.

———. *Don't Play Us Cheap!* New York, 1973.

Van Vechten, Carl. *"Keep A-Inchin' Along": Selected Writings of Carl Van Vechten About Black Art and Letters.* Edited by Bruce Kellner. Westport, Conn., 1979.

———. *Nigger Heaven,* New York, 1926.

Walker, George W. "The Real 'Coon' on the American Stage." *Theatre Magazine* (August, 1906), 224.

Waters, Ethel, with Charles Samuels. *His Eye Is on the Sparrow.* New York, 1978.

Williams, Bert. "The Comic Side of Trouble." *American Magazine* (January, 1918), 33–35.

Williams, Mance. *Black Theatre in the 1960s and 1970s: A Historical-Critical Analysis of the Movement.* Westport, Conn., 1985.

Woll, Allen. *Dictionary of the Black Theatre: Broadway, Off-Broadway, and Selected Harlem Theatre.* Westport, Conn., 1983.

———. *The Hollywood Musical Goes to War.* Chicago, 1983.

Woll, Allen, and Randall Miller. *Ethnic and Racial Images in American Film and Television: Historical Essays and Bibliography.* New York, 1986.

INDEX